LET SECTS AND PARTIES FALL

A short history of the Association of Churches of Christ in Great Britain and Ireland

By David M. Thompson

Berean Press
Birmingham

This book is dedicated to
the Churches of Christ in Great Britain
and Ireland
with gratitude

First published 1980
Berean Press
Distributed by
Tavistock Bookshop
86 Tavistock Place
London WC1H 9RT

ISBN 0 85050 012 5

Printed by Bookmag, Henderson Road, Inverness

CONTENTS

LIST OF ILLUSTRATIONS
(between pages 112-113)

1. Handbill announcing the opening of the meetings in Manchester, 1855.
2. Handbill advertising the Manchester church, 1855.
3. James Wallis.
4. David King.
5. John Crook.
6. Sydney Black.
7. Lancelot Oliver.
8. William Robinson.
9. Overdale College, Moseley, 1920.
10. Overdale College, Selly Oak, 1958.
11. Twynholm Hall, London, 1896.
12. East Kilbride, 1962.
13. James Gray.
14. Philip Morgan.

Love, like death, hath all destroyed,
Rendered all distinctions void:
Names, and sects, and parties fall,
Thou, O Christ, art all in all.

Charles Wesley (1707-88)
Hymns for Churches of Christ (1908) no 270
(*Methodist Hymn Book* (1933) no 720)

PREFACE

In 1971 I was invited by the Churches of Christ Publications Department to write a history of the Churches to replace the *History of the British Churches of Christ* (1948) by Dr A.C. Watters, which had long been out of print. I willingly accepted the invitation, since this was something which I had wanted to do for some time. What I did not foresee were the extra demands made upon my time in the last few years, which have delayed the book so long. I am grateful to the chairman and secretary of the Publications Department, Eric Spencer and James Garrow, for their patience, and their prodding.

I am aware of the defects of this book more than anyone. Although Churches of Christ are a small group of churches, there is a considerable mass of local material which I have not attempted to use. I soon realized that it was quite impossible in the time available to fulfil my original intention of writing a history which set the congregations of the movement in their local socio-religious context. I remain convinced that this approach is essential for a full understanding of the development of religious life in this country, and some day I hope to do what this book fails to do. Instead I decided to concentrate on the history of the corporate life of the Churches, and thus my main sources have been the magazines and Year Books. It is important to remember that they are not neutral sources. The Year Books consist of official reports and the minutes of Conference; and to understand what went on at Conference, it was essential to consult the reports of meetings in the magazines. These vary in completeness; they are fullest from about 1910 to 1939, which conveniently is one of the periods of maximum controversy. Even in these years, however, the reporting of debates is nowhere near *verbatim* and it is impossible to judge whether the reporters' view of what should be reported coincides with what the historian now would like to know. It is also clear that editorial policy over the publication of controversial correspondence has varied considerably from one editor to another. Although

5

successive editors have taken comfort from the fact that criticisms of their policies from both sides have tended to cancel each other out, again the historian has no way of judging the significance of what the editor chose not to publish. Another point at which editorial policy, or availability of material, has varied considerably concerns obituary notices. These are often the best sources for biographical details of leaders in the life of the Churches. Yet even such a simple fact as the date of birth is often not given, and it is sometimes frustratingly difficult to get the information one needs. Some of these defects in evidence could be remedied given more time: others can never be made good.

For these reasons there is much less than there could have been about the history of local churches and their leaders. I have also said relatively little about missionary work, because the Missionary Committee has its own plans for providing a public record of this. I realize in retrospect that I have written less about Sunday School and youth work than I probably should have done, though I doubt whether this is one of the areas where Churches of Christ have a distinctive history.

I am grateful to more people than I can name or remember for little pieces of information which have been valuable additions to the written word. My parents and my parents-in-law have brought past events to life by their memories in an invaluable way: I hope I have been able to make appropriate allowance for any bias in their points of view. Finally, I am grateful to my wife, Margaret, not only for her help in some of the more tedious aspects of research, but also for providing the constant stimulus to keep going: both she and my family will rejoice with me that 'The History' is now itself a thing of the past!

David M. Thompson
September 1979

INTRODUCTION

It is particularly difficult to write a 'denominational history' of Churches of Christ in Great Britain and Ireland. One obvious reason for this is that the Churches have never regarded themselves as a denomination but have always looked upon themselves as a movement. Cherishing the hope that one day all the Churches might be reunited on the basis of New Testament Christianity, they deliberately rejected denominational positions and limited themselves to what they thought could be proved essential from Scripture. But of course the question of whether a group is a denomination does not depend only on whether it thinks it is, and in many ways Churches of Christ have inevitably come to have many of the characteristics of a denomination over the years. The difficulties in writing a denominational history go deeper than this. Most denominations can be defined by reference to one or more of the following: a common founder, common origins, a common programme or theological position, and common support of certain institutions. With the partial exception of the last, all of these possibilities pose difficulties for the historian of Churches of Christ.

There was no common founder figure for Churches of Christ in Great Britain in the sense that John Wesley was for Methodism, or even in the sense that Alexander Campbell was for the Disciple movement in the United States. Certainly Alexander Campbell's writings were the focus for the new movement, but he only ever made one visit to Britain after his emigration in 1809, and by then (1847) the British Churches were already established. Leaders in the British Churches never accepted everything that Campbell said, and they never accepted anything he said simply because he said it. His writings were accepted because they were felt to express certain convictions of the early British leaders, particularly on the need to restore the ancient order of things in church life. To be fair to Campbell he would not have wished for anything else, but the fact that he lived on the other side of the Atlantic meant that he was an intellectual rather than a personal influence on the Churches. He was also constantly open to misunderstanding, because wherever the point of what he was saying was unclear the meaning had to be teased out through correspondence, inevitably a lengthy business, and damage was likely to be done before a reply was received. William Jones, for example, had been publishing his *Millennial Harbinger* for the best part of a year before it became clear that he and Campbell disagreed on crucial points. Only in a qualified sense, therefore, can Campbell be claimed as a founder of the British Churches of Christ. Yet there was no comparable native-born figure with the same influence in the early days. James Wallis played a crucial part by editing the *Christian Messenger,* but he was no theologian. In the next generation David King had a dominating influence: though more of a theological controversialist than Wallis, he had a narrower vision and was certainly not an original thinker. Moreover the Churches were by then already established, and could scarcely regard King as a founder figure, despite his important initiatory role in Manchester and Birmingham: and his domination of the Churches was never complete.

If there was no common founder, it is also clear that there were no common origins. In any case there is always a danger in writing histories in terms of origins. The important and distinctive thing about a new movement is what it becomes, not where it came from; and there is sometimes a temptation to claim a distinguished pedigree as a way of establishing the contemporary importance of a movement. The most important influence in the origins of Churches of Christ was that of the Scotch Baptists; and Scotch Baptist instincts remained important at certain points ever after — for example, there was a strong reluctance to go in for emotional revivalism, and an unwillingness to place great stress on a 'conversion experience'. But there were other independent sources from which the new movement drew strength, often attached to no denominational association, though invariably believer-baptist in practice. Many members of Churches of Christ were drawn from other denominations, particularly Methodism, which is not very surprising as the Methodists were by far the largest nonconformist group in nineteenth-century England.

Even if the first two points are admitted, surely, it will be said, there must have been a common programme. Certainly there was: the problem about the common programme is not that it did not exist, but that it was not unique to Churches of Christ. It therefore becomes just as difficult to use as a defining characteristic as the other two. Apologists for the Disciple movement on both sides of the Atlantic have tended to ignore the extent to which the programme of Christian unity on the basis of the Bible was part of the common stock of evangelical ideas in the early nineteenth century. It lay behind the burst of missionary activity overseas in the 1790s and 1800s: it was of obvious importance in the foundation of the British and Foreign Bible Society in 1804. But it did not last. In England first Anglican evangelicals and then Methodists abandoned the idea of undenominational evangelism, and by the 1830s separate Unions had been established for Congregationalists and Baptists. This new denominational sense took time to prevail, and in the field of evangelism particularly 'undenominationalism' was always apt to break out for the rest of the century: but a new course had been set. Even the Bible Societies were divided over whether the Apocrypha should be included in the Bibles they produced.

Despite these developments in the better established communions, there remained a strong and persistent minority tendency for small groups and individuals to hanker after the older ideal. Churches of Christ reflect one aspect of this development: the Plymouth Brethren represent another. But if one examines particular congregations 'on the ground', it is impossible to explain why they became what they did become in terms of theological programme alone. Why did one congregation join Churches of Christ and another join the Brethren? Why are there sometimes congregations of the Brethren and Churches of Christ in the same village? The answers here are to be found in terms of personal and social relationships, not theology; and so to define these groups primarily in theological terms is inadequate, if not misleading. For it has always to be remembered that most ordinary church life in a congregation of any denomination does not depend on distinctive denominational tenets. Sunday services, weeknight prayer meetings, and evangelism are all very similar in a nonconformist context. Churches of Christ were distinctive in their practice of weekly communion and believer's baptism by immersion — though the Brethren shared these characteristics. Churches of Christ also probably tended to

9

recruit their members more from other churches than by evangelism among the uncommitted, mainly because their position depended upon an intellectual view of the proper nature of the Church, rather than on the conversion of sinners. But even when this has been admitted, and it is very important, it remains true that theological definition is difficult, not least because Churches of Christ on principle never committed themselves to binding statements of belief. It is thus for the most part impossible to say what the 'official' Churches of Christ position is on anything. Significantly this position has only changed with the involvement of Churches of Christ in the modern ecumenical movement, when certain official statements have been approved.

It is therefore in the common support of certain institutions that the clearest definition of Churches of Christ is to be found. But these were slow to develop. The first General Meeting of the Churches was not held until 1842, nearly six years after James Wallis's group seceded from the Scotch Baptist church in Nottingham and more than ten years after Alexander Campbell's writings first became known in Britain. The Meeting did not become an Annual Meeting until after 1847, and support for common evangelistic work — the purpose of the Meeting — was slow to materialize. It was not until the 1860s and 1870s that it began to play a major part in the life of local churches. But it did serve the important purpose of developing the sense of a national fellowship, probably accentuated by the fact that the congregations inevitably felt somewhat isolated in view of their small size in any one place. This sense of a national fellowship has been the strongest binding force in Churches of Christ throughout their history. The Annual Meeting was a consultative body, and it refused steadfastly to act as a court of appeal in disputes between local churches. Membership was therefore voluntary. But the Churches also declined to limit their fellowship to those churches in membership with the Association. Thus although in one sense a Church of Christ may be defined by indicating whether it is 'on the list of Churches cooperating', in another sense Churches of Christ have never sought to define themselves in an exclusive way such as this. But the Annual Meeting did become the means by which the Churches acted collectively, first for evangelism, then for training and Sunday School work; and gradually other tasks were taken up as well — foreign missions, for example. The authority entrusted to the Annual Meeting in these collective

10

enterprises has often been considerable, certainly more than in the Baptist Union and the old Congregational Union. Because the Annual Meeting has represented the focus of the common life of Churches of Christ, I have made it the focus of this story. Theological development and the story of certain local churches will not be excluded — they cannot be. But a movement is not made by one church or one thinker; it is made by churches and people acting together. This therefore will be the theme of what follows.

1 ORIGINS

I

One Sunday afternoon in the summer of 1833 Peyton C. Wyeth, a young American portrait-painter, visited the Scotch Baptist chapel in Windmill Street, Finsbury Square, London. After the service he explained to one of the elders, William Jones, that he had been searching for a church with the same doctrine and worship as his own in Pennsylvania. Wyeth was looking for a church which had returned to the simplicity of New Testament Christianity, and he felt he had found this among the Scotch Baptists. He was admitted to membership of the Windmill Street congregation a few weeks later.[1] The American movement to which Wyeth belonged was that later known as the Disciples of Christ, of which Alexander Campbell was the leading spokesman. By his almost chance encounter with Jones, Wyeth provided an opportunity for the writings of Alexander Campbell to be made known to a British audience, and from this sprang the movement known in Britain as Churches of Christ.

Alexander Campbell was born in 1788, the eldest son of Thomas Campbell, who had recently become a probationer minister of the Anti-Burgher Secession Presbyterian Church in Ireland.[2] After some ten years spent in school-teaching and preaching to congregations without a settled minister, Thomas was called to the pastorate of a recently established church at Ahorey, near Armagh, in 1798. It was a difficult time in Ireland with both Catholics in the south and Presbyterians in the north agitating against the government in Dublin, which was dominated by the Anglo-Irish aristocracy and the Church of Ireland. This was also the year of an unsuccessful rebellion by the 'United Irishmen', led by Wolfe Tone, a Dublin Protestant lawyer. Thomas Campbell, unlike many Presbyterians, kept himself aloof from political involvement and made a reputation for open-mindedness and charity. He was also active in trying to reunite the divided groups in the Secession Church in Ireland, for the divisions inherited from Scottish experience were irrelevant

13

there. But his efforts were frustrated by the attitude of the Scottish Synod, to which the Irish Church was linked.

While at Ahorey Thomas Campbell continued as a schoolmaster, and in 1805 Alexander became assistant to his father in a new school which he opened in Rich-Hill. There was an Independent congregation in Rich-Hill, associated with the Scottish Independents through the work of the Haldane brothers; and this gave Thomas and Alexander opportunities to hear visiting preachers such as Rowland Hill, James Haldane, Alexander Carson and John Walker, for the Campbells were on good terms with the local Independent minister. Thomas Campbell also joined the Evangelical Society, which was founded to promote village preaching.

In 1807 Thomas's health broke down, and he was advised to take a long sea voyage. He was persuaded, somewhat against his will, to emigrate to the United States, and Alexander volunteered to look after the school until his father was settled in America, when he would bring the rest of the family over to join him. Just over a year later in October 1808 the rest of the family sailed from Londonderry, but after a storm were shipwrecked off the Isle of Islay on the Scottish coast. The family therefore proceeded to Glasgow, where they stayed until it was safe to make the Atlantic crossing the following spring. This gave Alexander the opportunity of attending classes at Glasgow University from November 1808 to May 1809. While the family were in Glasgow Alexander was greatly influenced by Greville Ewing, minister of the Glasgow Tabernacle, an Independent congregation set up as a result of the evangelical movement led by James and Robert Haldane. He accepted the Haldanes' view of faith as being essentially trust or confidence in Christ. He was impressed by the weekly celebration of the Lord's Supper which Ewing had introduced. Although by this time the Haldane brothers had adopted believer's baptism, Ewing broke with them on this point and Campbell remained a paedo-baptist. The opposition of the Church of Scotland clergy to such reforms, and to itinerant preaching, made Alexander increasingly disillusioned with Presbyterianism as such; and this culminated in his refusal to take the elements at the communion season in the Secession church which he still attended.

In the summer of 1809 Alexander and the rest of the family sailed for the United States. When they met Thomas Campbell,

Alexander discovered to his joy that a completely different train of events had led his father to a position somewhat similar to his own. Thomas had suffered censure from the Secession Presbytery of Chartiers in Western Pennsylvania because he allowed other Presbyterians to receive communion from him in view of the scarcity of ministers in the new country. When they went further and ignored his appeals to Scripture over against the articles of the Church, he withdrew from them and continued his ministry independently. In August 1809 those among whom he had been working resolved to form an association entitled the Christian Association of Washington. Campbell had been working on a Declaration and Address to set out its principles when his family arrived in the New World. The *Declaration* had been approved by the Christian Association in September, and was in proof when the Campbell family arrived. The *Address* was Thomas's justification and explanation of the Declaration and it culminated in thirteen propositions, the first of which was:

> That the Church of Christ upon earth is essentially, intentionally and constitutionally one; consisting of all those in every place who profess their faith in Christ and obedience to him in all things according to the Scriptures, and that manifest the same by their tempers and conduct; and of none else, as none else can be truly and properly called Christians.

In order that there might be no schisms in the Church, the third proposition asserted that

> . . . nothing ought to be inculcated upon Christians as articles of faith, nor required of them as terms of communion, but what is expressly taught and enjoined upon them in the Word of God.[3]

Alexander decided to devote himself full time to the propagation of the principles of this new movement. It soon became clear that there was little hope of promoting union between the existing denominations, and in May 1811 the Association constituted itself a church at Brush Run. Shortly after the birth of his first child in 1812 Alexander Campbell changed his view of baptism: he came to realise that, on the principles he now stood by, only the baptism of believers could be justified, and furthermore he decided that he himself had not been properly baptized. In June 1812 he decided to be immersed, and his father followed his example. From this point on, as Alexander's friend and biographer Robert Richardson observed,

Thomas in effect conceded to his son 'the guidance of the whole religious movement'.[4]

There followed a short period of fellowship with the Redstone Baptist Association, though there were no other Baptist churches in the immediate neighbourhood of Brush Run. In 1816 Alexander caused a stir at the annual meeting of the Redstone Association by his *Sermon on the Law*, in which he argued that Christians were not bound by the Law of Moses and that attempts to draw analogies from the Old Testament to justify church practices were misconceived. The latter point was, of course, supremely important for attempts to justify infant baptism by analogy with circumcision. This theme was developed in two public debates which Alexander held in 1820 and 1823. The first was with a Secession minister, John Walker, at Mount Pleasant, Ohio, when Alexander was pressed somewhat reluctantly to defend the Baptist position. His success in debate, however, removed some of the doubts which he, and particularly his father, had had about this method of defending gospel truth, and in 1823 the challenge which he had made at the end of the Walker debate to a further debate with any paedo-baptist minister in good standing was taken up by a Kentucky Presbyterian, W.L. Maccalla. The outcome of this debate considerably extended Alexander's reputation among the Kentucky Baptists. In the same year he began publication of his magazine, *The Christian Baptist*, in which as editor he displayed considerable controversial powers. The magazine also made clear some of the differences which existed between the Campbells and the Baptists generally, though an increasing number of Baptists were attracted to what became known as the "Reformers'" position.

Thus far the Campbells' Reformation had been mainly within the existing Churches. But in 1827 Walter Scott was appointed an itinerant preacher in the Western Reserve, and under his leadership the Reforming position had considerable numerical success. It was also brought into contact with Barton Stone's Christian Connection, which had very similar principles and was enjoying similar success in Ohio. From then on there was increasing cooperation between the two groups, and the Campbellite movement became actively involved in evangelism for the first time.

In 1829 Alexander Campbell debated with Robert Owen, the English social reformer, on the Evidences of Christianity. Quite apart from the boost which this gave to his reputation, the debate is significant for the development of an argument that Campbell had first used in a series of articles in the *Christian Baptist* in 1826.[5] He attacked the assumption that the idea of God could be derived from nature by the use of reason: only by revelation, he argued, did the idea of God appear, though once conceived it was supported at every point by the contemplation of nature. The Bible thus was essential as the record of revelation. In relation to Owen this argument was used to suggest that all his ideas about social progress were in fact derived from Christianity, and were not the result of natural reason. In the context of Campbell's thought generally, the argument was used to strengthen the position that the Bible, rather than any human system of theology, was the ultimate test of faith.

This became evident in the mounting crisis in Campbell's relationship with the Baptists. Increasingly the Reformers were being accused of denying Baptist doctrines by their refusal to acknowledge human creeds and their insistence on not going beyond what Scripture said on any point. The essential differences concerned the influence of the Holy Spirit in salvation and the relation of baptism to the remission of sins. Undoubtedly there was misrepresentation and misunderstanding of the Campbells' position on these subjects; but equally, after they had abandoned Presbyterianism, the Campbells had never really shared either the Calvinist or Moderate Calvinist views on these matters, which were still held by Baptists. From 1830 beginning in Kentucky there was a separation between Baptists and Reformers, and from 1832, again beginning in Kentucky, there was a coming together of the Reformers and Barton Stone's Christian Connection. The combined movement came to be known as the Disciples of Christ, and the decade which followed was one of rapid expansion.[6] This then was the movement which Peyton Wyeth described to William Jones in the summer of 1833.

II

In considering the relationship between Disciples of Christ in America and Churches of Christ in Britain, it is always necessary to remember that in Britain Alexander Campbell's ideas were grafted on to Scotch Baptist roots. What were these roots? The Scotch Baptists, as the name suggests, developed out of the

17

Scottish Independent tradition which had a different context and atmosphere from that of English Dissent. The leaders of the Scotch Baptists, Archibald McLean and Robert Carmichael, came from the Glasites (founded by John Glas after his deposition from the ministry of the Church of Scotland in 1730), who were the first group of Independents in Scotland. McLean and Carmichael had been members of the Glasite congregation in Glasgow, but in 1763 they withdrew because of a disagreement with Glas in a case of discipline. In reviewing the New Testament evidence on baptism in the following year McLean came to the conclusion that only believer's baptism was justified, and by 1765 he had converted Carmichael to his views. So there was formed the first Baptist church in Edinburgh, from which the Scotch Baptist movement developed.[7]

Like all Scottish Protestants in this period the theology of the Scotch Baptists was influenced by the Calvinism of the Westminster Confession, particularly in relation to the doctrine of election and the work of the Holy Spirit in conversion. To this they added the protest against an established Church and the emphasis on the New Testament as the only source of authority for church practice, following the Glasites. Thus they held to congregational government, a plurality of elders or pastors in each church (as distinct from a single minister), and a weekly celebration of the Lord's Supper. They differed from the Glasites in their belief in believer's baptism by immersion, in their more puritanical attitude to worldly amusements, and in their support for the missionary enterprise pioneered by the Baptist Missionary Society in 1792, which also brought them into contact with Baptists in England. Archibald McLean's book, *The Commission given by Jesus Christ to his Apostles* (1786), summarized his understanding of primitive Christianity.[8] The Scotch Baptists grew gradually in Scotland, and also spread into England and North Wales.[9]

After McLean's death in 1812, William Jones emerged as the leading figure among the Scotch Baptists. Jones was born in Gresford, Denbighshire, in 1762. His sister's husband belonged to a Baptist church in Chester which turned to McLean for assistance after the premature death of its pastor, Samuel Ecking,[10] in 1785. Jones was baptized by McLean when the latter was visiting Chester in 1786. In 1793 Jones moved to Liverpool and became a bookseller: he began a Scotch Baptist church there, and subsequently became one of its two elders. Then in 1812 he moved to London, where he became elder of the Scotch Baptist church in Windmill Street. He made a reputation as the editor of various theological journals for the Scotch Baptists, and also as an ecclesiastical historian through his *History of the Albigenses and Waldenses* and his *History of the Christian Church*. He also edited the works of Archibald McLean, and it was this which made him the main spokesman for the Scotch Baptists.[11]

The similarities between Alexander Campbell's American movement and the Scotch Baptists will now be clear: both sought the restoration of primitive Christianity. William Jones was also particularly interested to learn from Wyeth that Campbell's movement was not involved in the American emotional revivals which had been widely reported in Britain, but had been successful by a simple appeal to reason and Scripture. Campbell was known by reputation to Jones through his public debate with Robert Owen, and through Wyeth's introduction the two men began to correspond. Jones was impressed by what he read of Campbell's writings, and in 1835 he began to publish a new magazine, *The Millennial Harbinger and Voluntary Church Advocate*, to make these writings more widely known in Britain. The title of the new magazine is significant: 'The Millennial Harbinger' was copied from the title of Campbell's American magazine, though most of what was published in Jones's *Harbinger* was taken from Campbell's earlier magazine, *The Christian Baptist* (1823-30); 'the Voluntary Church Advocate' is a reminder that Jones came from that strand of early nineteenth century nonconformity, heavily influenced by Scottish experience, which blamed the union of Church and State for many of the troubles of the time. Such men were predisposed to look hopefully to the United States for evidence of a new and better order of things: thus on the very first page of his new magazine Jones wrote:

> In the present melancholy state of the continent of Europe, where despotism and bigotry have succeeded in establishing at least a temporary dominion, when in England itself the most vigorous efforts are making to uphold the unnatural alliance betwixt Church and State, and perpetuate the abuses of olden times, America possesses a stronger hold than ever on the hopes and affections of those who desire an amelioration of the general condition of man.[12]

Nor was this transatlantic interest confined to smaller groups like the Scotch Baptists: 1835 was the year when the Baptist and Congregational Unions sent deputations to the United States to report on religion in America.

It is clear, however, from the *Millennial Harbinger* that Jones was interested in Campbell's writings because they were powerfully presented versions of what he himself believed; yet in the first issue indirectly and in the second directly Jones made it clear that he did not agree with Campbell in everything. In succeeding issues the differences became more apparent and eventually in 1836 they led Jones to discontinue publication. Jones's *Harbinger* cannot therefore be regarded simply as propaganda on Campbell's behalf: but it was the means by which the name of Campbell became known in Britain, and its readers also began to buy and read Campbell's works for themselves, 'complete and unabridged', with important results. Jones was surprised and distressed that Campbell thought so little of the contribution of McLean and the Scotch Baptists towards the restoration of primitive Christianity. But this was soon replaced by more serious doubts about Campbell's orthodoxy: he expounded these in an appendix to his volume of sermons on *Primitive Christianity*, published in 1837. Jones was puzzled by Campbell's refusal to be dogmatic on points which were not explicitly touched on in Scripture; he was worried by his willingness to call 'dear brother' people whom Jones regarded as outright heretics; and he was sceptical about Campbell's joy in being emancipated from all human creeds and confessions. By 1837 William Jones's involvement with Campbellism was over.[13]

III

But the influence of Campbell's ideas among Scotch Baptists could not be quelled so easily. In his Sermons on *Primitive Christianity* Jones had singled out for criticism a book entitled *A Tribute to the Memory of the Apostles*, by Henry Grew. He said that this contained a direct attack on the doctrine of the Trinity and the personality of the Holy Spirit, and yet was commended by Campbell.[14] Grew's book came into the hands of a Nottingham draper, James Wallis, in June 1836 and was published by him.[15] Wallis had been born in Kettering in 1793 and after serving his apprenticeship as a tailor had joined the Particular Baptist church in Kettering in 1812. He moved to

20

Leicester in 1814 to avoid military service, and from there to Nottingham in 1816. In 1834 he left the Particular Baptists for the Scotch Baptists, and thus read Jones's *Harbinger* and learnt about Campbell. He received Grew's book from a former Particular Baptist friend, Joseph Harpham, who had emigrated to the United States, and he decided to publish it because he thought it well suited as an explanation of why he had decided to leave the Particular Baptists and join the Scotch Baptists instead. But it seems probable that its publication was also related to the controversy raging among Scotch Baptists as to whether the presence of elders was essential to a church, and in particular whether the Lord's Supper could be celebrated if elders were absent.

This controversy was not a new one. In 1810 the Scotch Baptists had split on the question, some arguing that a church was competent to do everything without pastors that it could do with them, and others, led by McLean and Jones, condemning this position. The issue revived in 1834 when an attempt to reunite the parties in Aberdeen intensified divisions elsewhere by raising the question of whether the reunited church in Aberdeen should be recognized as a sister church or not.[16] In publishing Grew's book Wallis was obviously taking the 'liberal' side in the controversy, for Grew argued that disciples had no right to neglect the commands of the Lord because they lacked an elder or a bishop. The significance of this is indicated by the fact that Wallis included with the text of Grew's work *A Query on Taking the Lord's Supper, answered by Alexander Campbell*. In this Campbell argued that it was more important that the Lord's Supper should be celebrated every week than that elders should preside. There should be elders in every congregation, and indeed no-one should act as an elder *pro tempore* for a single day except by the choice and appointment of the brethren: but the weekly celebration of the Lord's Supper came first.[17]

Wallis was obviously receiving Campbell's works direct from America by this time, because his copy of Campbell's *Christianity Restored* (published in 1835) is dated 16 July 1836.[18] This book, which may have sparked off Jones's doubts about Campbell's orthodoxy, was retitled *The Christian System* in its second revised (and subsequent) editions. This direct access to Campbell's writings is probably the background to the discussion which took place in the Scotch Baptist church at Park Street,

Nottingham between October and December 1836 on the question of whether baptism was for the remission of sins. Wallis and his friends followed Campbell in arguing that baptism was for the remission of sins; but others took the line which Jones was to follow in *Primitive Christianity* in 1837 by denying that immersion actually washed away sin. The division of opinion became so deep that John Bayley, the pastor, absented himself from the church on Sunday, 18 December 1836, and sent word that the church was not to break bread in her existing circumstances. This immediately reopened the question of whether a church could celebrate the Lord's Supper in the absence of an elder, and fourteen members of the church withdrew. On the following Sunday, 25 December 1836, these fourteen met in an upper room of a warehouse in Mount Street and broke bread together. The group was led by James Wallis and Jonathan Hine, the owner of the warehouse: their formation into a church created the congregation which was the pioneer of the movement later known as Churches of Christ.[19]

But it is a mistake to suppose that the Nottingham congregation, or even William Jones, is the only source for the Campbellite stream in Britain. The first group in the British Isles to hear of Campbell was at Dungannon in the north of Ireland. A church was formed here in 1810 by Robert Tener on the principle of requiring a simple faith in Jesus as the Son of God and immersion into his name. Tener's wife had been taught by Thomas Campbell as a schoolgirl. In 1825, Robert's son, Richard, was told by some of Campbell's Seceder relatives in Newry that Campbell's books would suit his father, and contact was established. In 1827 a Liverpool commercial traveller, Peter Woodnorth, visited the Dungannon brethren, and took some of Campbell's works to England, including those stressing that baptism was for the remission of sins. From Woodnorth the books found their way into the Scotch Baptist churches in Liverpool, Nottingham and Manchester. The Haldaneite Baptist church at Auchtermuchty in Fife came to know of Campbell in 1830, and one of its leaders, John Dron, visited Campbell in America in 1834. John Black, a former member of William Jones's congregation, gathered a group at his house in London to search the Scriptures for the divine order of things, and in due course also came into contact with the American movement.[20]

Another group which did learn of Campbell through Jones's

Harbinger, but which was not connected with the Scotch Baptists, was that led by John Davies of Mollington, Cheshire. At the age of sixteen Davies had become preacher of a church at Cox Lane, Denbighshire. On his removal to Mollington he founded two other congregations. In October 1835 one of the members brought news of Jones's *Millennial Harbinger*, which he had obtained from a Scotch Baptist friend in Chester, and the group were delighted to realize that they had brethren in America. Davies wrote to Campbell immediately, but it was not until October 1837 that they became aware of the other groups in England.[21]

Thus it can be seen that although the Scotch Baptist contribution to the new movement was crucial, it was not the only influence at work. Different groups were attracted by different elements in Campbell's work. What appealed to James Wallis in Campbell's writing was 'that the religion of Jesus is founded altogether upon the knowledge and belief of FACTS, instead of abstract influences and mystic operations upon the mind'.[22] John Davies was sceptical about the orthodox view of the work of the Holy Spirit in regeneration, and found Campbell's view more acceptable: the Teners were attracted by the Campbellite view of the design of baptism. All wished to restore a New Testament order. But apart from the split within the Scotch Baptists which did lead to a break of fellowship, many of these congregations did not feel precluded from enjoying fellowship with other Baptist groups which did not accept Campbellite principles. Each congregation was independent and could determine its own conditions of fellowship: this enabled them to envisage the achievement of Christian unity (in which they all firmly believed) in terms of a progressive broadening of fellowship until all man-made barriers were removed. This was after all a common evangelical view in this period, when denominational organization among non-Methodist dissent was only just beginning to appear.

IV

What held these diverse groups together? The answer lies in the magazine which James Wallis began to publish in March 1837, the *Christian Messenger or A Voice from America*; and this is also the explanation of the importance of the Nottingham congregation. As mentioned earlier, Wallis's first venture into publishing was Henry Grew's *Tribute to the Memory of the Apostles*. He had 1,500 copies printed, and 1,000 of them were in circulation within three months. As a result of this he received enquiries about Campbell's reformation from fifteen to twenty different places in England and Scotland. The Nottingham brethren decided that it was necessary to fill the gap left by William Jones's *Harbinger*, and so they resolved to publish a magazine to continue the work of publicizing the views and activities of the Campbellite movement. They estimated that they had material for four volumes, and significantly they added that whilst they wished the principles and practices advocated by Campbell to be widely known, they did not hold themselves responsible for them in every particular; nor did they wish to enter into controversy with their brethren on these subjects.[23] The reference to 'their brethren' here must mean that they envisaged their magazine circulating mainly among the Scotch Baptist churches. This is borne out by an examination of those who published it. The first volume of the *Christian Messenger* was published in London, Nottingham, Liverpool, Manchester, Leeds, Beverley, Leicester, Newcastle-upon-Tyne, Carlisle, Banbury, Huddersfield, Dunfermline, Stockton-upon-Tees, and Wrexham; and to this Edinburgh, Glasgow and Dundee were added for volume 2. Some of these publishers were the same as those who published Jones's *Millennial Harbinger*; most, if not all, were in towns where there was a Scotch Baptist congregation; and it seems clear that Wallis was able to exploit a Scotch Baptist circulation network for his journal.[24] It is no coincidence that booksellers were prominent in several local churches.

Most of the material published in the early volumes came from Campbell, including pieces from the *Millennial Harbinger* and earlier items from the *Christian Baptist* which Jones had ignored. There was also a series of specially written 'Letters to England', and the publication of the remainder of the Jones-Campbell correspondence, which clearly exposed the differences between the two men. Wallis took opportunities as they arose to clarify Campbell's views on the disputed points, and Jones's *Strictures on Campbellism* were answered.[25] In addition Wallis began to publish Campbell's works in England, beginning with the *Essay on Remission of Sins* (from *Christianity Restored*) in 1837, Campbell's version of the New Testament and the Owen-

Campbell debate on *The Evidences of Christianity*, both in 1839. The latter had the effect of converting one of the printers to Campbellism! In 1842 there followed the Campbell-Maccalla debate on *Baptism*, and the *Christian System* (the revised edition of *Christianity Restored*). A Welsh translation of the essay on *Remission of Sins* was published in 1840, the same year as the second edition of the English version.[26] Walter Scott's *Discourse on the Holy Spirit* was published in 1839 in an attempt to settle controversy on that matter, and a number of articles by Scott also appeared in the *Messenger*.[27] On the whole very little by Barton Stone, the other American leader, was published. This seems to have been due partly to the fact that Wallis did not receive Stone's journal at first: but a more important reason was that when he did receive it he found that Stone was prepared, for the sake of union, to advocate communion with Methodists, Episcopalians and Presbyterians.[28] Another early publishing venture by Wallis was his selection of *Psalms and Hymns*, published in 1841.[29] Though the sales of the *Messenger* were not equal to its costs, Wallis and his friends kept it going after the first four volumes had been completed because they had been encouraged by its success. From February 1841 Wallis had the assistance of John Frost, also of the Nottingham church, which was fortunate at the time of Wallis's illness later in the year.[30]

Through the unifying influence of the *Christian Messenger* the Churches developed in five and a half years to the point where in August 1842 the first Cooperation Meeting was held, at which some 50 churches were represented. This growth was due partly to the drawing in of the previously isolated churches mentioned earlier. John Davies of the church at Cox Lane, Denbighshire, corresponded with Wallis in the summer of 1837, and a letter from him was published in the *Messenger* for November 1837.[31] Davies was also made aware of the church at Wrexham led by Evan Jenkins, which similarly had no formal affiliation to any other Baptist group. Both were soon in contact with another church at Shrewsbury, which knew little of Campbell, but shared a similar ethos. Wallis discovered the little group in London, led by John Black, which also seems to have been an independent group, and one with distinctive views — for example, they held that the Lord's Supper should be celebrated on a Saturday evening, a possible link with early Seventh Day Adventism.[32]

Another group of churches came into being directly through

evangelistic efforts. One of Wallis's earliest visits was to Huddersfield, possibly on business; and a group began to meet there in August 1837 under the leadership of a Mr Stutterd, who, it was said, had been pleading for a reformation in the Baptist churches for more than twenty years. From Huddersfield further efforts were made in the West Riding and Lancashire, leading to the establishment of churches at Halifax, Delph, Cleckheaton and Bolton. Wallis's main efforts were concentrated in his own area. Work was begun in Newark in 1838 under the leadership of John Bell. In the following year a visit was made to Lincoln and Horncastle in July and August which led to the establishment of churches in these places and the winning of a Baptist minister, William Scott, for the cause. Scott subsequently devoted himself to evangelistic work in Lincolnshire, establishing further churches at Donnington, Louth, Spilsby, and eventually Hull in 1842. The Nottingham church, which had grown to a membership of more than 200 by the spring of 1839, purchased the old Barker Gate chapel from the Independents, and moved into it in September 1839. From Nottingham also a church was established at Loughborough in 1840, and in 1841 brethren were dismissed from the Nottingham congregation to form churches at Bulwell and Carlton.[33] In none of the places mentioned was the ex-Scotch Baptist element significant: in Newark and Lincoln Particular Baptists were the recruiting ground; in Yorkshire recruitment was often from various Methodist groups; and in Stockport General Baptists formed the main source. Further north, and particularly in Scotland, the Scotch Baptists were the main source, and this story is a more complicated one.

It is clear that the *Christian Messenger* circulated among Scotch Baptist groups, and in view of their divided state it does not seem to have proved any more controversial than other matters. Wallis made a trip to Edinburgh, Glasgow, Liverpool and Manchester in July 1839, and this must have been mainly among Scotch Baptist groups. Some had already been favourable — the church at Whitehaven, for example, was reported in April 1838 not to be afraid of Campbell's writings. Similarly John Parry in North Wales, a Scotch Baptist elder, appealed to his brethren to 'turn the word, the sword of the Spirit, against the enemy, and not against one another'.[34] Elsewhere conflict was more often found. John Briggs of Newcastle-upon-Tyne was forced out of the Scotch Baptist church, and began a separate Church of Christ, though he died within the year.[35] The battle was fiercest in Scotland. In 1837 J.B. Rollo reported from Ayrshire:

> The ancient order of things is gaining such rapid ground throughout the Connexion, that the old Elders who keep to the tradition of the Fathers, and who have long preached Calvinism, instead of the glad tidings of joy, blasting and withering the hopes of the self-abased and broken-hearted, are trembling for their 'Shibboleth'.[36]

But Rollo was too optimistic. It was another four or five years before it became clear that the advocates of the new position would have to leave the Scotch Baptists behind. In November 1841 Wallis reported that a correspondent in Scotland had remarked that the days of the Scotch Baptists seemed to be numbered. In 1842 a congregation at Saltcoats was cut off by the Scotch Baptists; reconciliation between the disciples and Scotch Baptists was shown to be impossible in Dunfermline; a congregation at Stevenson resolved to carry out the principles of the reformation; and a separate church was formed at Kilmarnock.[37] The decision to hold a Cooperation Meeting may have forced many to decide where they stood, for the Scotch Baptists never had any meetings or gatherings involving more than one local congregation.

In the 1870s William Thomson, a founder of the Church of Christ in Edinburgh, described his early experiences among the Scotch Baptists, and these may serve as a useful illustration of the whole process. Thomson was actually a member of William Jones's congregation in London when Peyton Wyeth made his historic visit, and learnt about Campbell from him. He pleaded unsuccessfully for reformation in London and, when he left soon after for Leeds, Jones sent a sixteen-page document to the brethren there warning them against Thomson; but they took no notice. Thomson subscribed to Jones's *Millennial Harbinger*, but gave up after a year when he realized that Jones was giving a false impression of Campbell. He then moved back to Edinburgh, where he found the Scotch Baptists divided on the question of celebrating the Lord's Supper without an elder present. He decided to join H.D. Dickie's congregation — the more 'liberal' one — not so much because he thought it right to break bread without an elder as because he thought he would have more freedom to study the scriptures. There he met James Stephen, an evangelist for the Scotch Baptists, whose contact with a member in Dumfries who had been in the States meant that he knew a little of what was going on. From him he heard about the publication of the *Christian Messenger*. As he absorbed Campbell's teaching he found himself increasingly suspect among the older brethren. Trouble came in 1839, when he and P.C. Gray (also of Edinburgh) visited Kilsyth at the time of the revival there, and preached that men should be baptized for the remission of sins. A Scotch Baptist elder from Glasgow preached about the need for faith, whereupon Thomson urged the company to obey Christ's command and be baptized. This led to a charge of heresy being laid before the elders in Edinburgh. After various vain attempts made by them to prevent his case being heard before the whole congregation (lest it start a public debate), Thomson was expelled by a small majority. He and Gray, who had separated from another congregation, thereupon began their own church, hiring a hall for holding meetings which they publicized with hand-bills headed 'The Ancient Gospel'. This was the beginning of the Church of Christ in Edinburgh.[38] The story that Thomson tells, although it clearly has an element of self-justification in it, illustrates only too sadly the truth of Campbell's criticism of the Scotch Baptists, that they were too apt to divide: as he sardonically put it in a letter to Wallis in 1837, 'They can make two churches out of one much more expeditiously than one out of two; and they grow incomparably faster in knowledge than in numbers'.[39] His explanation for this was that they desired unity in opinion rather than unity in faith. It has to be added with regret that Churches of Christ as they developed in Britain did not completely overcome the same tendency.[40]

There were other churches in Scotland that did not derive from the Scotch Baptists. Reference has already been made to the Dron brothers in Auchtermuchty, whose church dated back to 1809 and was formerly Independent (though the Dron brothers themselves had been Scotch Baptists). In 1838 a group of six brethren began to meet at Turriff in Aberdeenshire: their origin was quite independent of anything further south, though they were in touch with Wallis's publications. The great driving force in Fife and north east Scotland, however, came from Dundee. In 1839 George C. Reid, the pastor of the United Christian Church in Dundee — an independent evangelical congregation — was converted to the doctrine of believer's baptism. He and twenty-three others were thereupon baptized and formed a new congregation. It is not quite clear how Reid came to know of Campbell's writings, but it was probably through meeting the Dron brothers. He impressed the brethren so quickly that by April 1840, after a visit to Glasgow, J. Gowans was urging in the *Messenger* that he ought to be employed permanently as an evangelist.[41] Suggestions for the employment of evangelists had already been made earlier in the year by William Thomson in Edinburgh and E. Allenby at Lincoln.[42] Wallis's response on each occasion was to draw attention to the difficulty of raising money to support the work. He may also have been suspicious that this might mean a return of the one-man ministry system by the back door, particularly as the persons suggested had previously been pastors of congregations. Certainly other people suspected this. But G.C. Reid's dynamism soon began to make an impact. He made a ten-month tour of Scotland in 1840-41, followed by a five-month tour in 1841 which took in Carlisle, Chester, Wrexham, Wigan, Nottingham, Newark, Lincoln, Horncastle and London; and then in November 1841 he visited the churches in north east Scotland.[43] This gave him a first-hand knowledge of the state of the Churches in Britain, which even Wallis could not rival.

So from Banff in 19 November 1841 he wrote a letter reflecting on his experience, that decisively shaped the future of the British Churches. He warned the brethren against too much speculation on matters of secondary importance, referring particularly to the millenarian controversies; he urged the speedy election and ordination of an eldership in each church; and he urged 'a correct and co-operative plan for bringing out and continuing in the field of labour, efficient men to proclaim the glad tidings of salvation'. He considered two possible objections: lack of scriptural authority, and fear of an order of priests. The first objection, carried to a logical conclusion, would preclude even the circulation of the New Testament; and he referred to the fact that the Scotch Baptists were at death's door as a result of similar supineness. The second objection, he thought, could be met by asking the elderships at Nottingham and Dundee to work out a suitable system in cooperation with other congregations which felt able to support them.[44]

V

In April 1842 the *Messenger* included a report of a general meeting of messengers from thirteen congregations in Wellsburg, Virginia, held in 1834, as an example of the form which a Cooperative Meeting might take. This was the first time the title of Cooperative Meeting was used. Congregations of the disciples were invited to send letters 'stating whether they approve of the meeting or not, and whether, if approved, any of their number could probably make it convenient to attend'.[45] In the following month John Frost reported that the views of fifteen churches had so far been received, and all were in favour: and a letter from Reid was printed which heartily supported the idea but suggested that because of distance it might be better to hold one meeting in Nottingham and then another in Edinburgh. In June extracts from several letters in support of the idea were printed, and Frost noted that he had received only one letter against the meeting and upwards of twenty in favour. He also included a letter from a Scotch Baptist (place unidentified) saying that he did not think any Scotch Baptist church would take part, but he felt the idea ought to be supported in principle by individuals. In the July issue it was announced that several of the elders of the Nottingham church withheld their assent to the meeting taking place there, but that the elders of the church at Edinburgh proposed that the meeting should be held there on the third Thursday in August: Edinburgh was suggested because it was felt to be the most central and had the best communications.[46] (The main line railway network was, of course, still not complete.) Both the July and August issues carried articles by Campbell on 'Christian Organization', in which the duty of cooperative action was clearly stated.[47]

So on Thursday, 18 August 1842, some forty messengers from various congregations assembled in the South Bridge Hall, Edinburgh, for the first Cooperative Meeting of Churches of Christ in Great Britain. As well as the business meetings, the gospel was proclaimed each evening from Wednesday until the following Monday, and three were baptized as a result. Fourteen churches were represented by messengers, and eleven others by letter; and there were other brethren present who were not messengers but whose assistance was greatly appreciated. ('Messenger' was a traditional Baptist term for the representative of a Church.) John Davies of Mollington was appointed Chairman, and Peter Stephen of Dundee and John Frost of Nottingham were appointed secretaries. Statistics were collected from 43 churches, and a further 8 churches were noted as having sent no statistics. The total number of members reported was 1,233,[48] almost equally distributed between Scotland, and England and Wales. The eight churches which did not report, however, were all in England, and reference was made to other brethren in Wales of whom there was no exact account but supposedly totalling about 200. There were also one or two other churches, whose formation had been noted in the *Messenger* but which did not report at all — for example, the church at Carlton. The officially reported figure therefore is certainly an underestimate. By adding the figures reported at various times in the *Messenger* for the eight non-reporting churches, it is clear that they numbered nearly 200, so that with the other Welsh figures a total of 1,600 is easily reached.

Careful discussion took place on whether cooperation was justified, and it was concluded 'that if it is the duty of an individual congregation to do what they can in evangelising the world, it is equally the duty of the whole congregations to do it'. The first resolution, passed unanimously, was therefore:

> That this meeting deem it binding upon them, as disciples of Jesus Christ, to cooperate for the maintenance of evangelists to proclaim the gospel.

The principle behind this resolution has remained the foundation of the Association of Churches of Christ ever since. A committee of three was appointed to receive contributions for the support of the evangelists: Jonathan Hine, James Wallis and John Frost of Nottingham, with John Bell of Newark to act as treasurer. The other resolutions made it the responsibility of the leading brethren in the evangelist's church to advise the committee as to the needs of his family, so that they could be supplied; suggested that quarterly contributions be sent, each church being left to decide for itself how much it should send; laid down procedure for the selection of future evangelists; and made it the responsibility of the committee to communicate with the evangelists in making arrangements for where they were to work.[49] In the November issue of the *Messenger* an article by Campbell on the scriptural authority for contributing towards the support of men sent out to preach the word was included, with a note by Frost to make it clear that this was intended to clear away any remaining doubts about the scriptural justification for the Cooperative Meeting. He also urged churches to send in their contributions, saying that until this was done the committee could not call out several brethren upon whom their eyes were set. Next month several letters appeared from the churches which had contributed.[50]

By the end of 1842 therefore, Churches of Christ as they are known today were recognizably in being. The name as such was not yet widely used — New Testament Disciples, Christians, New Testament Reformers were all probably more common: but by meeting together at Edinburgh in 1842 the churches had taken a step towards a corporate existence which the Scotch Baptists never took. Their cooperation for evangelistic purposes also indicates that they had broken with the largely non-evangelical tradition of the Scotch Baptists. The reasons for this break are probably mainly personal. James Wallis, as a former Particular Baptist, would have fewer reservations about churches acting together in associations; G.C. Reid had an evangelistic drive quite different from the Scotch Baptist ethos; John Frost was an energetic young man and seems to have pushed the idea along in the *Messenger*. Alexander Campbell's role was to provide the scriptural arguments which enabled the action to be justified in terms of the restoration of primitive Christianity. It was a very cautious break, and as yet it was by no means final. These early years therefore show the importance of both the Scotch Baptist and the non-Scotch Baptist elements in the origins of Churches of Christ: the former provided a network for the spread of the new Campbellite ideas; the latter provided the stimulus of new groups also impressed by Campbellite ideas which made a new and separate movement inevitable. Both elements were indigenously British: the American influence came through ideas not people. Like the American movement the British churches were to have their tensions, but for the most part those tensions arose from domestic circumstances rather than American influences.

2 EARLY COOPERATION

Churches of Christ were born in a period of economic and ecclesiastical turmoil. The years 1836-42 were a time of economic depression and political agitation, culminating in the rise of Chartism. This was also a period of reform in the Church of England and the rise of the Oxford movement; it was a time when Methodism was increasingly racked by division and internal conflict, as nonconformity came to the end of the great membership boom which had begun with the evangelical revival. In a very real sense the beginning of the movement reflected the uncertainty and questioning of the time, and the hope that a new era might be beginning.

Some of the churches drew most of their membership from the poorer classes, and all of the churches drew some from that group. The congregation at Banbury had none who possessed 'much of the riches of this world'; the congregation at New Wortley, Leeds, reported in 1840 that their members were suffering from want of employment and the depression of trade; those at Bedlington said in 1842 that they were suffering much from poverty, because the iron works and the coal mines were all depressed together.[1] But fortunately there were others who, whilst not rich, were certainly better off. James Wallis was a draper in Nottingham: Jonathan Hine was a hosiery manufacturer and the Nottingham congregation first met in his warehouse. John Davies of Mollington was a surveyor and land agent, which made him unusual among Churches of Christ in having some links with the landowning aristocracy. These were men on the edge of the middle class. But they were essentially self-taught — as David King remarked in 1892:

> Our pioneers had no schoolmen among them and those added were like unto them. They were men of cloth and lace and leather, with here and there a 'commercial'.[2]

The commercial links of James Wallis gave him his opportunities for travel and evangelism. His annual visits to his suppliers in the cloth-producing areas of Lancashire and Yorkshire took him to the churches there; and his more frequent trips to his markets in Nottinghamshire and Lincolnshire were occasions to encourage the brethren locally. It is unlikely to be a coincidence that by the 1850s, just as the main line railway network was being completed, there were Churches of Christ strategically placed on a series of domestic trade routes. North Wales and Chester were linked to Liverpool by sea; and from Liverpool ships sailed via Whitehaven to Glasgow. Liverpool was also linked to Manchester by canal and railway, and thus to Yorkshire and the midlands. From Hull on the Yorkshire coast ships sailed to Newcastle and Edinburgh, and thence to Fife and Dundee, Aberdeen and the north east coast of Scotland. Ready access by sea was one of the attractions of holding the first Cooperation Meeting at Edinburgh. Liverpool, of course, was Britain's main Atlantic port at this time, having outstripped Bristol in the late eighteenth century. This was where the American mail came in; and this was where Alexander Campbell landed and embarked on his visit to Britain in 1847. Hospitality was provided for him by the local brethren.

With a background among small traders it is not surprising to find that there was little sympathy among Churches of Christ for Chartism and the violent politics of the industrial working classes. Henry Shaw of Huddersfield was unable to attend the Cooperation Meeting in Edinburgh in August 1842, because he had to stay at home and protect his warehouse from the Chartist riots.[3] James Wallis had a more practical objection to the Chartists: the nervousness over public order led to restrictions on all kinds of meetings, including religious ones:

> Since the Chartists, Socialists, and others have adopted a religious form of worship which altogether dispenses with the clergy, you cannot obtain a hearing in any public street without exposing yourself to the censure of the public authorities.[4]

But his remark also indicates that the movement was aiming at the kind of people who became Chartists — the literate artisans. The 'position and plea' for a restoration of New Testament Christianity was based on rational arguments. Articles in the magazines frequently defended the rational consistency and trustworthiness of the Bible. This was the foundation for the criticism of other Christian denominations: it was also the basis for the attack on Mormonism in the 1840s and 1850s, and on secularism in the 1860s and 1870s. David King followed the example of the Campbell-Owen debate and often debated with secularist publicists, including the two most famous in Victorian England, G.J. Holyoake and Charles Bradlaugh.

The love of public debate as a method of recruitment had two other consequences. One was that the people attracted tended already to have some kind of intellectual commitment: some were from a secularist background, but most came from other Christian denominations. Relatively few seem to have been converted to Christ for the first time. Sometimes indeed whole congregations of another denomination were won over. Not surprisingly the other denominations saw the matter differently: William McDougall was called a 'sheep-stealer' for baptizing a Primitive Methodist local preacher in Newcastle in 1848. The second consequence was that hostility from the clergy of other denominations (who were regularly attacked because they were paid for their ministry) often meant that it was difficult or impossible to hire public halls for meetings.[5] This made progress slow or difficult.

The early years were therefore primarily years of consolidation rather than dramatic advance. Indeed James Wallis's most significant achievement is probably the way in which he nurtured the tender plant of cooperation between the churches with a patience and a pertinacity that is quite outstanding. For although Churches of Christ rightly look back to the meeting in Edinburgh in 1842 as the beginning of their corporate existence, it was not obvious at the time that this meeting would have lasting significance. It was five years before another similar meeting was held, though the length of this gap was not intentional. It was decided in 1843 that nothing of sufficient importance had happened to justify another meeting; but the amount contributed for the support of evangelists had not come up to expectations, possibly because of the depression. Twenty-nine congregations contributed £150 in the first year, but £45 of this sum came from Nottingham alone.

II

Some of the obstacles to cooperation are revealed in a comment by Wallis, which had been prompted by a successful visit he had made to Halifax in April 1843:

> A more frequent interchange of brethren from different churches, and a more united cooperation of all the saints, regardless of our little selves, — of human opinions and dogmas, would have a great effect in promoting union among the disciples, as well as the more general spread of the gospel throughout the land. Some brethren cannot visit where the church does not use teetotal wine at the table of the Lord; others contend for the use of unleavened bread; others would not give a shilling for the support of the evangelists, even should the withholding of it prove the cause of thousands sinking into eternal perdition, lest, as they say, an hireling priesthood should be raised up amongst us.[6]

Here the problems which had always frustrated cooperation among the Scotch Baptists and the tendency for fellowship to be broken off on relatively minor issues are clearly seen.

But there was another problem too, which was to be debated in the Churches for a century. In November 1843 William Thomson, one of the evangelists, reported that people were beginning to feel that the evangelists moved on too quickly without staying long enough to build a congregation. In the following month G.C. Reid wrote a vigorous reply, arguing that local evangelism had no place in the New Testament and that such a system was bound to benefit the larger and wealthier churches at the expense of the smaller and poorer.[7] The reply may have had some effect as in April 1844 George Greenwell of Bedlington, one of the local evangelists criticized by Reid, was appointed as a third general evangelist and began work in Dumfries.

No Cooperation Meeting was held in 1844 either. In January Reid had written to Alexander Campbell on behalf of Wallis with an invitation to visit Britain to preach. Campbell replied saying that he was anxious to come, but would not be able to do so before the spring of 1845. Consequently the Evangelist Committee felt it wise to postpone a meeting until Campbell could be present with them.

By the summer of 1845, however, circumstances had changed considerably. The first change was the collapse of the system of cooperative evangelism. In the autumn of 1842 George Reid had contracted an illness which later developed into consumption. Despite this he carried on his evangelistic work until by the autumn of 1844 he was near exhaustion. He then resigned his position as an evangelist, and in April 1845 he sailed for New

York at the invitation of his son. He died peacefully in Milwaukee, Wisconsin, in January 1847 at the age of 43.[8] In March 1845 William Thomson resigned his position as an evangelist at the end of his tour of northern Scotland. Whilst affirming his conviction that much had been achieved since the Edinburgh meeting, he nevertheless questioned 'the propriety of taking a person from a congregation where he is doing good, as the loss sustained by the disciples in that place will not be fully compensated by the good done elsewhere'.[9] The Evangelist Committee sought the advice of the churches on what should be done next, and having received replies from 17 churches they suggested the formation of district associations to employ local evangelists. In September 1845 it was announced that George Greenwell, the one remaining general evangelist, would become district evangelist in Nottingham for the next twelve months. The final account of the Evangelists' Fund, published in November 1845, showed an income for the three years of £400, a quarter of which came from Nottingham. Only seven other churches contributed more than ten pounds.[10]

The other change was in the attitude of some of the British churches towards Campbell himself. He had already come under suspicion in the eyes of some when he founded Bethany College, even though he was careful to explain that it was to train evangelists and not pastors. Now there was a more serious objection: Campbell was accused of believing in open communion. When copies of Campbell's debate with the Presbyterian minister, N.L. Rice, arrived in England in 1844, some reviewers hailed his remarks on the importance of Christian union as evidence of a change of views. In May 1845 Campbell's own reply to these charges was published, and he stated that there was no practice of admitting unbaptized persons to communion:

> Professors of unblemished reputation, of Pedobaptist churches, are sometimes informed at our large meetings, *that we do not suppose all unimmersed persons to be absolute aliens from the family of God, nor are they absolutely excluded from any participation with us in prayer or in the Lord's Supper; on the contrary, if any of them take upon himself the responsibility, being satisfied in himself of his own baptism, to participate with us at a table which is not ours, but the Lord's, we have no power to forbid him, and would not withhold from him the symbolic loaf and cup.* But to make it a *practice* to receive such persons as members of our churches into regular communion, is a practice unknown to me in any one church in the Reformation.[11]

Campbell probably did not realize that his charity would be sufficient in the minds of some to constitute a 'practice'.

The subject of cooperation continued to be discussed in the pages of the *Christian Messenger* and in October the church at Nottingham invited others to join it in offering a definite invitation to Campbell from the British churches. The fuss over open communion may have convinced the Nottingham brethren that it would be wiser for the invitation to come from a church or churches officially rather than from private individuals, but they were fairly confident of a positive response, perhaps because of the visit Wallis and Frost had made to Liverpool, Wigan and Ireland at the beginning of September. When Wallis wrote to Campbell in January 1846 he was able to say that £170 had already been raised towards his travelling expenses by more than 27 congregations, which indicated that the communion controversy was dying down. He suggested four motives for the visit; the need of visitors from the U.S.A. to stir up evangelistic leadership among the feeble British churches; the hope for a system of closer cooperation between the churches; the desire for 'some bond of union and cooperation to be proposed, upon which all Christians can unite'; and the fact that sinners were perishing.[12] Because of family problems Campbell was not able to come in 1846, but word came in October that he hoped to be able to spend the summer of 1847 in Britain.

Whilst many seemed to agree on the necessity for closer cooperation, the diversity of opinion on the form that cooperation should take persisted, and was focussed by events in Scotland. In 1844 a division had taken place in the congregation at South Bridge Hall, Edinburgh, and other congregations in Scotland were affected. The cause of the division is unclear, though it is possible that it may have had something to do with speculation about the Second Advent. (The Baptist, William Miller, was the leading spokesman for the view that the Second Coming would take place in 1843-44. He influenced some of the Disciple leaders in America, and had quite a following in Great Britain too.[13]) In January 1846 a letter appeared in the *Messenger* from George Dron of Auchtermuchty saying that the leading brethren in Cupar, Dundee, Kirkcaldy, Perth, Newburgh and Auchtermuchty were convinced that cooperation was necessary to avoid the plague of schism. He referred to an article on 'Church Organization' by Campbell, which had been published the previous September, and suggested that 'all the churches of the reformation in our land' might indicate their approval of the suggestions made there on cooperation. In March 1846 representatives of the Fife churches met and agreed to adopt them for themselves. They read as follows:

> 1. Christian communities should cooperate in all things which they cannot so well accomplish by their individual enterprize.
> 2. As it is the duty of every congregation in any city or district of country to have respect to its influence upon the community in which it lives, being placed there as a candlestick; so it is the duty of all the congregations in any city or district to cooperate in accomplishing in that district, state, or nation, whatever they could not otherwise accomplish for the publication of the Word and the edification of the church.
> 3. To do this successfully, they must occasionally meet together, by deputies, messengers, or representatives, and consult together for the better performance of their duties. These meetings being voluntary expedients in matters of expediency, such persons have no authority to legislate in any matter of faith or moral duty, but to attend to the ways and means of successful cooperation in all the objects of duty before them.
> 4. Care, therefore, should be taken by all these churches to cultivate for each other the same kind Christian affections and confidence necessary to the cordial fellowship of a particular congregation.
> 5. When, therefore, any improper acts are committed by one congregation, affecting the moral or Christian reputation of a church, or when a church falls into a schism, it is the duty of the neighbouring churches, first by counsel and exhortation, voluntarily tendered, to correct those evils, and to prevent their consummation in alienation, estrangement, or separation; but in case of a failure to accomplish these ends by these means, then the church, desiring to be held in the fellowship of other churches, should refer herself to a committee of churches, the roots of bitterness or cause of discord and alienation existing each party, or all the members, as the case may be, obliging themselves to submit to such a tribunal as an end of all strife.
> 6. It would, therefore, be expedient that when a church actually falls into a formal schism and before these means have been resorted to, that neither party should be acknowledged or treated as a church by other congregations, until the case is adjudicated, and the matter of schism is either removed or fixed on one incorrigible party.
> 7. That so soon as one party is clearly ascertained to be an incorrigible faction, it becomes the duty of all other Christian communities to treat them as the leprous persons were treated under the law — as separated or cut off from the congregation of the Lord.[14]

Both Wallis and Greenwell (who was assisting him as editor at this time) were cautious about these proposals, and particularly the last three. Wallis was clear that cooperation was scriptural for the relief of distress and for the proclamation of the gospel: he also recognized the duty of discipline within the congregation, but was hesitant about the idea of a tribunal to judge matters of fellowship in a case of schism. He readily recognized the wisdom and prudence of counsel from sister congregations, but he rejected any suggestion that there should be brethren or churches recognized as supervisors of other congregations.[15] Greenwell supported him rather more trenchantly:

> We must either summon the universal church, which is impossible, or call a representative conclave, which is unscriptural and dangerous; or confine discipline entirely to single congregations, which is simple, Scriptural, and all-sufficient for every emergency.[16]

Further correspondence followed in subsequent issues, when it was pointed out that efforts at arbitration on the lines suggested had failed to heal division in Edinburgh.

Wallis's hesitation probably stemmed from his conciliatory nature, possibly from fears that similar schismatic tendencies would develop in Nottingham if these remedies were adopted, and almost certainly from his conviction that the scheme would not work. Doubt about the wisdom of the Scottish action may also explain why his proposal in May 1846 for a new scheme of evangelistic cooperation, to be launched at a meeting in Chester, was addressed to the English congregations: he noted that 'our brethren on the other side of the Tweed seem desirous to act by themselves'.[17] He was obviously disappointed that people still divided over matters of opinion:

> We have sometimes said, our Scotch brethren were the first to propose cooperation, union, and love, among all the disciples in these kingdoms, and also the first to divide — and that, too, on mere matters of opinion! From this fact it is practically certain, that some of those who profess to reject written creeds, divide about opinions and peculiarities, just as much as the creed-bound parties do — and the noble plea for the all-sufficiency of the Bible alone as a rule of faith and practice is dishonoured by the divisions of those who thus plead it.[18]

Wallis returned to the topic in May 1847, when he published a circular letter from the Fife churches 'to the congregations of the Disciples of Jesus Christ in the Reformation in Scotland'. This contained an account of a meeting in Auchtermuchty in March 1847 at which the resolutions of the previous year had been carefully revised so as to make clear that the right of other congregations to try to bring about unity and peace in a divided congregation derived not from any authority that one congregation has over another, but from the relationship in which they all stand to one another as members of the Body of Christ. It was pointed out that the term independency was not found in Scripture, and was incompatible with the unity and dependence of the body of Christ. Wallis commented that a scripturally ordered church with elders and deacons, possessing the Bible as a rule of life, had to settle its own affairs, 'even when in a state of dispute and strife, without any authoritative influence from other congregations'. He admitted that the term independency was not in the Bible — it resided with the Creator alone — but said that there was a voluntary self-government given to everyone, with which no-one may with impunity interfere; and the same applied to every scripturally-organized church and family on earth.[19] So Wallis put his trust in a system of rational individualism, with the Bible alone as the guide to matters of faith: it was an attitude entirely in accord with the rational philosophy of Alexander Campbell and the Scottish enlightenment.

III

Alexander Campbell, accompanied by James Henshall, arrived in Liverpool on Saturday 29 May 1847, where they were met by John Davies and others, who took them to Mollington. Wallis travelled to meet him there and an itinerary was arranged. Campbell began with addresses in Wrexham, Liverpool and Shrewsbury, and then travelled to London, via Nottingham, Derby, Newark and Leicester. He addressed audiences of 2,000 in the Mechanics' Hall in Nottingham — the Barker Gate chapel, which held only 800, being too small — and 1,000 in the New Hall, Leicester. The meetings in London were less successful, and Henshall complained that uncertainty was caused by a constant change of meeting places: he also regretted that the main audiences were composed of sceptics, a reminder that Campbell was mainly known in England through his debate with Robert Owen. After a week's rest the pair went to Banbury and then on to Manchester. This was followed by successful meetings in Huddersfield and Halifax, Sunderland, Newcastle and Berwick-on-Tweed. But in Edinburgh Campbell ran into trouble: he was trapped into saying that he did not believe that slavery was contrary to the Word of God and then found himself the target of placards from the Edinburgh Anti-Slavery Society, accusing him of being an 'abettor and upholder of manstealers'. The secretary of the society, the Rev. James Robertson, pursued Campbell with similar placards throughout his Scottish tour, and eventually sued Campbell for libel. Because Campbell would not give any security for his return from Ireland, he was imprisoned in Glasgow for ten days until his appeal to the Lord Ordinary in Edinburgh could be heard. The case was dismissed. A subsequent case brought by Campbell against Robertson was successful, but Robertson left the country before paying the costs. There is some evidence to suggest that this ploy by the Anti-Slavery Society was a deliberate attempt to distract attention from the real purpose of Campbell's visit and to discredit the infant Churches of Christ in Scotland. It was certainly an embarrassment to Campbell, and his visit to Ireland was curtailed as a result of his time in prison.[20]

The climax of Campbell's visit to Britain, however, was his presence at the second Cooperation Meeting of the British Churches at Chester on 1-2 October 1847. He was unanimously called upon to take the Chair. Forty-one messengers, representing 26 churches, were present and two other churches were represented by letter. In his preliminary remarks Campbell explained the purpose of cooperation. The Church of Christ was a community of communities, in which each church had certain obligations to its sister churches. The New Testament contained various examples of combined effort by the churches, particularly for the spreading of the gospel. He argued that the great and important subject to be brought before the representatives of the British Churches at that time was the ways and means for the effectual proclamation of the gospel. His answer was that:

> It can be done efficiently only by selecting qualified persons, entirely devoted to the work. None can excel in two businesses. Christ's work is also all-important, and ought not to be attended to as a merely secondary consideration . . . We must have then a valiant, a faithful, an educated corps . . . Let them be men mighty in the scriptures — men who can use the sword of the Spirit well. *Qualified* men. Men of *piety*.

The meeting unanimously resolved that the churches represented would agree to cooperate in contributing to the support of a general evangelist : £180 was promised. James Wallis, Jonathan

Hine and John Bell were again appointed the committee to carry the plan into effect. (John Frost, the fourth member of the original committee, had died in January 1846 at the age of 26.) Campbell was asked to select a suitable person from America to work in the British churches. James Wallis was urged to continue to edit and conduct the *Christian Messenger*, which he had said he would give up. Finally it was resolved to hold another meeting of messengers in Glasgow in September 1848.[21] On Sunday 3 October Campbell preached in Chester and Liverpool, and a special breakfast meeting was held in Liverpool on the Monday. Then on Tuesday afternoon about thirty friends accompanied Campbell and Henshall on board the paddle-steamer *Cambria*: when the bell rang to indicate that the ship was ready to sail, they shook hands and left in the small steam-boat, waving handkerchiefs 'till the showers from above and the mists from the sea' came between them. Alexander Campbell never visited his native land again.[22]

The 1847 meeting was a triumph for Wallis's beliefs about the nature of cooperation. Campbell's remarks from the Chair were concerned with evangelization rather than with matters of discipline and fellowship; though when pressed on that matter he did say that if a church received someone into fellowship who had been expelled by another church, that constituted renunciation of the other church as a sister church. The Evangelist Committee was reconstituted, though the hoped-for evangelist from America did not materialize. But the most important decision was probably the one to meet again in Glasgow a year later. A list of churches was also requested by the Chester meeting and published in November 1847. It contained 30 in Scotland, 39 in England, 2 in Ireland and 9 in Wales, making a total of 80. The membership was estimated at 2,300. Detailed figures collected in the spring of 1848 showed 85 churches with a total membership of 2,553. In five years therefore the number of churches and members had increased by about two-thirds, though it was to be another ten years before the 1848 figures were surpassed.[23]

IV

One of the main reasons for the halt to growth was the impact of another visitor from America, Dr John Thomas. Thomas was the son of an Independent minister (later a Baptist), who trained as a doctor in London. In 1832 the family emigrated to America and came into contact with the Campbellite movement. Thomas became a preacher and started a magazine called the *Apostolic Advocate*. Differences soon emerged between him and Campbell, particularly over millenarianism and the immortality of the soul. But the break between the two men was not final until 1847, when the followers of Thomas began to form the separate Christadelphian movement. Even then the loose structure of the Disciples in America made anything like a formal excommunication impossible: thus many Disciple congregations continued to receive him on his travels, even if they were aware of his split with Campbell (and, of course, not all of them were aware of it). As already mentioned, the interest of Disciples in New Testament Christianity often led to an interest in Prophecy and the Second Coming, though both Campbell in America and Wallis in Britain rebuked tendencies to make speculative interpretations of scripture binding.

In 1848 Thomas decided to visit Britain, prompted by the outbreak of revolution in Europe which was held by some to be a sign of the End. He obtained a letter of recommendation from a member of a Disciple congregation in New York, but he was already well known by repute in Britain. From its beginning the *Christian Messenger* had contained more articles by Thomas than any other writer apart from Campbell, though Wallis always added cautious footnotes to those on millennial themes. It seems that Wallis was pressed to include them by others and, like Campbell, he had a strong belief that truth would emerge from free and open discussion of controversial themes. When Thomas arrived in England, however, the officers of the church at Barker Gate declined to invite him to Nottingham, and Wallis warned his readers in July 1848 that Thomas had publicly abjured all connection with the churches of the reformation in the United States. Thomas replied to one of the Barker Gate officers that the British brethren had appealed to America for evangelists: Campbell had not been able to persuade anyone to come, but he had come of his own accord and offered his services for nothing. The congregation at New Radford, Nottingham, which had connections both with Millerite Adventists and Campbellites, immediately issued an invitation to Thomas to come and speak in Nottingham. Thomas also secured publicity through the columns of the *Gospel Banner*, which was a rival publication to

Wallis's *Harbinger** published by his former printer, H. Hudston. (Hudston had secured Campbell's permission to print his material when he was in England the previous year, at which time Wallis had been talking of giving up the *Harbinger*.) In this way Thomas gained access to both Millerite and Campbellite congregations and soon secured several invitations to preach.

When Thomas heard about the Cooperation Meeting arranged for September in Glasgow, he decided to go and secured a letter from the church in Lincoln nominating him as their delegate. At the meeting his credentials were challenged on the grounds that he was not a member of the church he claimed to represent. After some discussion the matter was referred to a committee, which reported by a majority of four to one that the church at Lincoln had acted injudiciously in appointing Thomas as their delegate. But the damage was done. His presence at the Glasgow meeting led to invitations to lecture in Glasgow, Edinburgh and elsewhere. Late in 1848 he returned to London where he wrote *Elpis Israel, an Exposition of the Kingdom and Age to come.* This led to some change of opinion among a number of the Campbellite followers. Thomas eventually returned to America in September 1850, but there is little doubt that the divisive effects of his two-and-a-half year stay weakened the movement in Britain. The Fife District Association at its annual meeting on New Year's Day 1851 noted that numbers had declined because of divisions and separations caused by Thomasite teaching. Thereafter the two movements grew apart and Thomas's followers took the name Christadelphians during the American Civil War. But attempts persisted by each to convert the other until the end of the century. David King, who had been involved in the original dispute with Thomas when he arrived in London in 1848, frequently lectured against the errors of Christadelphianism, and the fact that the two groups were often found in the same towns, particularly in the midlands, assisted this.[24]

The unhappy episode of Dr Thomas at the Glasgow meeting highlighted the problems of schism which the Fife brethren had discussed in 1845-46, but there was no attempt to persuade the meeting to adopt the kind of resolutions adopted in Fife. The nearest the meeting came to it was when it urged the divided Edinburgh congregation to seek the help of 'three or four

*The *Christian Messenger* became the *British Millennial Harbinger* in 1848.

brethren and wisdom and prudence' to bring about a reconciliation. In the columns of the *Harbinger* afterwards there was some
discussion as to whether the procedure could be improved. John
Davies of Mollington, who had presided at Glasgow, suggested
that it was unfair that decisions over the allocation of funds
should be voted on by all present, without regard to the number
of churches represented or the amounts contributed: he proposed
a scheme whereby only representatives of churches which
actually made contributions should vote on the allocation of
funds, and that the number of votes should be weighted in
proportion to the amount contributed. Davies doubtless noted
that only six churches had contributed to the Evangelist Fund in
1848. Wallis was sceptical about the suggestion, whilst J.B. Rollo
of Kilwinning was scathing in his criticism in the *Gospel Banner,*
saying it was an attempt on the part of the wealthy to keep control
of affairs. (Rollo was a pre-millennialist, and thus presumably
sympathetic to Thomas.)[25] When the Cooperation Meeting was
held at Sunderland in 1849 there was a preliminary meeting to
settle procedure: it was agreed to place John Davies's suggestions
before the meeting, but there is no record of their being acted
upon.

The Glasgow meeting in 1848 also urged the churches to
cooperate together in districts by periodic meetings for the
cultivation of unity and love and the promotion of evangelistic
activity; and it empowered the Evangelist Committee to assist
district evangelists as well as general evangelists until the next
meeting. The recommendation that district associations be
formed was repeated annually for the next few years, and became
more important as it became clear that general evangelists were
not forthcoming. Associations were formed in the north of
Scotland, Fife, London, and Newcastle by the time of the
Sunderland meeting, and the Lancashire Association was formed
soon after. The Nottingham Annual Meeting in 1850 commended the methods of evangelization employed by the
Lancashire Association, and also urged the churches to set aside
the offerings for the first Sunday in July for the support of the
General Evangelist Committee. When it was proposed to divide
the country into districts under a general board of management at
the Wrexham Annual Meeting in 1854, this was resisted by David
King and others on the grounds that much progress had been

made in the formation of districts under local initiative, and the proposal was dropped.

The early 1850s saw the gradual achievement of a consensus about the nature of the cooperation between the churches, and this was crystallized in the resolutions of the Annual Meeting in London in 1851:

> 1. That this cooperation embraces only the subjects of evangelization, and disclaims all intention of forming a body having power, or intention to receive or reject churches with reference to fellowship; and will receive messengers from any church recognizing the principles of our Lord — one faith, one baptism or immersion, one body, one spirit, one hope, and one God and Father of all, who is above all, and through all, and in all — and who attend to the positive institutions of Christ on the first day of the week. It also disclaims all power to hear or settle matters of discipline, or differences existing between brethren or churches.
> 2. That all churches wishing for union, have letters of recommendation from one or more sister churches; and that each church be requested to contribute, as the Lord may prosper it, not less than once a quarter, to the Evangelist Fund.
> 3. That all who are occasionally, or more constantly employed as evangelists, shall be recommended by two or more churches, besides those of which they are members, stating their qualifications and circumstances, that their necessities may be supplied accordingly.
> 4. That all churches not sending delegates to future Cooperative Meetings, be requested to send letters to such meetings, with an account of the number of members and officers, agreeably to a printed form, to be prepared and sent by that appointed Committee.[26]

The specific rejection of the idea that the Annual Meeting should judge or seem to judge questions of fellowship or discipline is clear, and doubtless the influence of Wallis was important here. But he continued to wish for a better and more comprehensive understanding of the subject of cooperation, as he wrote to Campbell in April 1853: and the context makes it plain that he was thinking about evangelism. The reason for his concern is apparent in an article like that of 'Adelphos' in the *Gospel Banner* for May 1851, which is entitled 'Evangelists weighed in the balance and found wanting' — part of a controversy which ran for most of the year on the question of whether pastors or evangelists should be supported by the church.[27] Despite his disappointment over evangelism Wallis's basic confidence in the good sense of the kind of cooperation adopted is reflected in his comments on the Wrexham meeting of 1854:

> Assuming no legislative functions, and abstaining altogether from any interference with the internal government of the churches represented, it was the subject of general inquiry what it was that had given to these annual assemblages of the brethren such a decidedly permanent character, the idea of their discontinuance finding no place. Every year, as the mere business duties of the conference became more and more matters of bare routine, the conference itself manifestly increases in vitality and power, and its continued existence becomes more and more regarded in the light of a positive necessity. The reason was rejoicingly discovered to be in the self-revealing power of the truth, unfettered, as it stands in relation to this movement by the clogging hand of human legislation.[28]

This was the confidence which lay behind mid-Victorian *laissez-faire.*

V

The year 1854 was nevertheless a turning point, though this was not apparent at the time. Since 1851 Francis Hill of Sunderland had been acting as an evangelist with the churches in Wales and in 1854 he was instrumental in persuading J.B. Rotherham, a Baptist minister at Wem in Shropshire, to resign his charge and become an evangelist with Churches of Christ. Rotherham was brought up a Wesleyan and became a minister in the Wesleyan Methodist Association after the division of 1848. Whilst serving in Stockton-on-Tees he first came across Wallis's *Millennial Harbinger*, but his conversion to a believer baptist position came as a result of reading Alexander Carson. This led him into the Baptist ministry in 1853. His conversion to the Campbellite position came on the question of the scriptural design of baptism and the relationship between baptism, regeneration and the gift of the Holy Spirit. Rotherham spoke at the Annual Meeting at Wrexham in 1854, explaining his change of views. After a brief stay with John Davies at Mollington, Rotherham took up residence at Newtown in Montgomeryshire in January 1855, and this became the base for his evangelistic work. In this he was assisted by Edward Evans of Llanidloes, who preached in Welsh whilst Rotherham preached in English.[29] Newtown was the centre of the Welsh flannel industry, but in the outlying villages the audiences addressed consisted mainly of farmers and their workpeople.

David King also made his first general evangelistic tour in 1854. King was born in Clerkenwell on 28 February 1819 and was converted under Wesleyan influences in the late 1830s, probably around 1837. In 1840 he first came across the writings of Alexander Campbell in a copy of Wallis's *Messenger*, but he did not make contact with the church in London until 1842. He was soon taking an active part in the congregation at Camden Town and further afield. In 1845 and 1846 he visited Maidstone to help establish a church there, and in 1847 he published his own *Bible Advocate* as a cheaper twopenny magazine than the sixpenny *Harbinger*. King was the main driving force behind the expansion of Churches of Christ in the south of England, but he was also a strong believer in district evangelism. This was made clear in his opposition to the proposals for a general board of management for evangelism at the Wrexham meeting. He was beginning to devote an increasing amount of his time to evangelistic work. From 1848 he spent Saturdays and Mondays on this, and in the early 1850s he was supported by the London Association on a full-time basis. His first preaching experience outside the London area had been in north east England after the Glasgow Annual Meeting in 1848, but in the spring of 1854 he agreed to spend three months in Fife at the invitation of the district association there. This was a sign of a new availability which was shortly to be exploited to the full.[30]

Lastly, 1854 was the year when plans were made to establish a new church in Manchester, a bold decision which indicated a new aggressive policy. At the Lancashire District Association meeting in Wigan on 12 November 1854, the association of churches at Ashton, Stockport, Halifax and Liverpool united with the Wigan churches. In the course of discussion on future plans Matthew Harvey of Ashton-under-Lyne said

> that as the next annual meeting was to be held in Manchester, it had occupied a good deal of his thoughts and attention whether some great effort could not be made for that city, the largest in Lancashire, and specially noted in the commercial, political, and religious world: and he was encouraged in these ardent desires by the consideration, that the matter was suggested by that last annual meeting, all the brethren in that meeting considering the desirability of making a great effort for Manchester, either at the meeting or previous to it.[31]

The proposal was warmly taken up and it was agreed by the meeting to raise not less than £200 to engage three evangelists to work together for three or four months before the Annual Meeting. Wallis endorsed the appeal in the *Harbinger*, saying that contributions could be sent either to Timothy Coop of Wigan who was treasurer of the district, or to the treasurer of the Evangelist Fund in Nottingham. In March 1855 it was announced that responses had been received from nearly 50 churches, and 33 churches had promised contributions amounting to more than £100. A committee of management had been appointed consisting of G.Y. Tickle of Liverpool, Matthew Harvey of Manchester, John Corf of Wigan, together with William Turner of Leigh and Timothy Coop of Wigan, who were secretary and treasurer of the District Association. Messrs Hill, Rotherham and King were engaged to work with George Sinclair, the Lancashire District evangelist, for an initial period of two months. Meetings began in the YMCA Lecture Hall, John Dalton Street, on 1 July 1855, but had to be transferred to Oldham Street Chapel after two days, because the YMCA withdrew permission for the use of the hall. (The reasons for the change of mind are obscure: it is possible that the Committee had originally thought that it was letting the hall to the Bible Christians.)

The Annual Meeting was held in Manchester at the beginning of August, and its report began by recalling that the original General Evangelical scheme had gradually been replaced by one of district associations; but now the new effort in Manchester had united the principal district associations in one grand effort. It was nevertheless agreed that the Nottingham Committee still served a useful purpose as a channel for the liberality of isolated churches and brethren, and as a reserve fund for district associations, so it was continued in being. There was general praise for the work of the Manchester Committee, and it was agreed to continue the work for a further three months with Messrs King and Rotherham. The accounts showed an income of over £160 with a balance in hand of nearly £50. Suggestions having been made in the *Harbinger* that a renewed appeal for help be made to America now that the Disciples' mission to Jerusalem had been suspended, a committee of four was appointed to draw up an address to the American churches in favour of sending evangelists to England.[32]

A church was formed in Manchester on 16 September 1855, and the Manchester Committee agreed to continue the work of

King and Rotherham until the close of the 1856 Annual Meeting and also to ask them to visit other churches in the district as often as they could. However, there were not sufficient funds to support two evangelists, and when difficulties arose at Newtown it was agreed that Rotherham should return there in January 1856 with the support of the Evangelist Committee. At the 1856 Annual Meeting, which was moved from Liverpool to Manchester, it was agreed, with the support of the London District, that King should continue in Manchester for a further three months. The request for evangelistic help from the American Christian Missionary Board was repeated, but it was pointed out that no evangelist from America 'in any way entangled in the subject of slavery' would be suitable.

In 1856 the churches in Scotland were strengthened by the adherence of Thomas Hughes Milner. Milner was born in 1825 at Springfield, Leith, seventh son of Dr Joseph Milner, a dispensing physician. Thomas's mother was Joseph's third wife, and had formerly been a member of the Haldanes' congregation in Edinburgh. Joseph died when Thomas was ten, and the boy joined his mother in her general drapery shop. He was converted and baptized at the Bristo Scotch Baptist church, Edinburgh, in 1842, and then joined a 'Morrisonian' congregation. When Francis Johnstone moved to Edinburgh from Cupar in 1846 to found a Baptist congregation with Morrisonian theology, Milner joined it, and began to preach in neighbouring country villages. He also edited a monthly magazine, *The Evangelist*, published by the Baptists. Difficulties arose in Johnstone's congregation in 1852 and these may have been connected with Milner, who was becoming increasingly critical of 'one-man' ministry. In 1855 Milner and his followers acquired Nicholson Street Hall and formed their own church. The numbers quickly grew, and in the summer of 1856 Milner was visited by John Dron of Auchtermuchty and James Ainslie of Dundee, who had heard about his work. As a result Milner was brought into contact with Churches of Christ. He planned a new magazine, *The Christian Advocate*, the first number of which appeared in January 1857, and was commended by a conference of messengers from the churches in Scotland, meeting at Cupar on 25 December 1856. Milner retired from business and devoted himself full time to church work. The church at Nicholson Street Hall first reported to the Annual

Meeting in 1857: in 1861 it moved to new premises in Roxburgh Place and the older congregation at South Bridge Hall united with it.[33]

Milner made a great impression on the Annual Meeting of 1857 in London, and it was suggested that King and Milner would make an effective evangelistic team. It was agreed that when King's extra time in Manchester was concluded, he and Milner should work together to establish a new cause in Birmingham, though in the end Milner was unable to go. It is doubtful whether Milner and King would have made an effective team, because both had strong personalities. Milner was more interested in preaching to the unconverted than King was: it was probably at Milner's instigation that the London meeting in 1857 agreed to recommend that brethren should stress the 'great fact of the love of God to man as manifested in the gift of his dear Son, as a propitiation for the sins of the world' in their preaching to the unconverted — a clear sign of Morrisonian emphasis. It is interesting that Milner never reprinted articles by Alexander Campbell in his *Christian Advocate*, and the magazine concentrated almost exclusively on Scottish news and events. His main difference from the older Scottish Churches of Christ lay in his views of cooperation and ministry. He was critical of associations of churches which had their own officers and funds: on these grounds he criticized the Baptist Association of Scotland in the first issue of the *Christian Advocate*, and he criticized the Fife churches in the same way in 1858. When a new system of cooperation between the Scottish churches began in 1861 with Milner as secretary, the eldership of the Edinburgh church was to act as the executive and the elders of other churches were to be corresponding committees; this was to ensure that the work remained in the hands of the office-bearers of the churches and to avoid forming 'any society apart from the churches'. Milner's attitude was clearly indicated in the letter he wrote to King for the Annual Meeting of 1861:

> Beyond the pleasure of seeing a few of the brethren, I have not yet got to see very much advantage in an annual gathering of two or three days. We have just arranged for a united effort at evangelization in Scotland, and have not thought it advisable to make a yearly congress part of the programme. I am for my own part very much satisfied, that the recognition of the eldership of the churches, instead of executive and corresponding committees, is the best way to attempt the work. But after all it is earnestness that must make the attempt successful.[34]

This suggests that the form of the scheme was a compromise with the views of Fife.

On ministry Milner was accused by King, in a phrase which was taken up in later discussion, of introducing a 'Plymouthian leaven' into the churches, because he seemed to suggest in his book *The Messiah's Ministry* that church members should themselves be judges of the gifts in ministry which they possessed.[35] King believed this judgement was the responsibility of the eldership. But King's opinion of Milner has been too easily accepted by later writers. If *The Messiah's Ministry* is considered as a whole, then it is difficult to see this view as a dominant one. What Milner has to say about the importance of evangelists and elders, and particularly what he has to say about the importance of training, makes it clear that in practice he was far removed from anything like a Brethren position, even supposing that King was right to describe this teaching as 'Plymouthian', which seems doubtful. Moreover, if King was right in believing that there was a disinclination to accept the leadership of elders, it seems unlikely that such a view needed Milner's support to make it popular; it is much more likely to stem from the cultural assumptions of an egalitarian, democratic approach to church life — a view abhorrent to Milner, King, Wallis and Greenwell alike, but nevertheless endemic in truly working-class nonconformity. It was the smaller, poorer churches that lacked elders — and perhaps needed them most.

In March 1858 King and Rotherham joined forces again to begin their work in Birmingham. There was a small church of four men and seven women. They hired a room in Cherry Street and began a series of meetings on the Manchester pattern, supplemented by open-air meetings in the Bull Ring. Encouraging progress had been made by the time of the Annual Meeting of 1858 which was held in Birmingham, when 37 members were reported. Once the cause was established Rotherham returned to Wales again, leaving King in charge. By the time of the 1859 Annual Meeting, also held in Birmingham, the membership had risen to 79. Towards the end of 1859 the Particular Baptist church in Bond Street, together with its pastor, S.J. Chew, decided to join the movement and the Cherry Street members united with them. But the union was short-lived. Chew was reluctant to become an evangelist rather than a pastor, and in August 1860 the church split and 129 withdrew to form a separate church. Chew remained at Bond Street.[36] Though Birmingham remained the centre of King's activities for the rest of his life, he continued to give assistance to neighbouring towns — for example, to the new church formed in Leicester in 1859 by James and Thomas Leavesley.

VI

In 1861 the Annual Meeting met in Leicester and this may be said to mark the end of the first phase of the history of British Churches of Christ. Its first action was to receive the resignations of Wallis and Hine as secretary and treasurer of the Evangelist Committee — Hine was now in his 82nd year. Both were thanked for their long and faithful service. The committee was reconstituted with a membership drawn from the Lancashire churches, rather than the eldership of a single church, and Timothy Coop of Wigan was to act as correspondent until officers were appointed. This represented a shift from the Nottingham-based origins of the movement to the more dynamic Lancashire area: Coop, in particular, wanted a vigorous programme of evangelism.

The second main action of the meeting was to redefine the nature and limits of the Cooperation. Three resolutions were passed which became in essence the constitution of the Association until the Rules and Regulations of the Conference were revised in 1911. Even the later revisions have only modified the details of the wording. The resolutions read:

> 5. That this Cooperation shall embrace such of the churches contending for the primitive faith and order, as shall willingly be placed upon the list of churches printed in its Annual Report. That the churches thus cooperating disavow any intention or desire to recognize themselves as a denomination, or to limit their fellowship to the churches thus cooperating; but on the contrary they avow it both a duty and a pleasure to visit, receive, and cooperate with Christian churches, without reference to their taking part in the meetings and efforts of this Cooperation. Also, that this Cooperation has for its object evangelization only, and disclaims all power to settle matters of discipline, or differences between brethren or churches; that if in any instance, it should see fit to refuse to insert in, or to remove from the list, any church or company of persons claiming to be a church, it shall do so only in reference to this Cooperation, leaving each and every church to judge for itself, and to recognize and fellowship as it may understand the law of the Lord to require.
>
> 6. That churches newly planted, and adopting the New Covenant order, and wishful to take part in this Cooperation, shall be placed

54

upon the list when proposed, and for that end approved by a General Meeting.

7. That in the event of division unhappily taking place in any church having part in this Cooperation, and the General Meeting consenting to examine the case, and declining further Cooperation with one or both parties until the breach be healed; and as all conferences and synods claiming power to control individual churches are unscriptural and evil, the decision of this Cooperation, in such cases, shall only relate to its associated action, and leave each church to determine for itself in all matters of fellowship and cooperation with the party withdrawn from.[37]

In view of the significance which these resolutions were later to assume, there was surprisingly little comment on them at the time. In the report it is simply stated that they were passed 'after much consideration' and there is no editorial or other comment either at the time or in succeeding issues. Milner makes no reference to the 1861 Annual Meeting in the *Christian Advocate*; and his disparaging remarks about the Annual Meeting in his letter to King have already been quoted. No representatives from Scotland are mentioned as having been present. The main changes from the 1851 resolutions came in the explicit disavowal of denominational status and the positive statement on the duty to cooperate with Christian churches outside the Cooperation. The 'primitive faith and order' is not defined in the 1861 resolutions as it had been in 1851, and the request to churches to contribute to the Evangelist Fund not less than once a quarter is omitted. Resolution 7 contains a more detailed statement of the Annual Meeting's attitude to divided churches than had been made before; and when the context is examined it becomes clear that the resolution is taking a stronger stand than had been taken before. Previously the Cooperation had simply disclaimed all power to hear or settle matters of discipline, or differences between brethren or churches. The power to *settle* such matters was still disclaimed in resolution 5, but resolution 7 clearly envisaged the possibility of such matters being heard and of the Annual Meeting itself reaching a conclusion on the view it took. The 1861 Meeting declined cooperation with two churches, one in Manchester and one in London, until they had settled the differences which existed between themselves and the churches from which they had broken away. What the 1861 resolution did was to make it clear that any such decisions of the Annual Meeting could not bind local churches, and this was affirmed

55

with the rather strong words that 'all conferences and synods claiming power to control individual churches are unscriptural and evil': these words were omitted when the substance of the resolution was embodied in clause 5 of the constitution of the Cooperation in 1911.

At the end of 1861 James Wallis handed over the editorship of the *Harbinger* to David King, who had been assisting him for some time. Wallis's health was beginning to fail and he was being urged to rest. It was a symbolic moment of transition, as both men recognized, for Wallis had been almost single-handedly responsible for ensuring the continued propagation of Alexander Campbell's writings in Britain after William Jones gave up. Now the object was different. The *Harbinger*, wrote King in the preface to his first volume in 1862, 'no longer exists mainly for the purpose of reproducing the thoughts of brethren who labour in distant lands . . . Brethren here speak through its pages'. King also reduced the price by a third — Wallis had always subsidized the magazine from his business, but King did not have other wealth to fall back on and therefore hoped to increase the circulation. There were other more subtle changes. Wallis's title had been *The British Millennial Harbinger devoted to the spread of primitive Christianity*: King's was *The British Millennial Harbinger devoted to the spread of Christianity as it was at the first and the defence and promotion of Biblical truth*. 'Primitive Christianity' did not have the same resonance as a phrase for King as it had for Wallis with his Scotch Baptist background. And there was a change in the cover text too. Since 1850 Wallis had put Revelation 14:6-7 (Campbell's translation) on the title page:

> I saw another messenger flying through the midst of heaven, having everlasting good news to proclaim to the inhabitants of the earth, even to every nation, and tribe, and tongue, and people; saying with a loud voice — Fear God, and give glory to him, for the hour of his judgment has come; and worship him who made heaven, and earth, and sea, and the fountains of water.

In 1862 King's text was Revelation 18:4 (A.V.):

> And I heard another voice from heaven, saying, Come out of her, my people, that ye be not partakers of her sins and that ye receive not of her plagues.

In 1863 it was his favourite text from Jeremiah 6:16 (A.V.):

> Ask for the old paths, where is the good way, and walk therein, and ye shall find rest to your souls.

Wallis's belief in New Testament Christianity would never have allowed him to use an Old Testament text in this way. King varied his texts from year to year until the format changed in 1875, but they are generally rather more 'sectarian' in tone than Wallis's had been. All this was part of the change in atmosphere that was coming over the leadership of the churches.

James Wallis died on 17 May 1867 aged 73. John Davies of Mollington had died in 1865 and Alexander Campbell died in 1866. The first generation of the Churches was passing. Paying tribute to Wallis, David King said that

> in our recently removed brother we have had not a merely devoted Christian but one who, in the providence of God, has been enabled directly, or indirectly, to promote a return to the faith, order, and discipline of the Church of Christ, to a larger extent than any other, living or dead, whose name has been enrolled with those, in this country, who during the last twenty-five years have pleaded a return in all things to the good laws and right statutes of the Apostolic Church.[38]

King praised him for his willingness to follow the word of God wherever it led, and for the way in which his work for God and the church was part of his business. He also remarked that Wallis was characterized by faith in God, faith in Christ and faith in the church — a significant trio. But, he added:

> His faith in the church was not a substitute for charity. He did not think that every man outside the church would go to hell. He had no doubt of there being Christians in the sects, but he knew they had no proper business there. He knew that their being there could not make the sects Christian, and also that a church of Christ is something more than a company of Christians. Hence when a party of believers call themselves a church and disregard the constituted order of the church of Christ, he was not prepared to recognize them.[39]

In his last sentence King probably took a harder line than Wallis. Certainly Wallis would have said that those who disregarded the constituted order of Christ were in need of reformation, but he seems always to have been open to them in such a way as to make it doubtful whether it is true that 'he was not prepared to recognize them'. He remained a friend of William Jones to the time of the latter's death, and seems always to have treasured hopes that the Scotch Baptists would join the reformation. He was also convinced that many of the churches of the reformation still had some way to go to attain the primitive order, especially in ministry. But from the 1860s for a generation it was to be the harder line of King that dominated the movement.

3 TOWARDS THE JUBILEE

I

Between 1861 and the jubilee of the Association in 1892 the membership of Churches of Christ increased more than threefold and the number of churches nearly doubled. It was a period of growing confidence, and it was dominated by one man who epitomized the new mood — David King. The corporate life of the movement developed, as the Annual Meeting took on additional responsibilities and new committees were formed. But it was also a period of controversy, particularly over the Communion question, and this led to separation from the American Churches. Indeed this was the period in which a distinct group of churches was formed as a result of work by American ministers. Nevertheless by the early 1890s there were signs of a more liberal mood emerging, which burst forth after David King's death in 1894.

The significance of the thirty years from 1861 to 1892 as a growth period may be seen from the fact that half the churches still in membership with the Association in the 1970s were founded during this period. In part the growth reflected larger churches: in 1892 there were 31 congregations with a membership of more than a hundred; in 1861 there had been 7; and the average size of churches rose from nearly 40 to just over 60. But there was also a change in the distribution of churches. Only about fifty of the eighty or so churches in existence in 1861 were still in being in 1892, which meant that two-thirds of the churches in 1892 were less than thirty years old: in fact, one third were less than ten years old. The period also saw a much more rapid expansion of the churches in England than in the rest of the British Isles: the membership in Wales actually fell. The areas of most rapid growth were the north east of England and Yorkshire, but these only accounted for about 15% of the membership. The real strength of Churches of Christ by 1892 lay in the Midland and Lancashire and Cheshire divisions, where nearly half the membership lived. The other area of strength was

Scotland which also had a membership just topping the 2,000 mark; but the notable fact about Scotland was the relative decline in its influence in the movement in these first fifty years. In 1842 half the membership reported had been in Scotland — a clear tribute to the Scotch Baptist origins of the movement: in 1861 rather more than a quarter lived in Scotland and in 1892 the proportion was about one-fifth. The reasons for this change are not clear. It is true that a significant number of Scots emigrated, but this was also true of England and there does not seem to have been disproportionate emigration from Scotland. The explanation probably lies in the fact that there were fewer evangelists working in Scotland, and none at all before 1859; but it has also to be remembered that nonconformity of all kinds found expansion in Scotland difficult, and the vast majority of the Scottish population were divided between the three main Presbyterian denominations: the Church of Scotland, the Free Church of Scotland and the United Presbyterian Church.

Nevertheless these years did see the opening up of several new areas. J.B. Rotherham served in Scotland as an evangelist in the early 1860s, working with Charles Abercrombie. Abercrombie was brought up in Airdrie, where he became a Baptist. After ten years in the U.S.A. he returned to Scotland in 1858 and became a schoolmaster at Drumclair, near Slamannan. Here he conducted a revival in 1859, with some eighty baptisms in this mining village during the year. He was brought into contact with Milner, who persuaded him to become an evangelist. Through his efforts much work was done at Drumclair, Bo'ness, Grangemouth, Bathgate, Armadale and Crofthead. Nevertheless the Scottish Committee was doubtful about the value of itinerant evangelists. In 1870 they remarked that if elders were more prepared to engage in preaching in neighbouring churches and there was an evangelist to look after visitation and other matters connected with church organization, it would be easier for the churches to be centres of evangelization. But this does also sound rather like a desire for a full-time ministry. In the 1870s work continued in the fishing communities along the Banffshire coast and James Anderson began work in the Slamannan District, where he was to spend most of his life as an evangelist.[1] Outside the towns miners and fishermen were the main source of support for the Scottish Churches: both involved movement. James Anderson wrote in 1912: 'Drumclair is in ruins, so are other villages at which I used

60

to preach. Pits do not last for ever; and the miners must move when the minerals are exhausted'.[2] This was to be true of other parts of the country too after the First World War.

In England, as has been noted, the main growth came in the midlands and north. In Nottinghamshire churches were established in the coalfield at Riddings, Underwood, Eastwood, Hucknall, Ilkeston and Selston. There were also new churches in Birmingham, Nottingham and Leicester. In Yorkshire churches were established in Leeds, Liversedge and Sheffield in the 1870s and at Dewsbury, Doncaster, Harrogate and York in the 1880s. Doncaster and York were railway towns, and there were also churches in Crewe and Swindon: the Swindon church was founded in 1892 by ex-Primitive Methodists who had joined the Church of Christ in York. In the north east churches began at Broomhill, North Shields, Blyth, Gateshead and Percy Main. A cluster of churches was founded down the north west coast from Carlisle at Aspatria, Cleator Moor and Workington. James Anderson, whose early life was divided between Lanarkshire and Cumberland became a member of the Church of Christ in Whitehaven, which was the centre for much of this evangelistic activity in the mining areas of West Cumberland. Further south the Furness churches were mainly a product of this period too. The church at Kirkby-in-Furness was originally connected with the Baptist church at Tottlebank, but separated when that church adopted open communion: it was discovered by the evangelist Francis Hill in 1854 and brought into the Cooperation. In 1874 William McDougall of Wigan conducted a revival at Kirkby, increasing the membership from 38 to 101 in two years, which led to the building of a new meeting house at Wallend in 1876. From Kirkby churches were founded at Askam, Lindal, Ulverston and Dalton. The church at Barrow had a different origin, having begun on Walney Island as a result of contacts with a fisherman from Whitehaven.[3] The development of the Furness peninsula in this period was again the result of mining, in this case for iron ore rather than coal. The remaining areas of expansion in Lancashire were around the towns of Liverpool, Wigan and Manchester.

In nearly all these places the essential method was the same. A group would be gathered by meetings held in a hired room, or sometimes in the open air. The topic for discussion would be connected with New Testament Christianity, sometimes taking the form of a debate. Usually there would be a small core of

61

members associated with a nearby church. If the meetings held by the evangelist were reasonably successful then a church would be established, and after a period in hired rooms, provided success continued, a chapel would be built. Not surprisingly this approach still tended to appeal more to those who already had some sort of Christian conviction. In the earlier period many had been Baptists of some kind: in the later period more seem to have come from Methodism, though given the numerical predominance of Methodism in English nonconformity this is perhaps not too surprising. In Lancashire in the 1850s there had been systematic attempts to capitalize on the internal problems of Methodism. Both William Turner of Leigh and Timothy Coop of Wigan were former Methodists. David King, also a former Methodist, attempted to draw on the Wesleyan Reformers in his Manchester campaign.[4] Methodism was an easy target in so far as it had considerable appeal among the kind of social groups, to which Churches of Christ appealed in general: and theologically Methodists having been led to conversion and study of the Bible could often be persuaded to 'follow the Lord more perfectly' in Churches of Christ. In this second period of Churches of Christ growth, expansion did take place mainly as a result of the conversion of individuals. After 1860 there were hardly any instances of whole congregations changing their denominational allegiance or of isolated congregations being discovered and persuaded to join the Cooperation.

II

The Cooperation was also changing. For upwards of twenty years there had only been one committee — the General Evangelist Committee — and in 1861 the object was defined as evangelization only. But as David King remarked in 1874, 'the truth is, that our general cooperation, with its yearly meeting, fund, and committee, is a growth, and is still growing'.[5] Twelve years later Alexander Brown in his Chairman's address compared 1886 with 1866 by naming 'a few things now prominent which were then entirely absent':

> We had then no Reference Committee, no Reporting Committee, no Social Meeting Committee, no Training Committee, and no Publication Committee . . . Again, we had then no Sunday School Conference, no Temperance Meeting, and no Sisters' Meeting. If the

numbers were deducted that have come chiefly for these three, there would be a felt reduction, in every way, of our present gathering. Again, we had no Annual Meeting Paper, occupying a whole afternoon in delivery and discussion; and we had little of the present complete arrangements to utilise the services of visiting brethren in holding forth truth before others.[6]

Significantly 1886 was the year of publication of the first *Year Book*, thanks to the initiative of John Crook, secretary of the General Evangelist Committee and the organizing genius of the last quarter of the century. The *Year Book* grew out of the Annual Meeting supplement of the *Christian Advocate*, first published in 1884.

The crucial decade for these changes was the 1870s. The Reference Committee, first appointed in 1871, was set up to do three main things: firstly, to consider new applications for evangelistic help and make recommendations to the Annual Meeting; secondly, to consider 'all communications addressed to the Annual Meeting by districts, committees, societies, persons, or churches other than those churches recognised by the last Annual Meeting'; thirdly, to consider any matters of difficulty referred to it by the Annual Meeting.[7] The first function picked up a task performed by an *ad hoc* committee since 1869: the second and third functions recognized the fact that applications for recognition as churches on the List sometimes arose from divisions in existing congregations. This was always a delicate matter, despite the attempt in the 1861 resolution to disclaim judgement in matters of fellowship between churches. The Reference Committee consisted of the Evangelist Committee with certain additional members. Its size gradually increased, until it was abolished and its functions transferred to the Central Council in 1942.

The establishment of the Reference Committee was the most obvious example of a number of changes which facilitated the conduct of business at the Annual Meeting. In 1866 J.K. Tener presented the Minute Book. The election of the Chairman and Vice-Chairman also became less of a spontaneous decision at the beginning of the Meeting, being first passed to the Reference Committee in 1880, and then being conducted by ballot of the whole conference from 1888. From 1877 the Reference Committee was appointed a year in advance, and expected to prepare their recommendations, as far as was practicable, before the Annual

63

Meeting began. Much of the initiative for this smoother organization came from John Crook and he prepared the first compendium of Rules and Regulations. By a resolution of 1880 it became a duty of the secretary of the General Evangelist Committee to keep this up to date. In 1878 a Reporting Committee was appointed to prepare a report of the proceedings for the magazines.[8]

The Evangelist Committee itself underwent a series of changes in these years. At the beginning of the period there was still some suspicion of the committee in certain places. Robert Dillon reported on a visit of David King to Bath in May 1862 and added:

> The journey of our dear brother has been doubly prosperous, seeing that he has removed by his plain scriptural teaching, that kind of Plymouthian prejudice which previously existed against organized evangelistic co-operation . . .[9]

King expressed his own understanding of the relative roles of committee and evangelists later in the year when he wrote that

> The evangelist may receive advice from individuals, churches, or committees, but, as he is responsible to the Lord, those who advise may not command.

The Committee, however, belonged to the region of expediency not scriptural requirement: its task was to collect and disburse funds for the support of evangelists, but not to arrange and supervize their work.[10] The report of the Committee for 1863 actually suggested that it be empowered to guide the evangelists in the locality and duration of their labours, and it was probably this which led King to say that he could not engage himself to the Committee or the Meeting for the year following, but that the recommendations of each would receive 'his careful and prayerful consideration, and have in the formation of his decisions considerable weight'.[11] When in 1869 the Annual Meeting resolved by a majority of five to recommend him to work in Liverpool for the next year, he resigned his connection with the Committee and took up an appointment as evangelist with the Birmingham District Association which had been formed for this purpose.[12]

An article in the *Harbinger* for April 1866 suggested that there would be many advantages if evangelists were located in districts rather than travelling far and wide over the country, as the

Birmingham church had proposed in its letter to the 1864 Annual Meeting. In the next few years several district associations were founded: Nottingham, and Cumberland in 1866, Lancashire, Yorkshire and Cheshire in 1868, Birmingham in 1869, and a separate Yorkshire District in 1872. In 1873 the Evangelist Committee report raised the question (often discussed before and after) as to whether longer periods of service in one place by evangelists might be more effective, and to this end the Annual Meeting resolved to form districts for evangelistic effort (renamed divisions in 1874). Scotland, which had had its own Annual Meeting since 1861, was regarded as a division and five divisions were created in England — the Southern, Midland, Yorkshire, Lancashire and Cheshire, and Northern (subsequently divided into North East and North West).

In 1875 the divisions were encouraged to engage their own evangelists were funds allowed, leaving the General Committee responsible for breaking new ground and assisting weak districts. The General Committee was reconstructed in 1877, so that it had three or more members from one locality, and consulting members from each division: eight were appointed in the first instance. Discussion continued on the relative merits of district and general evangelism, with the evangelists, not surprisingly, expressing a preference for longer stays in one place. Bartley Ellis, supported by James Grinstead, suggested a three-year placing on the Methodist model in 1880: but David King steadfastly opposed any tendency towards centralization, perhaps more vehemently now than twenty years earlier because of the problem of relations with the American Churches. (One American response to British criticisms of their practice over communion had been to criticize the British Annual Meeting as a body with ecclesiastical power.)[13]

In the long run, however, the changes in the roles of evangelists and the Evangelist Committee were implicit in the expansion of the Churches. In 1861 there were three evangelists: in 1892 there were fifteen receiving a salary from the G.E.C. In the hands of John Crook the organization of and the publicity for the Committee had been considerably improved: quarterly reports from the Committee had been introduced, which supplemented the reports sent in from churches. The other change in the later 1880s was a rising concern for aggressive evangelism, which will be discussed at the end of this chapter.

III

The work of the Evangelist Committee led to interest in two other directions: building chapels for new or growing congregations, and training evangelists to gather new congregations. Both raised the question of the extent of cooperation and the form it should take, but the answers produced were, for the rest of the nineteenth century at least, different. One of the signs that Churches of Christ were coming of age in the 1860s and 1870s was the increasing number of new chapels being built. The churches were moving out of hired halls and cottage meetings into chapels of their own. In 1864 the Wakefield church raised the question of a committee to gather funds for chapel building, and a committee was appointed to investigate the matter, including the problem of trust deeds.

The committee reported in 1866. The main problem it found was that any scheme whereby the chapel property was held by trustees required a trust deed with a definition of the religious views held by the body concerned. This they judged awkward because of the general opposition of the brethren to creeds and the strange interpretations given to doctrinal statements in the law courts. Two alternatives remained which avoided the necessity of a trust deed: leasing a chapel from a private individual who had been induced to build it, or leasing a chapel from a group of shareholders which could consist of members of the church, or neighbouring churches, in their private capacities. The former possibility they thought unlikely to happen frequently (although seven of the sixteen churches which supplied information were in this position), and so they were inclined to recommend the shareholder pattern (already followed in Manchester and Birmingham) as the most feasible.[14]

In 1872 the Evangelist Committee recommended the formation of a Chapel Building Committee to examine plans with a Loan Fund to assist the churches, and the Annual Meeting commended the suggestion to the churches. As a result of this in December 1873 a Lancashire Chapel Building Fund was established, and the 1874 Annual Meeting recommended that it be extended to the whole country, proposing that its trust deed be discussed clause by clause at the Annual Meeting of 1875.[15] In July 1875 David King wrote an article on the Chapel Building Fund in the *Ecclesiastical Observer* in which he criticized three features of its constitution: its doctrinal statement; the stipulation that a church whose membership fell below ten could be required to hand over the chapel to the Fund; and the fact that the Fund was controlled by its subscribers rather than, say, the Annual Meeting. The last point revealed a characteristic voluntaryist suspicion of anything which looked like becoming an endowment in private hands, but whilst King avoided making any judgement on the desirability of a doctrinal statement it was fairly clear that this would be the main point at issue. His way of summing up the significance of the previous year's resolution was calculated to rouse feeling: 'We are, then, to be invited next August, to compile a creed, which shall go forth as accepted by the Annual Meeting.'[16]

At the Annual Meeting the Lancashire Committee withdrew its offer to extend the scheme, but said it would be glad for the doctrinal statement to be discussed: the Meeting, however, preferred to proceed to the next business. The Annual Meeting did not assume responsibility for a Chapel Building Fund until 1923: it did, however, in 1876 give the General Evangelist Committee the job of investigating appeals from churches for money for chapel building before they were commended to the brotherhood generally. This reversed an earlier decision of 1870 that the Annual Meeting should not be involved in such appeals.[17]

The question of training evangelists led to a rather different answer. In 1856 after the beginning of the new work in Manchester the Annual Meeting asked the Evangelist Committee to circularize the churches to discover whether there were any potential evangelists who might benefit from working with a more experienced evangelist to give them experience and confidence to work on their own. But nothing seems to have resulted from these enquiries. In November 1863 T.H. Milner wrote an article in the *Christian Advocate* suggesting the establishment of an education fund: a letter of support appeared in August 1864 and by the time of the Scottish Conference in July 1865 four or five people had indicated their willingness to train. The Conference agreed to set up a fund and place it under the control of the executive.[18] Also in July 1865 David King published the second of two articles on 'The Harvest and the Labourers' in which he referred to the need for more evangelists and offered to train any who wished to offer themselves. There was no immediate response. When, however, T.H. Milner died in 1866, the Scottish Conference agreed to merge its education fund with King's. King was present at the Conference and able to explain how it would be used. As a result John Strang moved to Birmingham in September 1866 and stayed for a year. Daniel Scott joined him in December 1866. Both had previously worked with Charles Abercrombie in Scotland under the terms of Milner's scheme.[19]

Both Milner and King were suspicious of college-training, partly because of the stories circulating about developments in America, but mainly because they regarded it as unnecessary. They argued that there already existed adequate institutions for a secular education, and for specifically evangelistic work practical experience was best. David King described the course of instruction in 1867 as follows:

> English Grammar and Composition at the Midland Institute, under highly qualified instructors. Reading under the guidance of a competent Brother. House Visitation and exchange of Tracts weekly. Topical Study of the Doctrine of Christ and the Apostles. Each is required to classify the entire testimony of Scripture on the topic in hand as, *faith, repentance, baptism, election* &c, &c. Mutual Instruction class for reading and speaking, in which each is called upon to point out errors and defects in language, manner, and matter. Public preaching and exhortation, with subsequent private examination and correction in regard to the same. Preaching in-doors and out in the neighbouring places without such oversight. It is not intended to include either Greek or Hebrew. Not that the study of the languages of Original Scripture is deemed unimportant, but because brethren coming here are likely to be far behind in other respects and not likely to remain long enough to compass more than above indicated, to which, where the time will allow, there should be added considerable attention to the Evidences of Christianity and Church History.[20]

Joseph Adam from Dundee was the next student to arrive in January 1869 and he completed his training in 1870. T.K. Thompson of Leicester was the first Englishman to go for training under the new scheme in 1871.

The question of training for evangelism illustrates the wider problem of attitudes to culture. In 1871 the Annual Meeting resolved 'that it is desirable that some effort be made to attract to New Testament ground, more than has hitherto been done, men of education and culture'. The idea behind the resolution was to get someone to write scholarly articles in first-class periodicals which would reach the educated classes, but it was taken by some who were not at the Meeting to involve the risk of accommodating the gospel to the wise and wealthy. George Collin, G.Y. Tickle's brother-in-law, who never did have much time for books, attacked the resolution for seeking to appeal to a particular social class. It is interesting that David King, although he never tired of criticizing college education, defended the resolution and criticized the careless use of 1 Cor. 1:27:

> Some men quote this text and preach foolish things enough to confound the wise, could they be thus confounded; but the result is not gained and the wise are merely disgusted. God's 'weak things' include strong men, who so use and set forth His truth that strong philosophers are humbled.[21]

It was for this kind of reason that King spent so much time debating with secularists: and he, and George Greenwell, used the columns of the *Harbinger* and the *Observer* to criticize the work of Darwin, Renan, Strauss and others, carefully examining the extent to which the evidence available supported the conclusions drawn.

The idea of a training institution, however, continued to be advocated. Joseph Adam suggested one in 1871 and Bartley Ellis did the same in 1875, giving as one argument that provision needed to be made for 'persons of education in our midst'. On each occasion David King added a note to the effect that he wanted nothing to do with a college, and he was particularly critical of Ellis's plea for the educated children of well-to-do members, suggesting instead that they ought to become evangelists.[22] It is not surprising therefore that the committee appointed by the Annual Meeting in 1874 'to consider and, if possible, to prepare a scheme for a permanent training institution' for evangelists did not report. The committee, with one change, was reappointed in 1875 'to mature a plan for the better training of preaching brethren'. Its report was unanimously adopted in the following year. The objects of the scheme were to train those who wished to devote themselves wholly to the work of evangelization and also to train brethren of proven ability who wanted to improve their usefulness, while following their ordinary calling. The instruction was to vary with individual requirements, and generally followed the pattern already established by David King. G.Y. Tickle, in a paper submitted to the committee, argued that the plan for a college was utopian, given the present state of the Churches, but in any case, he said, the place for training evangelists was the church, not an institution of human devising. The Annual Meeting appointed an Evangelist Training Committee to supervize the scheme in 1876.[23] David King trained Lancelot Oliver and John M'Cartney (both later involved in training work) under the new scheme in 1878-79, and in 1879 Alexander Brown conducted a training class while he was evangelist at Bedlington. His removal to Glasgow in 1880 limited the training resources at the committee's disposal, and the work of the Training Committee was handed over to the Evangelist Committee for two years. In 1882 a new Training Committee was appointed, but it had to report in 1883 that it had not been able to accomplish anything. David King no longer had time to train students and Alexander Brown, though willing to undertake the work, was not able to make suitable arrangements with the committee. A new committee, consisting entirely of Scots, was appointed in 1883, and engaged Alexander Brown and Lancelot Oliver to conduct the work. Apart from breakdowns in health Brown remained responsible for training until his death in 1893, with the periodic assistance of Lancelot Oliver who succeeded him.[24] Unlike chapel building, therefore, the training of evangelists became a direct responsibility of the Annual Meeting.

The other work which began directly through the Annual Meeting in these years was publishing. In 1883 the Charles Henry Street church, Birmingham, drew attention to the need for cheap copies of the movement's publications, which tended to be rather expensive because they were imported from America. But, due to an oversight, the schedule was not forwarded to the Annual Meeting. It was submitted in 1884, and a committee was set up to consider the matter. Its report was adopted by the Annual Meeting of 1885, when the cooperation was extended to include publishing. A Publications Committee, standing in the same relation to the Annual Meeting as the Evangelist Committee, was appointed, consisting of five brethren from Leicester and seven consulting members. A proposal for a trust fund for the committee with a trust deed had been submitted and rejected — another sign of pure voluntaryism. The first items published by the committee were a tract, *Sincerity seeking the Way to Heaven*, J.W. McGarvey's *Commentary on Acts* and Moses E. Lard's *Commentary on Romans*. The latter two were offered for sale at 3/- each (in cloth): in 1879 King had been charging 6/- for

70

McGarvey and 13/- for Lard in the American editions.[25] The committee's reports in the first few years show that interest was not as great as has been hoped: in 1890 the committee suggested that its work be transferred to the new Magazine Committee, but the Annual Meeting rejected the suggestion. Eventually in 1905 the Publishing Committee took over the work of the Magazine Committee.

IV

The other extensions of cooperative work all began with initiatives from outside the Annual Meeting. The most important of these was Sunday School work. At the invitation of a group of members in Birmingham a Sunday School Conference was held in Birmingham on Sunday and Monday 20-21 November 1865.[26] Sunday schools had existed in a number of churches for many years, but there was some doubt as to whether they were scriptural, particularly if secular education was a primary component. In his editorial for January 1870 David King foresaw the need to remodel the Sunday Schools in the new educational era presaged by the Education Bill:

> We shall gather children to teach them the way of salvation, and not, as now, do the work of the nation by imparting the first elements of common school learning.[27]

Joseph Adam wrote a letter from Leicester, published in April 1871, in which he suggested a Sunday School Conference, either separately or with the Annual Meeting, and a year later when the Annual Meeting was held in Leicester the local Sunday School teachers invited others to join them in a conference which was held every morning from 7.00 to 8.00 a.m. In 1873 the Conference asked David King to alter *The Sunbeam* (a children's monthly magazine begun by T.H. Milner in 1857, which he had taken over on Milner's death) to make it more useful for Sunday School purposes. King also responded to the request of the 1874 conference to produce a new Sunday School hymn book. In 1876 a Sunday School Committee was appointed to plan the conference for the ensuing year and handle business connected with Sunday School work.

The first Sunday School statistics collected in 1873 showed that 45 churches had schools and 33 did not: there were 406 teachers and 2,884 scholars (1,814 of whom were under 14); 289 scholars were members of the church, 91 of whom had been baptized during the preceding year. In the same year there were 107 churches on the list, and 82 of them reported a membership of 4,115. From 1875 notes on the International Series of Sunday School lessons began to appear in the *Ecclesiastical Observer*, and this led to the publication from 1877 of suggested bible readings for church services on Sunday as well. The Sunday School work grew steadily in size and importance. In 1887, when the work was transferred to the superintendence of the Annual Meeting there were 100 schools with 1,009 teachers and 9,131 scholars, roughly three times the numbers 15 years earlier. Church membership had doubled in the same period. The Sunday School Committee regarded 'this extension of the Annual Meeting as a formal recognition of the true place of Sunday Schools among the evangelizing agencies of the Churches'.[28]

The same recognition was not so readily accorded to the other two separate meetings which sprang up alongside the Annual Meeting. These were the Sisters' Meeting and the Temperance Meeting, both of which were held for the first time during the Annual Meeting at Huddersfield in 1880. The Sisters' Meeting was less controversial and may be considered first. It began with a memorandum on a rough slip of paper, which was sent up to the Chairman and read at the close of the business session on Thursday afternoon. The memorandum read:

> Impressed with a feeling which has arisen during the Annual Meeting that the sisters from the various Churches should have had, at some suitable interval, a conference as to their own ability to help forward the Lord's work, at which they could have stimulated and interested each other with account of efforts made in various towns, we invite all the sisters, who feel interested in having such a conference another year, to meet together in the Ladies' room at six o'clock this evening.

It was signed by nine ladies, with Sarah Black of Chelsea, a daughter of James Wallis, as the secretary *pro tem*. The meeting was duly held. Mrs King was invited to preside and Mrs Black gave an account of the work done by women in Chelsea: others added their own experiences, Mrs Mary Tickle of Liverpool was appointed corresponding secretary.[29] These Annual Sisters' Conferences very quickly became successful: over a hundred attended the second at Manchester in 1881, where Louise King told them that 'Woman's star is now somewhat in the ascendant' and said that the new positions being taken up in society should find their parallel in the Church.[30] Mrs King continued to preside at the Conference until the death of her husband in 1894, after which she rarely left Birmingham.

That women's work could be a matter of controversy as well as congratulation was shown in 1889 when Sydney Black read the Conference paper on 'The Position and Work of Sisters in Evangelization'. With characteristic verve, which still makes th paper exciting to read today, he swept aside the traditional texts about women being in subjection and keeping silence, and stated his conviction that the Churches

> are losing incalculable blessing and power by keeping our beloved sisters in such an unscriptural and senseless position. We must . . . get them out of that 'Sisters' Corner' to which they have been consigned in the *Christian Advocate*, and that right speedily![31]

The speakers in the discussion, who included Joseph Adam, Bartley Ellis, R.K. Francis, George Collin and David King, were critical of the extreme position which Black had taken up. The paper was printed with an explanatory footnote lest it be thought that it represented the views of the Churches as a whole; and David King wrote that it should not have been printed in the *Year Book* 'as not in its main contention harmonizing with our faith and order'.[32] It was not until the 1900s that views like those of Sydney Black began to be adopted by any number in the Churches. The Sisters' Committee was not given equal status with other committees until 1937, although women became eligible to sit on other committees when Miss L.K. Dawson was elected to the Sunday School Committee in 1903.

The Temperance question was controversial not so much because there was disagreement in the Churches over teetotalism, but because there was disagreement about adding to the tests of fellowship prescribed in the New Testament. Not surprisingly the main protagonist here was David King. In 1863 there was discussion in the columns of the *Harbinger* over whether someone engaged in the sale of intoxicating drinks could be a deacon or pastor in the church, and whether a church member could hold office in a Temperance society. King was inclined to say that selling drink was only an obstacle to church membership if the person concerned kept a public house or a beershop. But he was quite clear that a Christian should not belong to a

Temperance society because it involved being joined with unbelievers and implicitly suggested that a Christian could have other loyalties than the Church. The only Temperance society he would approve was one confined to church members, and that he thought unnecessary.[33] It was clear that his attitude surprised people.

The first temperance resolution passed by the Annual Meeting came in 1868, when a resolution in favour of Sunday closing was passed in response to a memorial from the Central Association for Stopping the Sale of Intoxicating Liquors on Sundays. In 1869 the Annual Meeting urged all church members to abstain from intoxicating drinks and advised church officers to provide unfermented wine at the Lord's Table. In 1871 a general resolution supporting movements to persuade people towards abstinence was passed, whilst in 1873 it was resolved:

> That while we disapprove of the liquor traffic, we do not think it needful annually to pass a resolution in reference to it, and we deem the resolution of former meetings sufficient for the present.

After a lull of two years, however, the pressure built up again. Sunday closing was condemned in 1876, drink in general in 1878, and unfermented wine was even more strongly urged in 1879.

When the Temperance Conference was inaugurated in 1880, therefore, one result was a resolution congratulating Sir Wilfred Lawson on the success of his local option resolution in the House of Commons. It was also agreed that the next Conference paper should be read by G.Y. Tickle (jnr) on 'The Duty of the Churches in regard to the Drinking Customs of the Land'. This immediately indicates the difference of view between David King and the younger generation on the whole subject, as is illustrated by the way in which the introduction of the Temperance Conference was noted in the magazines. David King wrote:

> Friends deeply in earnest upon the Temperance question, held an early morning meeting, which they seem disposed to view as the commencement of some annual action of that sort.

In the *Christian Advocate*, edited by G.Y. Tickle (snr), the Reporting Committee's version read:

> On Wednesday morning, a wish that has existed in some minds for many years past, was gratified in the assembling of a number of brethren and sisters attending the Annual Meeting, to confer on the Temperance question.

74

A Temperance Committee was also appointed consisting of the members of the Sunday School Committee and two others.[34]

G.Y. Tickle's paper the following year was regarded by the Temperance Conference as a great success, and they looked forward to an increase in temperance work amongst the Churches. David King remained sceptical and in an editorial in March 1884, entitled 'Whited Walls', he criticized the faith put in social reform and argued that the only antidote to social evil was Christ. H.E. Tickle defended the Christian's duty to work for righteous and just laws, to which King responded sharply by saying that

> if the devil wills to bring to nothing the activities of earnest labourers in the church, he can do nothing better than run them through election contests, and give them a seat in the Town Council.[35]

Further controversy broke out in the Annual Meetings of 1888 and 1889. At the 1888 Meeting there was a long discussion over whether the Band of Hope column in the Sunday School schedule should be continued, this being now a question for the Annual Meeting following the absorption of the Sunday School Committee into the General Cooperation. David King objected on the familiar ground that Bands of Hope were outside organizations and said that the 'continued ability of himself and others to cooperate would depend upon the cooperation being simply, as heretofore, for evangelization'. James Grinstead objected to the implied threat, and remarked that King had not objected when a deputation from the Peace Society had been sent to the Annual Meeting, and had assured them from the chair of the support of the Churches. But it was agreed to appoint a committee to look into the matter, and to drop the items in the meantime. The Temperance Conference also asked the Temperance Committee to consult with the General Evangelist Committee about the possibility of incorporating its work into that of the Annual Meeting.

These matters duly came back to the 1889 Meeting, and discussion of them was preceded by a schedule from the Manchester church, objecting to a resolution passed at Glasgow in 1887 to the effect that the Annual Meeting strongly felt that it was highly improper for drinksellers or owners of public house property to be retained in church-membership. Charles Greig argued that this imposed an unscriptural test of membership, but someone moved the next business. This was the report of the special committee which, by a majority, recommended that temperance work continue to be carried on separately from the Annual Meeting. A contrary view failed to gain support.[36] King's view therefore prevailed, and it was to be 1920 before the Temperance Committee became a full committee of the Annual Meeting. Thus, although the corporate life of the Churches was developing, the line which was drawn between cooperation for evangelization and cooperation for other reasons was still quite rigid: and although David King was the most articulate spokesman of the narrower position, it would be wrong to think that he was alone. The threat to withdraw from the Cooperation, though extreme and itself an indication of the strength of the pro-temperance group, could not have been carried out by a single man, not even David King.

V

Many of the issues which have been discussed so far assume a new significance if they are set against the background of the issue which agitated the Churches more than anything else in this period — the Communion question. In fact, as will be explained, it was more than a Communion question: it might be better described as 'the American question'. But it crystallized over the issue of the admission of persons not baptized as believers to communion. Reference has already been made in chapter 2 to the unfavourable impression made by the reports of Alexander Campbell's remarks in the Campbell-Rice debate of 1844. Rumours that the American Churches admitted the unbaptized to communion persisted through the 1850s and in 1859 the Annual Meeting asked its chairman, G. Y. Tickle, to write to Campbell to ascertain the truth of the matter. Campbell was away from home when the letter arrived and did not find it until June 1860. His reply, published in the *Harbinger* for September 1860 stated:

> I can say, so far as my knowledge extends, we have no such custom. In all my travels abroad, I have not witnessed such an occurrence. That unbaptized persons may have sat down to the Lord's table amongst our brotherhood without invitation, is not wholly improbable; but I know of no church that has formally invited them to participate with it on such occasions. We do not, indeed, on any such occasions, known to me, '*invite*' or '*debar*', in the usual currency of these words, any one

76

unbaptized to participate with us in any act of social worship. Communion, indeed, is not confined to any one ordinance; — Lord's day, Lord's supper, prayer, or praise. We can preach to all men, and pray *for* all men, whether they pray or do not with us, but we cannot praise or commune *for* all men in any act of social worship. Such have been my convictions, time out of mind. All men have not faith, nor repentance, nor devotion of heart; and, therefore, all such are evidently of the world and not of the church, nor within the pale of Christian communion.[37]

Not all were convinced by this reply, but it was not easy to challenge Campbell's word.

It should also be remembered that there was an English background to the question. The question of open communion was a controversial one among English Baptists for most of the first half of the nineteenth century, as the majority of Baptist churches gradually adopted the practice. Scotch Baptists and their spiritual heirs among Churches of Christ were disinclined to follow in the same direction, and open communion became a regular item in criticisms of Baptists in this period. In 1861 the *Harbinger* published a series of articles by George Greenwell criticizing the work of Robert Hall, who had been the leading exponent of the position. The question was topical in the late 1850s because of the St Mary's Chapel case, when a group of members of St Mary's Chapel, Norwich, sued the minister, the Revd. George Gould, in the Court of Chancery for breach of trust in introducing open communion. J.B. Rotherham, while visiting relatives in East Anglia in the late summer of 1858, preached to this group on two successive Sundays. The suit failed, however, and in so doing marked a significant step forward in the progress of the 'open membership' principle among Baptists.[38]

The question became a live issue within the British Churches with the arrival of Henry Earl in 1861. Earl was an Englishman who had graduated at Bethany College and returned to England with letters of recommendation from Alexander Campbell, Robert Milligan and Robert Richardson. When he first attended a service at Camden Town in London he took with him his mother, who had not been immersed, and was surprised and hurt to discover that she was not offered the elements at communion. Shortly afterwards he visited Leicester for the Annual Meeting and indicated that he would be willing to spend some of his time in England as an evangelist. He made a good impression on some of the older brethren, but was asked what his position on the communion question was. Having at first indicated that he was not willing to debar anyone from communion, he was subsequently persuaded to adopt the closed communion position, and served acceptably as an evangelist for nearly three years. When he left for Australia in May 1864 he had been responsible for 331 additions to the British Churches.[39]

At the Annual Meeting of 1864 in Wigan the Evangelist Committee were urged to correspond with the Board of the American Christian Missionary Society, to follow up an appeal made to the Board (and published in the *Harbinger*) by James Challen of Philadelphia that they should send evangelists to England. G.Y. Tickle moved an amendment that such an appeal was not expedient in present circumstances because the A.C.M.S.'s funds were too low. The division of people for and against, and the arguments used, were very interesting. James Wallis was against the idea because of the instability of converts made by American evangelists. David King was in favour, being prepared to trust the American brethren. The main argument against the proposal was not that the Americans were unsound on the Communion question, but that they placed too much trust in preaching and college training, and not enough emphasis on mutual edification. The amendment was carried, and Americans were not invited.[40] In 1865, however, the Annual Meeting, having heard through King from Benjamin Franklin of Cincinnati 'that two reliable evangelists are ready to come over to this country', empowered the Evangelist Committee to make the necessary arrangements; but nothing was done because the necessary money was not forthcoming from the churches.[41]

The question of evangelistic help from America was nevertheless discussed at the Nottingham meeting in 1866, and, according to King's report in the *Harbinger*, two things became apparent:

> 1. The catholic feeling of the Assembly, inasmuch as that an earnest loving faithful preacher, sound in the faith and firm in adherence to the order of the Church of God, would be gladly received without regard to country or clime.
> 2. That any Evangelist, whether American or English, who in any way advocates communing at the table of the Lord with unbaptized persons is to be considered as repudiated by the general meeting of the churches.

It was therefore resolved:

> That we learn with deep regret that some Evangelists in America
> commune at the Lord's table with unbaptized persons, who without
> formal invitation, and, as it is alleged, on their own responsibility
> partake; and we hereby decline to sanction Evangelistic cooperation
> with any brother, whether from America or elsewhere, who
> knowingly communes with unbaptized persons, or who, in any way,
> advocates such communion.[42]

Clearly this was the strongest statement so far and it was not a
unanimous view: Timothy Coop who was treasurer of the
Evangelist Committee dissented from it, but the reports of the
episode were themselves overlaid by subsequent controversy.
W.T. Moore, one of the American evangelists who subsequently
worked in Britain, alleged in his *Life of Timothy Coop* that all the
Evangelist Committee voted against the resolution and that
James Wallis was not in sympathy with it; but this version of
events was denied by others who were present.[43] The situation
was also complicated by the increasing diversity of the movement
in America. The Civil War had been a difficult time and although
it was always proudly claimed by American Disciples that they
were one of the few Churches not divided by the War, patterns of
separate development appear from this period. The death of
Alexander Campbell in 1866 removed the main unifying
influence and various leaders laid claim (though never openly) to
his mantle. There was therefore room for genuine doubt as to
what American practice was and there is no reason to disbelieve
King's claim that he always believed that the majority of
Americans were perfectly sound. The leaders he most admired,
J.W. McGarvey at Lexington and Benjamin Franklin, editor of
the *American Christian Review*, were on the conservative side of
the movement: the latter has been described as being 'outside of
the mainstream of the movement' by the early 1870s.[44]

VI

Nevertheless the real difference of practice between Britain and
America was not communion but preaching. In the autumn of
1866 T.J. Gore, an American evangelist on his way to Australia,
visited Britain and stayed more than a week with King in
Birmingham. He described his impressions to Benjamin
Franklin:

The practice of the brethren in this country differs materially from the practice in America. By no means do they have *preaching* on Lord's day mornings. The morning meetings are for the purpose of attending to the Lord's Supper, and for mutual instruction and edification. We have been very much pleased, so far as we have seen, with this order. It is certainly nearer the ancient practice than ours. It exalts the importance of the Lord's Supper, and brings out, to a very great extent, the talent of the Church. At night the gospel is preached to the world.[45]

The relationship between the two issues lay in the fact that an emphasis on preaching in the morning made it more likely that strangers would be attracted, who would then be present for the Lord's Supper at the end of the service.

In 1868 David King decided to write a series of letters to Benjamin Franklin to correct what he felt to be misrepresentations of the British position in America and to explain the criticisms which the British Churches had of American practice. The first was published in the *American Christian Review* for 2 June, and they were subsequently reprinted in the *British Harbinger* in the autumn. It is probable that King was prompted to do this by the discussion on 'Expediency and Progress' which began in the American periodicals that spring.[46] In these letters criticisms of college-trained preachers and neglect of mutual edification came before the Communion question, but it was the latter that generated the heat. The essence of King's criticism came in his fifth letter when he referred to the use made by American writers of 'the Logic of the Heart' to soften the hard logic of God's positive commands, illustrating the point by reference to Robert Richardson's *Memoirs of Alexander Campbell*. For King heart-logic had its place in the region of unordained things, but on a matter like communion 'to the "Law and to the Testimony", not to our own hearts must the appeal be made'.[47] Not surprisingly the letters provoked controversy in America, and they also became entangled with the discussion of personalities, particularly Henry Earl: but it is significant that Franklin wrote that 'Br. King's letters have *generally* been well received in this country'.[48] It was perhaps unfortunate for his image in England that Henry Earl travelled to America in the spring of 1870 as the authorized financial agent for a proposed Bible College in Australia, another reminder of the relevance of the wider question of ministry to the whole discussion.

David King's articles on 'Ministry in the Church of Christ'

(subsequently reprinted in the *Memoir of David King* and influential in the British Churches until the inter-war period) were published in the *British Harbinger* during 1870: and they sought to steer a middle course between the sacerdotalism which seemed to reach a new peak with the declaration of the First Vatican Council on papal infallibility and what King always called 'the Plymouthian leaven' — the view that anyone could do anything — which he associated, somewhat unfairly, with T.H. Milner. As King expounded his view of scriptural ministry, however, the American Churches lay in the background, providing the most immediate contrast of all.

While the controversy rumbled on in the magazines there was a lull at the Annual Meeting. In 1868 a committee had been appointed, consisting of David King, G.Y. Tickle, William McDougall and William Linn (whose brother lived in Detroit), to prepare a statement 'in reference to certain differences between the Churches in America and Great Britain'; but it never met and no such statement was prepared. Perhaps David King's articles, which had already begun, were thought to be sufficient.[49] Then in 1872 at the Leicester Meeting the whole issue blew up again. The Evangelist Committee had urged the Meeting to secure the evangelistic services of Henry Exley, formerly of the Wakefield church who had been working as an evangelist in the U.S.A. for some years and was now back in Britain, and also to take up an offer of help from Benjamin Franklin and John F. Rowe, which King had secured. The Meeting decided after considerable discussion not to take up the offer from Franklin and Rowe. No reason was given, but in view of the fact that King had made the approach it can hardly have been because they were unsound on communion: it may have been because the balance in hand was only some £12, compared with £115 a year earlier. Next day the Meeting considered the question of engaging Henry Exley. Questions were raised concerning his practice over admission to communion and a deputation of three, David King, Robert Black and William McDougall, was appointed to talk to him. When it was reported that he had adopted the American practice, it was resolved not to act upon the Evangelist Committee's suggestion.[50]

Again, however, it is clear that at the Leicester Meeting there were more things about American developments than their communion practice that were troubling the brethren. G.Y.

Tickle read a Conference paper on 'The Causes, Consequents and Prevention of Divisions' in which his main argument was that division was a result of departure from New Testament simplicity, particularly in matters of ministry and church order: and he saw danger not only in the American position but also in some trends in the British Churches:

> While our churches are looking away too much from the power with which the church itself is invested, for self edification, to the evangelists, who should be altogether relieved of church work in the labour of saving souls, except in the setting in order of infant churches: across the Atlantic the brethren seem to have got considerably ahead even of that position. The college-educated pastor is fast assuming a sort of presidency over the elders as well as over the church.

He also went on to attack a writer in an American magazine, the *Christian Quarterly*, who had emphasized that the study of the primitive church was a study in embryology, because there was no completed system of church order in it. 'There you have at one fell swoop all the ground swept from under us upon which, in America and England, we have been endeavouring to build for year,' he wrote.[51] This is in a nutshell the difference between the patterns of thought in the British Churches in the nineteenth century and those in the twentieth. The position Tickle rejected has subsequently been adopted by the majority in Churches of Christ, but contrary to his expectation this has not swept the ground from under them because, being freed from the necessity to restore a New Testament order in every detail, they have been enabled to concentrate on embodying the principles of New Testament order in an appropriate contemporary form. In fact, most of Tickle's paper was a discussion of precisely those principles, as he identified the desire to be great among the brethren as the root cause of division, and submission to Christ and to one another as 'the spring and essence of unity and peace in the body'. But in locating the cause of division in the practice of ministry and discipleship in the Church rather than in theological and doctrinal speculation, Tickle was making an emphasis characteristic of the whole movement to which Churches of Christ in Britain belonged.

VII

The last phase of the 'American question' began in 1875. In that year the Foreign Missionary Society was organized in America and Henry Earl was present at the Convention in Louisville. He indicated that he intended to return to England to work in new areas and asked for recognition as a missionary. The officers of the Society tried to persuade him to go elsewhere, as they did not think that the American Churches would regard England as a foreign field, but Earl's mind was made up. So the Society resolved to appoint him a missionary to England, and he was set apart for the work by prayer and the laying on of hands.[52] When he arrived at Liverpool, he was met by the General Evangelist Committee and two or three others, who ascertained that he intended to work in the south of England. After visiting Bath, he moved to Southampton where he hired the Philharmonic Hall and was soon preaching to audiences of between one and two thousand: by September he had formed a church of 33 members, 30 of whom he had baptized. His doings were reported in the British magazines, but without comment. Earl also attended the Annual Meeting at Leeds and objected to the adverse comments on American methods of evangelism made by David King in his Conference paper on 'Evangelization'.[53]

The calm did not last for long. By the spring of 1877 the membership of Earl's church at Southampton had passed 100, and his letters to America stated his conviction that a great harvest could be reaped by American evangelists in England. In April he was visited unexpectedly by Timothy Coop, James Marsden and Robert Black, and, according to Earl, they 'expressed themselves much pleased with what they saw and heard'. John Aitken, editor of the *Christian Advocate*, though he still felt disappointed that the American Society had not consulted the British brethren before sending Earl, was inclined to wish him God speed in view of his success: but he was anxious to know what *methods* Earl had adopted, to see whether they could be adopted by the British Churches, and thus save the Americans the trouble of sending more missionaries. Others were less open-minded.

At the Annual Meeting in Birmingham the church at Charles Henry Street (to which King belonged) submitted a resolution proposing the appointment of experienced brethren 'affectionately to expostulate' with the brethren in America concerning their deviations from apostolic practice. Despite opposition from Earl and a defence of American practice, this resolution was carried and William Linn, G.Y. Tickle and David King were appointed to carry out the task. Alexander Brown, who had been in the chair, subsequently wrote in the *Ecclesiastical Observer* that the work in Southampton need not have been mentioned if Earl had not raised it himself: but it was quite clear that Earl had imported undesirable practices from America and that one of the three who had visited Southampton had said that the work was not all he could wish. Brown also noted that only one of the British evangelists had spoken in favour of the resolution and some had almost seemed to be against it: he said, however, that he knew that these brethren did not sympathize with American methods and warned everyone to be vigilant. The four letters prepared by the committee were published in the *Ecclesiastical Observer* in January and February 1878 and covered substantially the same ground as David King's letters ten years earlier.[54]

They had very little effect. In January 1878 a second missionary from the F.C.M.S., Marion D. Todd, arrived in Chester and began a campaign there, capitalizing on the work of Moody and Sankey. The church in Chester, which had dwindled in size and was lacking in leadership, identified itself with the new work, and in 1883 its name was removed from the list 'the brethren having ceased to cooperate'. Timothy Coop now decided to give his support to the American effort. He visited America and offered to add £1,000 to every £2,000 the F.C.M.S. would contribute towards supporting missionaries in Britain. In response to his appeal, W.T. Moore, minister of Central Christian Church, Cincinnati, one of the largest and most influential in the U.S.A., offered to return with Coop. He did so, and was subsequently established as minister of the church at Mornington Road, Southport, whilst the brethren who had met there returned to their chapel in Sussex Road which was given to them by Coop as redemption for his mortgage of it. Coop resigned from the Evangelist Committee in 1878, and was thanked for his work.[55]

Although the British Churches had not liked the work in Southampton, it did not compete with any existing church. The establishment of churches in Chester and Southport aroused much more antagonism because they seemed to be set up in direct competition with existing churches. In 1881 the American-founded churches formed themselves into the Christian Association, and for the next thirty-five years developed along separate lines. W.T. Moore moved to Liverpool; then to London in 1881, where he became minister of the West London Tabernacle, an independent congregation, and founded the *Christian Commonwealth*. Personal relationships continued to exist: James Marsden was Timothy Coop's partner in business and his son-in-law; J.B. Rotherham wrote for Moore's paper, and published a pamphlet on the 'Communion Question' in 1879, in which he said that he regarded it as an 'untaught question'. But the general attitude was one of suspicion and hostility, and there were now two distinct groups in Britain both claiming to plead for Christian unity on the basis of New Testament Christianity.

This division was disastrous for the Churches of Christ in Britain, but with the Communion question a central issue, it was inevitable. It was not helped by the fact that men like W.T. Moore were on the very liberal side of the American movement, whilst the British Churches as a whole were closer to the conservative side. The F.C.M.S. became associated with laxity as was illustrated by an ironic incident in the 1880s. From 1877 the Society supported an ex-Catholic, M. Jules DeLaunay, in a mission in Paris. But he proved a difficult person to work with; there were constant financial problems; and in 1886 the Society withdrew its support. DeLaunay had visited Britain several times, and though at first suspect because of the American connection he gained the support and sympathy of many in the British Churches. He also adopted the British position on Communion, and there is a sad little postcard, simply addressed to John Crook, Southport, England, written from his sick bed just after celebrating his 73rd birthday in December 1886, in which DeLaunay said of his dismissal, 'The bone of contention is the closed communion q. — everything else is only a pretext'.[56] Whether he was right or wrong, the impression this created among the British leaders confirmed their view of developments in America.

The disaster of the division, however, lay in the fact that more was at stake than communion. David King vigorously criticized all the methods used in the Southampton venture, including instrumental music, open collections, and a choir which was not confined to the membership. With them all methods of aggressive evangelism seemed to be on trial, and the Conference papers of the 1870s and 1880s echo with defences of the traditional position on ministry and evangelism. Both Tickle and King were involved in this, which is important, for the fatal defect in the 'anti-King' analysis offered by W.T. Moore in his *Life of Timothy Coop* is his under-estimation of the role played by G.Y. Tickle. Tickle was chairman of the Evangelist Committee and had an official position of leadership which King never had; he had been in the movement from the beginning and came of impeccable Scotch Baptist stock; and his editorial role in the 1880s was quite as important as King's, because the *Christian Advocate* was then a livelier magazine than the *Ecclesiastical Observer*. Tickle's account of the breach between the Evangelist Committee and the American group is more telling than King's trumpet blasts because of its characteristic combination of grace and firmness. [57]

VIII

Alexander Brown's reference to the quietness of the evangelists during the discussion of 1878 may reflect their unease that everything from America was being criticized. Reference has been made earlier to the growing conviction among them that longer periods of service with each church would be more productive. George Greenwell, one of the first three evangelists to work for the Annual Meeting, read a Conference paper in 1879 on the Eldership, in which he pleaded the claims of a separated pastorate — not to rule the other elders, but to work with them; and he criticized the stress placed on mutual teaching:

> The truth must be spoken, though it should be spoken in love. That liberty of prophesying, or freedom of mutual exhortation, which we believe has some foundations in ancient supernaturalism, as well as in synagogue usage, has been with us a decisive failure. Among hungry and thirsty congregations men rise up and talk without teaching, so that the sheep are not fed. [58]

David King devoted three weeks to criticizing this paper. Against Greenwell's accusation of 'decisive failure', King wrote:

> We claim decisive success! And we are willing to submit the claim to stringent tests. We insist that our members, generally, know more of the Bible than those of churches, anywhere, which possess the hired pastor. That they are far more formidable in Bible enquiries, in meeting men who oppose the truth, than are those who have been charmed every week by the preparations of the best men hired for what our friend calls pastoral work. We would be very sorry to say a word implying satisfaction with our modes of applying this liberty as if there were no need of improvement. But with all our faults (not *its* faults) we love it still, for manifest good results, which will bear the strongest tests that can be applied.

So King retained his conviction that 'the hired pastorate has been a failure all along the line', without apparently realizing that he had completely missed Greenwell's point.[59]

King was also put on the defensive in another way. He was criticized for operating a 'one-man' system himself in Birmingham, since none of the churches had elders, allegedly because there were no suitable candidates. In 1880, five elders were ordained by King at Geach Street, Birmingham, and in 1882 he resigned his oversight at Charles Henry Street. In the latter case, however, a Provisional Executive was formed, because there was no immediate likelihood of elders being ordained. King retained his membership at Charles Henry Street, but always regarded himself as ineligible for election as an elder because he had no children. The report of the occasion stressed the efforts he had made to involve others in the life of the church so much, that he must have felt defensive about the Birmingham situation.[60]

Also in the 1880s the pressure for more aggressive evangelism was beginning to mount. In 1883 Sydney Black, son of Robert Black of London, began his own evangelistic work in new areas. He founded churches in Leominster, Ross and York, but did not work under the direction of the G.E.C. In 1885 he suggested that the subject of the Conference paper for 1886 be 'Aggressive Christianity', and his wish was to some extent met by Bartley Ellis's paper of 1887. Ellis did stress the need for greater giving to support the G.E.C., but David King opposed Halstaff Coles's resolution at the Annual Meeting of 1890 to raise the income of the G.E.C. by £5,000 p.a., lest it encourage a hireling ministry. The resolution was passed none the less.[61]

This indicates the way in which the mood of the Churches was changing. The older generation was passing. In April 1888 G.Y. Tickle died. George Greenwell, who had emigrated to Australia in 1880, died in 1886. William Linn of Glasgow died in 1887, as did Timothy Coop. Coop died in America, but John Crook spoke at the memorial service for him in Southport, and Bartley Ellis spoke at a similar service at Rodney Street, Wigan — an indication that personal feelings towards Coop on the part of his old friends were not affected by differences over policy. Of the leaders in the 1850s and early 1860s only King and J.B. Rotherham were left.

It was hardly surprising therefore that the 1891 Annual Meeting asked David King to prepare a paper for the Jubilee

Conference on 'Fifty Years' Work and the Lessons it suggests'. Most of the paper was historical, though no opportunity was lost to emphasize that the British Churches had remained true to the position of Alexander Campbell. His conclusions were defensive: that the largest numerical success was at the beginning before there were full-time evangelists; that too much emphasis on raising money to support evangelists could lead to lack of effort on the part of individual church members; that complete adherence to aim and purpose was more important than numerical success; 'that to "*Hold the Fort*", is a first essential; preserving, intact, every element of the Faith and Worship of the Church of Christ . . . but refusing to surrender a single item of HIS, even to convert a continent'.[62]

The Jubilee Conference itself was a very harmonious occasion: it was held in Edinburgh like the first meeting in 1842. David King was honoured by an affectionate biographical sketch in the *Year Book*, together with his photograph. But the times were already changing. A new magazine which began publication in 1891, *The Young Christian*, criticized King's favourite exhortation to 'hold the fort' in its first issue:

> It is not a very brilliant achievement to 'hold a fort', which, in some instances, the devil does not take the trouble to storm, simply because he discerns within its own citadels the elements of spiritual suicide.[63]

By the time of the jubilee the future for British Churches of Christ lay with that point of view rather than with David King's.

4 WIDENING HORIZONS

I

David King died on 26 June 1894 at the age of 75. It was the end of an era. The generation which followed was increasingly outward-looking. This showed itself in various ways: in the 'Forward Movement' for evangelism and social reform at home; in the new concern for missions overseas; in a new willingness to grapple with theological change, and particularly biblical criticism. Towards the end of the period there was a new openness to other Christians, and a reconciliation with the Christian Association: and finally there was the foundation of Overdale College for the training of ministers in 1920. Before this happened, however, Britain had been transformed by war. From this time new divisions began to appear in the Churches, and the world in which they had to work and witness was changed almost beyond recognition.

These changes were of course beginning before King died. Younger men like Halstaff Coles and Sydney Black were pressing for a Forward Movement in the late 1880s; and they achieved some success when the Annual Meeting of 1890 at Leominster — scene of Sydney Black's first evangelistic success — agreed to raise £5,000 to form a substantial fund for the increased development of evangelistic work. The sum of £800 was immediately promised, and the income of the G.E.C. for 1890-91 was nearly £3,000 — three times the amount for 1889-90. Although £1,000 came from four individuals, it is clear that a great effort had been made; but in the following year the income had dropped by half.

David King did not conceal his disapproval of these developments. He opposed the Coles-Black resolution in 1890. In July 1891 he wrote:

> 'Aggressive Christianity', 'Forward Movements', 'The Church of the Future', and like phrases, are plentiful just now. But there is more than slender ground for fear that going forward may amount to going out from apostolic doctrine and practice; that the contemplated 'Church

of the Future' may not be the Church of Christ, and that 'Aggressive Christianity' may be little more than loud and superficial Revivalism.[1]

At the 1891 Annual Meeting he opposed the movement towards foreign missions, suggesting that the commission to 'go and preach the gospel to every creature' was addressed to the Apostles and not to the Church. He also thought that work at home should take priority.[2] His fear that concern for temperance and social questions could divert the church from its main task has already been noted. Yet King's opposition did not stop either the Forward movement or the beginning of foreign missions; and it did bring the liberal movement into the open when in January 1891 they started their own magazine, *The Young Christian*.

In 1889 the Annual Meeting had decided to publish an official magazine for the first time, which was to replace King's *Ecclesiastical Observer* and the Scottish-sponsored *Christian Advocate*, formerly edited by G.Y. Tickle. The new magazine, the *Bible Advocate*, began in January 1890, and David King was appointed editor-in-chief. Halstaff Coles was in charge of the Sunday School section, but not for long. In October 1890 David King attacked a pamphlet published by Coles, in which the latter had suggested that 'too much effort has been expended upon the work of proselytising and not enough upon that of conversion of sinners'. He had also criticized the insinuation that other bodies of professing Christians had no claim to be called Churches of Christ. This, of course, was a red rag to King:

> We answer that not any one of the sects, as such, from Rome downward, including the Salvation Army, is entitled to be so designated. So it has been held from the early utterances of A. Campbell down to the present hour, by every one numbering with us, who has understood the principles to which he had allied himself . . . Taking the ground of the writer, our existence as a people cannot be justified.

Coles replied in a letter to the editor in the next issue, regretting King's 'spiritual insularity'.[3] In the December issue his name disappeared as the one in charge of Sunday School notes, and in January 1891 the first issue of *The Young Christian* was published, with Coles as editor and John Crockatt of Leeds as publisher. The exchange between Coles and King was a more trenchant version of one between Coles's father (who had served as an evangelist both in Australia and Britain) and G.Y. Tickle in the *Christian Advocate* just before the latter's death in 1888, when Coles rejected and Tickle supported the view that members of the sects (Baptists possibly excluded) were 'not in union with Christ'.[4]

'*The Young Christian* is a magazine with a mission. That mission is to give a 'forward' impetus to the advocacy of Apostolic Christianity.' With these words the new magazine declared its purpose. An article on 'The Forward Movement' stated that 'the vast majority of our most educated, cultured, and earnest young men and women' were discontented with the limited vision of so many in the Churches:

> To such an extent had this dissatisfaction proceeded, that some little time ago quite a number of devoted, liberal, Christ-loving young men and maidens in our ranks had almost decided to fling themselves, spirit, soul and body, into some form of purely social and philanthropic enterprise, whilst still, in all faithfulness to their Lord, filling up their places in their respective congregations for the communion of saints and the quickening of spiritual life.

The movement launched at the Leominster Meeting had filled them with new hope. New areas were being opened up by the G.E.C. and Sydney Black was shortly to commence a new work in London. The article ended with a confidence that catches the spirit of this late-nineteenth-century movement:

> This great kingdom shall yet rejoice in a united church which shall evangelise the world . . . The obstacles in the way of final victory are but two — sectarianism and alcohol![5]

The difference between these younger men and King is clear.

When David King died, therefore, the tribute in *The Christian at Work* (as *The Young Christian* had become in 1894) was somewhat more muted than those given elsewhere. John Crockatt, who was now editor, referred to the biography prepared for the Jubilee Year Book by Joseph Collin, the same writer's sketch in the *Bible Advocate* for 15 July 1894, and 'the many tender tributes which love and admiration have prompted to lay on his grave'. He continued:

> To many they will come as a revelation of the one departed. Known to thousands only by his writings, they would fail to discover in them anything of that tenderness of character to which so eloquent and unequivocal testimony has been borne. Therein, they find a statement of truth indicative of keen perception and intense conviction on the

part of the writer, expressed in the most lucid terms, with its logical issues unflinchingly applied. The '*fortiter in re*' is present in all his writings; we could wish that the '*suaviter in modo*' had not frequently been wanting . . . That he was a wise, pure, and courageous leader is thankfully acknowledged. To say he was not a perfect leader, is but to say that he shared the frailty and limitation of humanity. We have sometimes thought that his syllogisms though true, were very inadequate, and touched but the surface of the subject dealt with; and so completely had he the goal of truth ever in his mind, that even in judging those who had traversed a long distance in that direction from error, he could but call attention to the space which yet intervened. His habit of directing the gaze upon the error in men and systems, and ignoring that which was admirable was neither generous nor just, and in the minds of many was his most serious failing. He was a man of war from his youth up. And unfortunately some amongst us have caught those habits, who lack the ability and redeeming features present in his case.[6]

The value of these comments is that they pinpoint exactly the problem which confronts the historian. Judged by his writings alone, King is not an attractive figure, though no-one could doubt the power of his mind. Yet the tributes paid by those closest to him, and particularly his students, revealed a different side. T.K. Thompson recalled that as a teacher King never pressed his conclusions on others, and he also referred to 'his patience, thoughtful kindness, and encouragement'.[7] T.J. Ainsworth probably put his finger on the point when he said, 'perhaps we of the younger generation did not understand him; it may be that he did not understand us'.[8] Certainly relations between the younger men and the leaders seemed to become easier after King's death, and at the end of 1894 *The Christian at Work* ceased publication, saying that there was less need now of a periodical to supplement the official one. The implication was obvious.

The leading figure in the 'Forward Movement' was undoubtedly Sydney Black. Reference has already been made to his early evangelistic work in the 1880s, when he was enabled by his father's help to be financially independent of the churches. In May 1888 he returned to his native London, and hired the Chelsea Town Hall for evangelistic meetings. This was the beginning of his conviction that he was called to work in London permanently, a conviction strengthened by contacts he made with a working lads' mission in Fulham and by getting to know Mary Hugill, who ran a Rescue Home for Women and was baptized as a result of attending his meetings.

In September 1889 Sydney Black went to Oxford to equip himself for further work by taking a course of private tuition under Professor Fairbrother of Keble College and Principal Fairbairn of Mansfield College. This Congregational college had recently moved to Oxford from Birmingham to become the first nonconformist theological college in either of the two ancient universities. He studied in Oxford for a year and was then much involved with the arrangements for the 1890 Annual Meeting at Leominster.

After spending the autumn of 1890 touring the country on deputation work for the G.E.C.'s £5,000 appeal, he sailed for Australia in February 1891 on the first stage of a round-the-world trip to raise money for his London mission. He visited Australia, New Zealand and the U.S.A., returning to Liverpool in November 1892 with more than £1,000 for the new work. He began services in Fulham Town Hall, whilst the 'Queen Anne' Coffee House at Fulham Cross was adapted for its new purpose. The building was bought by Sydney Black for £2,250, his father contributing £1,000 towards it, and renamed Twynholm Hall after the Scottish village in which his father had been born. As remodelled, it contained an assembly hall for 500 people, a basement schoolroom and soup kitchen, with class rooms, clubrooms and a coffee bar as well. The church formed at Fulham Cross was added to the List of Churches in 1894, and in 1900 the remaining members of the church at College Street, Chelsea united with it.

The programme at Twynholm Hall was typical of the institutional churches of the time, with a host of activities every night of the week: Bible Classes, Band of Hope, Women's meeting, Working Lads' Social Club, Singing Class, Sewing Class, Free Breakfasts for Working Men's children, and a nurse available six mornings a week. To this can be added the work of the Orphanage which was founded soon after his arrival. Sydney Black also became involved in the public work of the neighbour-hood: he was a member of the Fulham Free Church Council; in 1899 he defeated the vicar of St Albans church in the election for the Fulham Board of Guardians; and in 1900 he was elected as a Progressive candidate for the Chelsea division of the London School Board. He drove himself so hard — he still conducted

missions in other parts of the country for a week or so at a time —
that his health broke down, and he died in October 1903 at the
age of 43.[9]

Neither Sydney Black nor the church at Fulham Cross (which
by 1900 was the largest in the brotherhood with a membership of
over 400) were typical of Churches of Christ in this period.
No-one else had Black's combination of personal gifts, and the
type of work in which he specialized was largely confined to
London, even among other denominations. But in a unique way
he symbolized the spirit of the 1890s, and the aspirations of the
younger generation. Thomas Ainsworth, who wrote Black's
biography, was one of his contemporaries, and belonged to the
same group of enthusiasts. The difference between this group and
the older generation may be seen by comparing Ainsworth's
biography of Black with James Anderson's *Outline of my Life*.
Anderson spent most of his life in Scotland, but it is not just
geographical distance which explains why, at the time Sydney
Black was gathering in the poor of Fulham, James Anderson was
debating with Christadelphians, Jehovah's Witnesses, Seventh
Day Adventists and Brethren about the correct interpretation of
the New Testament. The way Anderson helped the small church
in Belfast in the 1890s seems to belong to a different world from
Black's methods at Fulham Cross.

II

The second great broadening influence was the establishment
of overseas missionary work. There had been spasmodic interest
earlier. For a few years after 1851 several of the British Churches
supported the efforts of Dr Barclay, an American Disciple who
worked in Jerusalem (taking Luke 24:47 literally). Then in the
1860s David King collected money from the Churches to support
the development of Churches of Christ in Jamaica. In 1876
William Hindle, an evangelist who worked in both Britain and
Australia and caused some controversy with his 'Bible carriage',
suggested that a group of Christian men (with their families if
possible) should be sent out

> to preach the grand old Gospel in its New Testament simplicity and
> fulness to the people of Uganda. The company selected should include
> a carpenter, a blacksmith, a tailor, a man who understands practical
> farming, one or two preachers, and, if possible, a competent

day-school teacher, male or female, or one of each, with farming implements, joiner's and blacksmith's tools, outfit &c.[10]

David King liked the plan (apart from the preachers, who he thought should be able to work as well) but said that zeal was not enough.

The real father of the overseas missions of Churches of Christ in Britain, however, was John Crook. He was the son of a Baptist minister in Wigan, and spent some time in America before returning at the time of the Civil War. His widowed mother had been attracted to take up membership at Rodney Street, Wigan, by the ministry of William McDougall, and on his return to Britain he followed her example. In 1872 he became a member of the General Evangelist Committee, and rapidly became its secretary, an office which he held for 27 years until 1900. The reports of the G.E.C. for 1881 and 1882 noted the absence of foreign missionary work in the British Churches of Christ: but the turning point came with his four articles on 'Foreign Missions' in the *Christian Advocate* for 1886.

Crook explained his deepening conviction of the importance of foreign missions in this way:

> A missionary spirit infused into our churches, a spirit to care for others in a wider circle than has ever yet been within our vision, a spirit which will teach us self-sacrifice in a larger measure than has ever yet been possessed by us, would not only enable us to occupy our right position as lights in the world, but would be the best of blessings to ourselves, for in watering others we should be watered by refreshing rills flowing from many lands.[11]

Subsequent articles provided practical information about possible areas, and he concluded by suggesting that the Annual Meeting take steps to consider the possibility of a movement in this direction. The question was raised directly in the report of the General Evangelist Committee, but it was resolved that no action could be taken in view of the large demands on limited resources at home. In 1887 Bartley Ellis returned to the matter in his Conference paper on 'Aggressive Christianity'. Despite the difficulties which would be raised, he believed 'the time has fully come when something of a practical nature should be done in this direction', and he cited Carey as an example of someone who had encountered exactly the same criticisms. But nothing was done until the Annual Meeting of 1890 appointed John Crook to read a

Conference paper the following year on 'Foreign 'Missions and our Relation thereto'.[12]

At 2.00 p.m. on Wednesday 5 August 1891 Rodney Street chapel, Wigan was 'over-filled with eager friends' to hear John Crook read his paper. He said the occasion was unique in the history of the Churches. The resources of the Churches were now enlarged, both in money and men, and they were therefore in a position to implement the Nottingham resolution of 1886 and carry out the Lord's commission to evangelize the world. 'If we are to be Apostolical, we must be a missionary people.' The rest of the paper was taken up with a review of missionary history and the areas of the world which might provide suitable openings. George Collin opened the discussion by referring to Alexander Campbell's criticism of missionary societies and their failure so long as they relied on preaching men. This fired Arthur Black to defend the success of missions, and particularly their reflex influence on work at home. He was followed by his brother, Milner Black, who had come as a delegate from Churches of Christ in Victoria specifically to seek the cooperation of the British Churches in the work they had begun in India. A number of others spoke in favour of action, the only one to take a contrary view being David King. The climax came in John Crook's reply to him:

> Bro. King said those who said 'Go,' did not go themselves. Well, he had said, 'Go,' and, if they were willing to accept an old man, he would go.[13]

Next day Halstaff Coles moved, James Marsden seconded and Milner Black supported a resolution affirming 'That in the opinion of the Conference the time had arrived for definitely undertaking Foreign Mission work'. George Collin moved an amendment to the effect that 'earnest consideration' should be given to the subject, and after some discussion this was carried. To mark the sense that a great step forward had been taken the Meeting sang a verse of 'All hail the power of Jesu's name'. David King then moved that a committee be appointed to consider the matter and report back, and although James Marsden hoped that the committee might have the power of making a small beginning King's proposal was carried.

Nevertheless it was a victory, for delay did not in fact make much difference (though it explains why protagonists of the

Forward movement felt so strongly about the 'old guard'). The Committee of Inquiry interviewed various people, including W.S. Caine, M.P. for Bradford, who knew India, and Dr Richard Glover of Bristol, who had recently visited B.M.S. stations in China. They also had a letter from S.M. Cooke, a missionary in Nigeria supported by one of the American churches. The recommendation to begin foreign missionary work was carried in 1892, with several of the arguments of the 1891 debate being repeated: but it was already clear that feeling in the churches was in favour, since 93 out of 110 who replied to a circular from the committee had indicated their support for a deputation to Central India and Burma to find a suitable field. Only about three people voted against.[14] The Foreign Missionary Committee appointed consisted of James Marsden, Robert Black, George Collin, John Crook, W. Richardson, W. Chapman, G.Y. Tickle (jnr), A. Ferguson, T. Jenkins, Lancelot Oliver, James Nimmo, David King and W. McLintock, a representative cross-section of the leadership.

All but one were present at the meeting in Wigan on 12 October 1892, which decided to begin work in Burma. Work in central India was considered but rejected, probably because the Disciples were already working there and the committee did not wish to be associated with the Foreign Christian Missionary Society. On 31 October the first three missionaries accompanied by John Crook sailed from Liverpool to Rangoon. The three who had offered themselves were William Forrester of Shipley, A.E. Hudson, a Glasgow engineer, and Robert Halliday of Hamilton. After visiting various places it was decided to start a mission at Ye in the province of Tenasserim, a town of about 3,000 people and a centre of the Talaing race. William Forrester had to return almost immediately because a hearing deficiency made it difficult for him to learn the language.

At the end of 1893 the two men were joined by their families, but within six months Mrs Halliday died, and Mr Halliday and his two children returned home in February 1895. It was in that month that the first convert in Burma was made. Then the Hudsons also had to return home because of Mrs Hudson's illness. These difficulties might have tempted the committee to give up, in view of the hesitations which had surrounded the venture from the beginning. But the commitment once made was not lightly given up, and in September 1896 Robert Halliday returned with his new wife, Lizzie. She was a daughter of James Anderson, the evangelist, and had undertaken some medical training before going out. The early work was mainly educational — a boarding school was opened — and medical, and the task of translating the scriptures into Talaing was begun. In 1900 Alfred Hudson returned to Burma for two years on his own, whilst two other men were in training: John Wood of Dalton-in-Furness for industrial work, and Percy Clark of Blackburn for evangelistic work. The Hallidays had their first furlough in 1902, returning in the autumn with Percy Clark, Agnes Campbell who was to marry John Wood, and G.F. Munro, M.A., of Banff, who was to take over the school.

Hudson decided to stay a little longer and in 1903 crossed over into Siam to develop work with the Mons, who spoke the same language as the Talaings. He was subsequently joined by Clark, who took over the work with his wife, Mary, when Hudson had to return to Britain in 1906. The headquarters of the work in Siam was established at Phrapatom (later known as Nakom Pathom). Meanwhile John Wood had resigned in 1904 because of the difficulties of the industrial work, and George Munro resigned in 1907. The Hallidays, having had furlough in 1909, then spent time in Siam to give the Clarks a chance to come home. While there they decided that the prospects were better than in Burma, so that in 1912 the Burmese mission at Ye was transferred to the American Baptists.

Other fields were opened up in the 1900s too. In 1903 the Foreign Missions Committee in cooperation with the Australian Churches of Christ sent out R.K. Francis to help the few small churches in South Africa. He worked in Capetown and Johannesburg and also went as far north as Bulawayo. The idea had been mooted for several years, and was related to the increase in British and Australian emigration to South Africa in the 1890s. Fred Cowin and Bartley Ellis also spent time in South Africa on behalf of the committee. In 1906 the New Zealand Churches of Christ took over responsibility for the Bulawayo mission. Two years later George Hollis and George Hills from Capetown, both of whom had fought in the Boer War, established a mission in Nyasaland, and in 1909 the Foreign Missions Committee gave it their support. The work was carried on from two stations at Chikunda and Zomba. Hills soon had to withdraw and Hollis worked alone until joined by Mary Bannister (from Burnley) in

1912, and Henry and Etta Philpott in the following year. A.C. Watters had also completed a course of training for work in Africa when war broke out in 1914.

The last area in which work was undertaken was India. In 1909 the committee took over a mission at Daltonganj in Palamau, which had been begun by Paul Singh, an Indian pastor in the Methodist Episcopal Church. He had been converted to the position of Churches of Christ by R.H. Parker, who had been working as a free-lance medical missionary in the Central Provinces. Robert Halliday visited Daltonganj on his way home on furlough, and was able to recommend the work to the committee. R.H. Parker, who the committee had hoped would assist, went to Melbourne, Australia, where he persuaded G.P. Pittman and his wife to go out to India. In 1914 the committee were offered another mission station at Dudhi by the London Missionary Society, and so Archie Watters and his wife were sent there instead of Africa. By the outbreak of war, therefore, John Crook's vision had been more than realized, and overseas missions had become a full part of the life of Churches of Christ in Great Britain.[15]

III

The Forward movement and the interest in foreign missions represented a broadening of outlook among the Churches. But fundamental change depended on a new theological outlook, and the key issue here was biblical criticism. This sharply exposed some of the ambiguities inherent in the position taken up by Churches of Christ. From one point of view their attitude to the Bible had been traditionally radical: they did not look to the Bible to justify particular credal or confessional statements, and were therefore free to look for the natural sense of the words. This made them sympathetic to the view that the words of scripture had to be understood in their historical context. Their antipathy to priestcraft, and anything that smacked of a professional ministry, also made them suspicious of any interpretation of scripture that seemed designed to bolster ministerial claims. It was this combination of views that gave them such a good debating position in encounters with secularists: they shared much of the anti-clericalism and theological iconoclasm which was the secularist stock in trade, but still defended the reasonableness of Christianity. James Grinstead illustrated the point neatly in his Conference paper of 1895:

> At the close of a recent lecture I delivered in the Albert Hall, Bristol, a man said to me, 'Ah, Mr Grinstead, those very things you have been exposing and denouncing to-night were the very things which drove me into infidelity. I bless God that ever I came to hear you in this hall.' . . . Having no other standard than the Bible, we are at liberty to learn, teach and practise whatever the word of God authorizes; and we are at liberty to unlearn and discard whatever is unauthorized by the Bible.[16]

Here the influence of Alexander Campbell, himself indebted to the Scottish Enlightenment and John Locke, was crucial.

But there was another side. The alternative proffered by Churches of Christ was a restoration of the New Testament order, which entailed the belief that the New Testament was both a reliable and a sufficient guide. Here the influence of the Haldane brothers and Alexander Carson, all in different ways leaders in the development of the new biblical literalism of the nineteenth century, was important, though never ultimately victorious. Thus the more radical New Testament criticism which began in nineteenth-century Germany was a threat. George Greenwell had read D.F. Strauss before English translations were available, and criticized his views in the *Christian Messenger* in the early 1840s. Later he wrote on Renan, Colenso and other writers who were adopting a critical position on the New Testament. David King did not show the same interest in biblical scholarship, and this was one of the sad consequences of his dominance in the later nineteenth century. T.J. Ainsworth said this of him:

> Strong himself in all questions that related to faith, unmoveable in the principles of the New Testament, he regarded the growth of the later theology with a stern antagonism, and in his writings gave no quarter to teachings he considered Anti-Christian. It may be that his opposition would have been far less stern had he given more time and consideration to the books he combatted. He seemed to derive his knowledge of the writers he objected to second-hand, for no really capable article against the New Theology and Higher Criticism came from his pen, and what references there were, indicated but an inadequate knowledge of present-day thought.[17]

In this he differed both from his contemporary, J.B. Rotherham, and from the younger generation which Ainsworth represented. When Rotherham left full-time evangelistic work in

1868, he began work on a new translation of the New Testament and in that year published his version of Matthew's Gospel with the help of Samuel Prior, a business man connected with the Grosvenor Street church in Manchester. The first edition of *The New Testament Critically Emphasised* was published by Bagsters in 1872, and a second followed in 1878. He then turned to the Old Testament, and had almost completed it when Ginsburg's new Hebrew text was published: so he revised it completely, just as he revised his New Testament on the basis of the Westcott and Hort text rather than the Tregelles text he had used earlier. This work took most of the 1890s. Rotherham was probably the best biblical scholar that the British Churches of Christ produced.[18]

He was nevertheless a rather isolated figure. Living as he did in London for the latter part of his life, he was somewhat on the fringe of the Churches' life, though he did still visit other parts of the country to preach from time to time. His relationship with David King had been an uneasy one since their time in Manchester together, and his willingness to write for W.T. Moore's *Christian Commonwealth* made him suspect in some quarters because of its American associations. At the end of his life in his *Reminiscences*, he wrote a revealing section entitled 'Revised Conclusions'. It was prompted by the question, 'How far am I satisfied still to remain in a position taken up more than fifty years ago?' That he could ask the question is significant in itself: his answer is even more so. He characterized the effect of his change of views in 1854 (when he left the Baptists) with the words, 'Now I have found room to grow!' But it followed from this that he must have subsequently revised the conclusions provisionally accepted fifty years before:

> I submit that it is inconceivable that our pioneers . . . should have thought out all Bible questions with such thoroughness and accuracy as to come out right in everything, or even in everything of importance, leaving nothing material to be modified by those coming after them . . . Many questions had not then been mooted which have since attracted anxious consideration. Not only so, but the discoveries, investigations, and conclusions which now range themselves under the head of 'textual criticism' had scarcely been started then; and the Reformers of 1808 and onward accepted, and occasionally argued, from texts which we now know to be spurious. How was it possible for them to anticipate labours not at that time begun? How, then, could they think out *for us* problems which had not in those days been raised?[19]

At the time when the Manchester church, which he had helped to start, celebrated its jubilee in 1905, he went to speak as the only survivor of the four pioneer evangelists. In his address on 24 September 1905 Rotherham expounded some of his revised conclusions in public. His first point was that Christianity should be regarded as a mighty faith rather than as a logical system:

> I had in the intervening years heard much of the 'Christian System' . . . But it is surprising, to those who have not yet gone thoroughly into the subject, how little of logical method is discoverable in the way in which any great theme of Revelation is taught in the Bible. Take the subject of the Atonement for human sin effected by the death of Christ — where, in all the Bible, is there given a complete and connected view of the whole subject? Nowhere. Or, turn to the very different subject of Church government, and come down under that head to the ministries authorised in Christian assemblies; and, still further, to the necessary qualifications of Elders — everyone knows that several apostolic deliverances have to be carefully pieced together in order to obtain a complete view of the instruction given . . . From all of which the lesson is, that as there is no revealed 'Christian System' logically developed and arranged, so surely must any systematised exhibit, as such, be a human production.[20]

Rotherham's use of the phrase 'Christian System' must have been deliberate, as the Publishing Committee had reprinted Campbell's book of that title the year before. In his Manchester address he was applying Campbell's critical insights to the teaching of Campbell himself: the movement was becoming self-critical.

Rotherham's expertise, however, lay in textual, or 'lower', criticism. The questions which were beginning to press in the 1890s and 1900s also concerned 'higher criticism' — the analysis of sources, dating and authorship. *The Young Christian* was notable for the way it brought some of these issues before the Churches of Christ public. At the Jubilee Conference of 1892 Lancelot Oliver, who had just begun to take over the training of evangelists, delivered an address on 'Biblical Criticism' on the Wednesday evening. The position he took was fairly conservative, as is indicated by the fact that David King felt able to print the whole address in his halfpenny magazine, *The Old Paths*, for October 1892, so as to secure for it a wide circulation. *The Young Christian*, not surprisingly, regarded Oliver's address as a 'very cautious performance', though it rejoiced that he had not condemned biblical criticism out of hand. Nevertheless

> while it is advisable to lay hold of such results of criticism as *confirm* traditional views, it is well to be equally ready to accept such as to *rectify* tradition provided, of course, that these are of reliable character.[21]

And there was disappointment that Conference had rejected the suggestion of Biblical Criticism as a topic for a Conference paper, particularly as no alternative had been put forward.

The Young Christian had already begun a series of articles on 'The Higher Criticism' by Joseph Smith, a young man from Newcastle who had just finished a course of training under Alexander Brown. Joseph Smith was born in 1865, eldest son of a Cumberland farmer. He hated farming and served an apprenticeship as a mechanical engineer in Salford. In 1886 he moved to Newcastle-upon-Tyne and became a member of the church there. He was selected for special training in 1890 and was given twice the normal period of six months because he was such a promising pupil. From 1891 to 1893 he served as an evangelist under the direction of the North East Divisional Committee. He then resigned and went back to engineering, serving for some years on a tramp steamer to get the necessary practical experience of ship engines at sea. This enabled him to rise to the position of foreman in Armstrong's Yard in Newcastle, where he worked until he was called to be a Tutor at Overdale College in 1923. Even in these years he was not theologically idle: he attended lectures by Dr W.H. Moulton on New Testament and won first prize in the local Congregational Lay Preachers' examinations in New Testament. (Before the examination he had compiled a list of the books he wanted as his prize!)[22]

The seven articles in *The Young Christian* for 1892 were some of the first of Jo Smith's writings to be placed before the churches. They show what was always characteristic of his later writing — clear, concise exposition. The main theme was the documentary structure of the Old Testament, generally following Driver rather than Wellhausen as was typical in Britain at that time. In the following year a series in reply was written by R.P. Anderson, another young evangelist, but the moderate nature of its conservatism is striking by comparison with the older writers.

When *The Christian at Work* ceased publication at the end of 1894, open discussion of biblical criticism tended to disappear again. However, in his Conference paper for 1910 on 'Ways of staying the Alienation of the Masses from the Church', Joseph Smith returned to the same theme. He referred to the change which had taken place in the attitude, even of ordinary people, to the Bible in the previous 25 years:

> In circles of the highest learning the old theory of inspiration has given place to a more accurate theory, based not upon dogmatic prepossessions, nor upon a *priori* conceptions as to what the Bible ought to be, nor upon the *necessities* of ecclesiastical controversy, but upon a careful, exact, and exhaustive survey of the whole of the actual facts disclosed in the sacred volume . . . Of course, it is perfectly simple and easy to ignore all this, and in supreme and ignorant confidence to maintain on the platform the 'from cover to cover idea', but such an attitude neither convinces nor deceives anyone, because it fails to come to grips with the evidence upon which the newer view is based, and is out of harmony with the fundamental postulates of literary research and scientific method.

It was therefore necessary to adopt a different approach, if any impact was to be made on the reflective working man:

> The point of attachment is found not in proof-texts describing the nature and needs of man from this or that point of view, but in those deep, ever-recurring longings for something which neither science nor socialism nor biblical criticism can satisfy. Proclaimed with religious fervour, intellectual grasp and honesty, moral power and spiritual insight, the message of the Cross, disassociated from primeval views of the cosmos, patriarchal ideas of the construction of society, and unproved dogmatic conceptions of the record of Revelation, will still find its way to the heart of man.[23]

The paper was described as one of the most fearless ever read in Conference, and what is striking to the modern reader is the way in which Smith simply left behind so much of the kind of argument of the past.[24] It was decided that the following year's paper should be on the effects of Higher Criticism on New Testament Christianity, and Charles Greig of Manchester was appointed to read it. It was a judicious and balanced review, leading to a hopeful conclusion:

> It has often been a great joy to the writer that Biblical criticism, rightly understood, leaves New Testament Christianity — in other words 'our plea' — so unimpaired. Accepting the views here put forward . . . the Deity of Christ and the inspiration of His Apostles stand forth confirmed in many respects and shaken in nothing . . . It has ever been the aim of the churches of the Restoration to keep the Old Testament, the Gospels, and the Acts and Epistles in their true relative positions. This has been sound criticism. It has its gains today.

Greig's regret was that, at a time when he believed critical study was actually preparing the ground for the sowing of the seeds of New Testament truth, Churches of Christ did not have people fittingly equipped to take advantage of it.[25] Nevertheless the report in the *Bible Advocate* commented laconically: 'An animated discussion followed, which showed that there was little disposition to accept the leading of the higher critics'.[26] Indeed James Anderson's autobiography published the following year by the Publishing Committee had a concluding chapter in which he attacked both Higher Criticism and the theory of evolution: and events at Overdale in the 1920s were to show just how much division of opinion remained. The renewed pressure for an improved scheme for training evangelists was, however, a result of the thinking stimulated by these papers.

IV

One effect of these theological changes was the beginning of a more open attitude to other Churches. As already noted, this was precisely the point at issue between Halstaff Coles and David King in 1890. The '*Young Christian* group' supported the unofficial conferences of church leaders organized by Sir Henry Lunn at Grindelwald in the early 1890s, and Arthur Black attended the one in 1892. King's editorial on the conference was sceptical. After a few rather barbed compliments, he wrote:

> Still, we cannot but hold that all this is distant from the oneness taught by the Apostles and by the Saviour, and may not, in any measure, lead thereto. Though the Grindelwald friends have oneness on their lips, they give little or no proof of acquaintance with the only process by which it can be brought about.[27]

A month later *The Young Christian* referred to an article by the leading Baptist, Dr John Clifford, on Disciples of Christ in Lunn's magazine *The Review of the Churches*. It noted that Clifford's discussion was confined to Disciples of Christ in America and the American Churches in Britain, and made no reference to the older British movement. Why?

> Simply because of the 'stand off' attitude it has adopted towards other religious communities. Its leaders have kept themselves, as far as possible, out of the current of spiritual life flowing through the age. They have inculcated the view that all faithful disciples ought to occupy the same position. They have avoided association with all

believers in Jesus not of their own company. In short, they have done whatever could be done to keep the movement from coming into amiable contact with the bulk of religious organisations with which it is contemporary. This isolating policy has had its natural results. After 'Fifty years' work', the foremost men in the religious world of England are ignorant of the movement and uninfluenced by its existence. Surely there is a lesson in this![28]

The younger men therefore wanted to take advantage of new contacts between the Churches in order to share their confidence in the compelling force of 'the position and plea'. Sydney Black was very much of this opinion. On his voyage to New Zealand from Australia in November 1891, he met Charles Berry, the Congregational minister who did so much for the English Free Church unity movement, and enjoyed much conversation with him. Six years later, when he was President of Conference, Black used his presidential address to make a considered reply to Berry's address as Chairman of the Congregational Union a month or so before. Berry had argued that the unity of the Church did not require a single organization: against this Black set out his vision of New Testament churchmanship:

> For some few years past some of us have been led to cherish the glorious hope that at length many of the most influential and far-seeing minds in religious journalism, and in both Roman and Protestant sects, had gripped the scriptural idea, not only of the *desirability*, but also of the *possibility* and *pressing necessity* of organic Christian union, in order to the speedy and successful evangelization of human society on every continent.

After reviewing Berry's argument for an invisible unity in which separate denominational traditions would continue, he asked how it should be met. It was necessary to meet it *destructively* by demonstrating its scriptural inadequacy, but also, he said:

> We must meet it constructively by pleading everywhere and always for the 'One Flock, One Shepherd' ideal of the early Church; by contending for an unqualified restoration of Primitive Christianity in all its pristine simplicity and purity; by showing that all the apostolic Churches rejoiced not in uniformity of details of working, but in uniformity of organisation and constitution; by pleading for the organic Christian union of all obedient believers in Jesus Christ upon the seven-planked platform constructed by the great Apostle to the Gentiles, under the direct superintendence of the Divine Spirit, and brought to view so clearly in Ephesians iv.4-6; and by demonstrating that the oneness for which our dear Lord so earnestly prayed, in His intercessorial pleading with the Father, instead of being realised by

inter-denominational amenities and courtesies, can alone be effected by the extinction of all dividing barriers and schismatic hobbies, together with the rallying of all the disintegrated forces of Christendom in one glorious army under the blood-stained banner of the Cross. This alien world will never believe until the Church is organically one.[29]

The quotation is important, both for the rhetoric which gives a clue to its style, and also because it shows quite clearly that the fundamental belief, that restoration of New Testament Christianity is possible and unproblematic, remains unaltered. It certainly should not be supposed that Sydney Black was compromising in his attitude to other Churches. A revealing sentence in his obituary states:

Among his fellow-religionists on the Fulham Free Church Council and elsewhere, he was opiniated and obstinate to a degree that helped to isolate the Church of Christ at Twynholm in a way that even its constitution did not necessitate, but again one must qualify the statement, for there was no acerbity in his composition: he used the cudgel in debate with a free enough hand but tabooed the treacherous stiletto.[30]

The most searching test of changing attitudes to Christian unity in this period was the relationship between the Cooperation and the Christian Association. W.T. Moore wrote of the formation of the latter body:

From this time forward the plea for *Christian unity* was to be made a prominent feature in the movement, and in making this plea it was proposed to emphasize points of *agreement* rather than points of *difference*.[31]

This was not far from the attitude taken by some of the 'Young Christian group'. At a personal level the breach between the two groups had never been complete, and there were often friendly relations at local level. In 1901 the Christian Association Conference passed a resolution in favour of closer cooperation with the older body of Churches, and the General Evangelist Committee appointed a group of seven representatives to confer with a similar group from the Christian Association. A two-day conference revealed that the two sides were still a long way apart on the Communion question, but it was nevertheless decided at the Annual Meeting of 1902 to continue the conversations. Eventually it was acknowledged in 1905 that no further progress was possible. The discussions had covered more than the

Communion question: other issues included the position of the pastor or evangelist, the wisdom of accepting offerings from non-church members, the use of instrumental music, and 'the constitution of certain missionary societies'. But a more important difference between the two sides was over the goal: the G.E.C. was thinking of closer cooperation in terms of a common practice, whilst the Christian Association representatives thought in terms of an exchange of preachers and mutual transfer of members, with the continuation of separate conferences. It is interesting to note the way in which the G.E.C. representatives stressed that uniformity of practice in essential matters was a precondition of cooperation: the Christian Association, on the other hand, defended its variety of practice on the grounds of the inalienable rights of the local congregation.[32]

Local contacts continued as before, and by 1910 pressure had built up to the point where a new committee was appointed to investigate the possibilities. A number of American Disciples had been delegates at the Edinburgh Missionary Conference of 1910, when some of them became aware of the older British Churches of Christ for the first time. The British Churches were not represented at Edinburgh, but the *Bible Advocate* reported the conference sympathetically. The renewed discussions with the Christian Association did not produce any better results, so the committee was discharged in 1913.

A new initiative in ecumenical affairs generally began a year later. The Conference paper in 1914 was entitled 'What Churches of Christ might do to promote unity among baptized believers', a topic suggested by John M'Cartney. He had been President in 1912 and in his presidential address he had referred to the quickening of interest in Christian unity in the past twenty-five years. He declared his belief that Churches of Christ could make an invaluable contribution towards the solution of the problem, but, he asked, 'Are we ready for the occasion, should it suddenly emerge?' Would visitors to the Churches recognize the practice of New Testament Christianity if they entered one Lord's day?[33] M'Cartney thought the answer was by no means certain. Lancelot Oliver was the man chosen to read the paper of 1914. Though of quiet and retiring disposition he had in the previous twenty years become an influential figure. He had succeeded to two of David King's leading roles: the editor of the magazine and the man in charge of training. In 1911 he had written a book on

New Testament Christianity, which represented the moderate conservative position then prevailing among the leadership of the British Churches.

Oliver's paper took note of the new situation created by the movement to establish a World Conference on Faith and Order, and he also referred to the work of Peter Ainslie among Disciples of Christ in America, especially his book, *The Message of the Disciples of Christ for the Union of the Church*, published in 1913. The paper did not show much sign of movement over the position which Churches of Christ might take up, but it made two practical suggestions of great importance. One was the appointment of a committee 'to represent the Churches to deal with all practical questions *re* union with others — the Committee for *Christian Unity*'; the other was the need of unity among Churches of Christ — 'If we would persuade others to unity we must manifest unity among ourselves'.[34] The Annual Meeting did appoint a committee of seven to carry on such representative work in relation to the World Conference on Faith and Order, and also American Disciples and the Christian Association. The members were James Marsden, J.W. Black, S. Wolfenden, Lancelot Oliver, W. Richardson, R.W. Black and H.E. Tickle: they were, in effect, the first Union Committee, though it did not become a standing committee of Conference until 1926.

In 1916 the President of the Christian Association Conference, George W. Buckner of the church at Southport, urged that fresh consideration be given to cooperation with the British Churches, and as a result the following resolution prepared by William Price, minister of the church at Lancaster, was approved:

> That in view of the atmosphere of unity, coupled with larger sympathy through a common sorrow, we follow our President's suggestion for larger cooperation, leading, we trust, to unity, with our brethren who hold dear the restoration of primitive Christianity.

Discussions were resumed with a new urgency now that a complete union in a single Co-operation of Churches was proposed. Reporting to the 1917 Annual Conference, the committee stated their view that

> the matter becomes one, not so much for the continued discussion of differences, but for such an adjustment of them as should at once

satisfy conscientious scruples on both sides, and speedily result in joint conformity to a common standard.

The agreement reached was expressed in six resolutions. The first two concerned foundation principles:

(1) The great confession of the Christhood and Divinity of Jesus of Nazareth as the basis of man's relation to God through Him, and the foundation on which the Church is built.

(2) The great commission of the risen Christ as the basis of man's assurance of pardon, and of his relation to the Church, built on the rock foundation.

The other four tackled the differences over communion and ministry:

(1) That we come into Christ, and therefore into His Body, the Church, by faith in Christ, repentance from sin, and, upon confession of faith, immersion in water, in the name of the Lord Jesus Christ.

(2) That the Lord's Supper is an ordinance inside the Church, and, according to our understanding of New Testament practice, scriptural qualification to participate therein is attained by compliance with the above conditions.

(3) That it is our duty to do everything in our power, and as soon as possible, to induce any unimmersed believers who present themselves at the Lord's Table to obey Christ in believer's immersion.

(4) That it is our duty to develop the abilities of all the members of the Church capable of taking part in the Lord's work, and to afford them suitable opportunities.

It was clearly stated that the statements were not intended as a credal standard. The Committee concluded:

We have not surrendered anything, nor have we made a compromise with aught of what you or we disapprove.

Arrangements were also made to combine the assets of the two Associations, and to make provision for three extra members of the G.E.C. to be elected from Christian Association churches for a transitional period of six years to handle the distribution of funds from the F.C.M.S.[35]

The Christian Association Conference at Cheltenham accepted these proposals unanimously in July 1917. The Churches of Christ Annual Conference at Leicester approved them by 115 votes to 12.[36] The feelings were described by the President of the Christian Association as follows:

'They were all with one accord in one place' waiting for a deputation to come from the Annual Meeting assembled in Sir Edward Wood Hall, a short distance away, to convey to us the result of our application as Churches to be received into the co-operation. The intervening time was spent in hearing a synopsis of the Presidential Address of Mr A.J. Elwes by one of our brethren who heard it in the morning . . . Some time was also spent in prayer, in which several took part. Then someone near the window was heard to ejaculate: 'They're coming!' And sure enough a motor-car conveying J.W. Black, W. Richardson and H.E. Tickle was seen hurrying to our hotel. Bro Black was the spokesman, and in few words announced that our application had been acceded to by an overwhelming majority, and he also said that the Conference was waiting to give us a welcome. We hurried to the street below, where tram-cars were immediately requisitioned, and in a few moments our whole party were in the Conference Hall, and given such a welcome as will not soon be forgotten by those privileged to welcome it. Those of us who were honoured with a place on the platform were greatly moved by the scene in the body of the Hall. Numbers were seen wiping tears from their eyes. The *Bible Advocate* truly remarks:— 'The welcome to the platform of the Christian Association's representatives made a scene which may well be regarded as historic.'[37]

Fifteen of the seventeen Christian Association churches joined the Cooperation, with a total membership of 1,341. Two churches, stayed out: the church at Southampton, which was 50 or 60 miles from the nearest Church of Christ and very much absorbed in its own growth and activity; and Neston (Cheshire), an independently founded church of immersed believers, which had only joined the Association in 1911.[38]

One consequence of the union which was not so favourable for ecumenical progress concerned relations with the Free Church Council. In explaining the union to the American Churches Leslie Morgan, the General Secretary of the Christian Association, gave as a second reason for it, after 'the spirit of unity created by the war':

> An embarrassing situation arising from the fact that for the first time the two groups of churches, both pleading for Christian union, were each represented, but separately, in an important conference called to consider the union of the Free Churches. Hitherto this field had been left almost exclusively to the churches represented by the Christian Association.[39]

The leaders of the Christian Association had been very active ecumenically since the Edinburgh Conference of 1910: they were the first body in England to appoint a commission to the World Conference on Faith and Order. Another aspect of their involvement had been participation in the discussions about a new move towards Free Church unity. The older Churches of Christ had given a cool reception to the enquiries of the National Free Church Council in 1912, saying that they could not contemplate organic connection with the Council as they were not a denomination.[40] In 1916, when J.H. Shakespeare's proposals for a United Free Church of England raised the matter again, the Conference agreed to appoint James Marsden and R.W. Black 'to consider whether and on what basis union is possible'.[41] At the time the Christian Association churches were welcomed in 1917, however, James Marsden noted as a proof of their genuineness that 'in order to join, as they were doing in joining us, a *close* communion body, they had withdrawn from the Federation', notwithstanding the fact that one of their number was secretary of one of the committees.[42]

The problem for Churches of Christ about the proposed Free Church Federation lay, as James Marsden had indicated, in the proposal for inter-communion. The first of the resolutions passed by the conference of Free Church representatives held at Mansfield College, Oxford, in the autumn of 1916 was as follows:

> That in any Federation of Churches it is essential that communicants who are in membership with any of them shall be admitted to the communion of the Lord's Table in any other and all of the federating Churches.[43]

The two representatives of the older Churches of Christ dissented from this resolution, which clearly stood no chance of acceptance at that time. Perhaps if there had been some recognition of the significance of baptism as a theological issue, the outcome might have been different. In an article on 'Churches of Christ and the Free Church Council' in the *Bible Advocate* for 7 March 1919 the Editor, R.K. Francis, wrote that Churches of Christ would very much like to join the Free Church Council but felt unable to do so because of three fundamental differences — on the nature of faith, baptism and conversion: he also repeated the traditional objection to a professional ministry, but it was the cluster of issues surrounding baptism that was decisive.[44] It should also be remembered that many of those involved in the formation of the Federal Council of Free Churches saw it as the

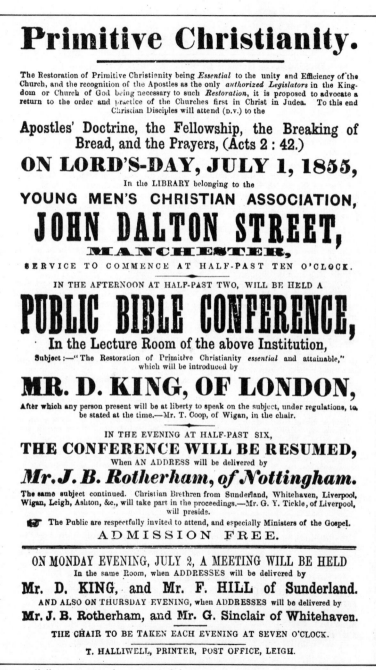

Primitive Christianity.

The Restoration of Primitive Christianity being *Essential* to the unity and Efficiency of the Church, and the recognition of the Apostles as the only *authorized Legislators* in the Kingdom or Church of God being necessary to such *Restoration*, it is proposed to advocate a return to the order and practice of the Churches first in Christ in Judea. To this end Christian Disciples will attend (D.V.) to the

Apostles' Doctrine, the Fellowship, the Breaking of Bread, and the Prayers, (Acts 2 : 42.)

ON LORD'S-DAY, JULY 1, 1855,

In the LIBRARY belonging to the

YOUNG MEN'S CHRISTIAN ASSOCIATION,

JOHN DALTON STREET,

MANCHESTER,

SERVICE TO COMMENCE AT HALF-PAST TEN O'CLOCK.

IN THE AFTERNOON AT HALF-PAST TWO, WILL BE HELD A

PUBLIC BIBLE CONFERENCE,

In the Lecture Room of the above Institution,

Subject :—"The Restoration of Primitive Christianity *essential* and attainable," which will be introduced by

MR. D. KING, OF LONDON,

After which any person present will be at liberty to speak on the subject, under regulations, to be stated at the time.—Mr. T. Coop, of Wigan, in the chair.

IN THE EVENING AT HALF-PAST SIX,

THE CONFERENCE WILL BE RESUMED,

When AN ADDRESS will be delivered by

Mr. J. B. Rotherham, of Nottingham.

The same subject continued. Christian Brethren from Sunderland, Whitehaven, Liverpool, Wigan, Leigh, Ashton, &c., will take part in the proceedings.—Mr. G. Y. Tickle, of Liverpool, will preside.

☞ The Public are respectfully invited to attend, and especially Ministers of the Gospel.

ADMISSION FREE.

ON MONDAY EVENING, JULY 2, A MEETING WILL BE HELD
In the same Room, when ADDRESSES will be delivered by

Mr. D. KING, and Mr. F. HILL of Sunderland.

AND ALSO ON THURSDAY EVENING, when ADDRESSES will be delivered by

Mr. J. B. Rotherham, and Mr. G. Sinclair of Whitehaven.

THE CHAIR TO BE TAKEN EACH EVENING AT SEVEN O'CLOCK.

T. HALLIWELL, PRINTER, POST OFFICE, LEIGH.

1. Handbill announcing the opening of the meetings in Manchester, 1855 (see page 50)

THE RESTORATION OF PRIMITIVE CHRISTIANITY.

Disciples having the above for their object, assemble in the late Baptist

Chapel, Oldham Street, Manchester.

SYNOPSIS.

1. THE existence of numerous dominations, alienated from each other, having distinctive names, creeds, and rites, is anti-scriptural and carnal. 1 Cor. iii. 4. John, xvii. 21.

II. The Redeemer's preparatory work having been completed under the Jewish dispensation, in order to the introduction of the *Christian Economy*, or Kingdom of Heaven, on the day of Pentecost next following his resurrection—the Gospel, ordinances, and polity of the present dispensation, must be learned from the book of the Acts of the Apostles and the Epistles written by them to the churches. Matt. xix. 28. 1 John iv. 6, Heb. ii. 3. 4.

III. Legislative authority having been committed to the apostles, and they having, under the direction of the Holy Spirit, entirely perfected and delivered, *once for all*, the faith, or *Christian system*—a strict and faithful adherence to the things preached and taught by them would prove alone and fully sufficient for the union of all who love the Saviour.

IV. That, as the rise and consummation of the Papacy, all sectarianism, and want of union, are direct and legitimate results of deviating from that system, the union of Christians, and the realization of the full use and power of the church depend upon its restoration.

V. Such restoration would distinguish the one body of the Lord from unauthorised sects, by the following, among other characteristics :—

Its numerous congregations would have but one name, one creed, one polity (Eph. iv. 1, 6.)—co-operating for great objects, each would manage its own affairs, guided by the apostolic writings, and uncontrolled by sister churches, synods, or conferences.

The many congregations would not compose divers sects, but together from the one church, or party of the Lord.

Persons believing on the Lord Jesus, and confessing his name, and only such, would be entitled to membership. Rom. x. 8-15. John i. 12.

Thus begotten of God by the word of truth (James i. 18)—without regard to human creeds or difference of opinion, being constituted members of the one body, by an immersion in the name of Jesus, (Acts ii. 38), into him, (Gal. iii. 27), and into his death. (Rom. vi. 3).

On the first day of every week each congregation would worship God, not only in spirit, but with due regard to the divine order, (Col. ii. 5), attending stedfastly to mutual prayer and praise,—mutual teaching and exhortation,*—the fellowship† and the breaking of bread. (Acts ii. 42. Rom. xii. 5—8.

For efficient oversight each congregation would ordain elders, pastors, or bishops—and for various services deacons,—all of whom would be chosen from the church in which they labour, and not have official standing in other congregations. In order to the extension of the kingdom, brethren would be appointed to proclaim the gospel, and to plant and set in order churches.

---

* Every brother, competent to edify the body, having liberty to teach or exhort.

† The Fellowship, involving the presentation of a free-will offering by each member, according to his prosperity, and being the authorised arrangement for aiding the poor and the proclamation of the Gospel, would render unnecessary begging sermons, and the other love-destroying schemes of modern parties.

MEETINGS.

LORD'S DAY MORNINGS, at 10½, to worship God after the Apostolic order.
LORD'S DAY AFTERNOONS, at half-past Two, Public Discourses.
LORD'S DAY EVENINGS, at half-past Six,   Ditto.
MONDAY EVENINGS,   } at half-past Seven, Public Meetings & Conferences.
THURSDAY EVENINGS, }
          SEATS FREE.—Contributions not expected from Strangers.

2. Handbill advertising the Manchester church, 1855 (see page 50)

3. *James Wallis*

4. *David King*

5. John Crook

6. Sydney Black

7. *Lancelot Oliver*

8. *William Robinson*

9. Overdale College: the first building in Moseley, 1920

10. Overdale College: the second building in Selly Oak,
after reconstruction, 1958

11. *Twynholm Hall, London, 1896 (The poster says, 'Mr Sydney Black preaches the Gospel of Christ here every Lord's Day at 7 p.m. and every Wednesday at 8 p.m. 500 seats free: no collections.') (see page 93)*

12. *East Kilbride Church of Christ: the opening ceremony, 1962 (see page 170)*

13. James Gray

14. Philip Morgan

first step to a United Free Church of England: certainly this was J.H. Shakespeare's vision.

The hesitation felt about the Free Church Council did not, however, extend to the proposed World Conference on Faith and Order. Peter Ainslie had met with Churches of Christ leaders in London, Leicester and Edinburgh during his visit to Britain in 1913-14 and had enlisted their support for the Conference.[45] In 1918 the Conference paper was given by H.E. Tickle on the Formularies to be presented to the Preparatory Conference on Faith and Order, which led to 'a profitable discussion'.[46] Three representatives — H.E. Tickle, J.W. Black and W. Robinson — attended the Preparatory Conference at Geneva in 1920, a delegation which compared favourably with that of other English Free Churches (two Wesleyans, two Congregationalists, one United Methodist and one Baptist). The Conference made a great impression on the representatives, and they made some impression on it.[47] It was William Robinson's introduction to the Faith and Order movement to which he made an important, though often incognito, contribution. But the unexpected death of H.E. Tickle in April 1921 has tended to obscure his vital contribution to the beginnings of ecumenical involvement for Churches of Christ. William Robinson wrote of him:

> Perhaps no one ever represented the plea for union, on the basis of a return to New Testament Christianity, with such dignity and charm as Henry Tickle. . . . His chief work, however, was in connection with the Geneva Conference. He was largely responsible for the Formularies which he presented to the Conference last August. . . . At Geneva he came in contact with the world's leaders in the Christian Union movement, and moved with grace amongst them. . . . My own experience of the Geneva Conference — rich as it was — could not have meant to me what it did but for the fellowship of this man of God.[48]

Henry Tickle, younger son of G.Y. Tickle who had remonstrated with Alexander Campbell over open communion, had the experience and enjoyed the trust which were each required to lead Churches of Christ into the new ecumenical age. In committing themselves to unity, rather than federation, as the goal (as the Formularies clearly stated), the Churches were destined to discover that the way was harder than they had hitherto supposed.

These developments took place against a background of continuing expansion in the total membership, even though the rate of growth slowed down. The total membership in the jubilee year of 1892 was 9,954: in 1917, just before the Christian Association churches joined, it was 15,101; and in 1920 it was 16,011. In other words the quarter-century after the jubilee saw a growth of about 50% compared with about 150% in the quarter-century before. The deceleration is not surprising, and the growth rate achieved compares very favourably with that of the major nonconformist denominations in this period: but contemporaries were very much aware of the fact that many more joined the church than remained in its membership.

In 1912, Bartley Ellis, the evangelist, read a Conference paper entitled 'Some Main Causes of Separations, and suggestions for staying this serious drainage from our numbers'.[49] Ellis noted that 26 years earlier H.E. Tickle had read a paper on the same subject.[50] What strikes the modern reader is how similar the analysis was in each case. Ellis calculated that in the ten years from August 1901 to August 1911 there had been a total of 12,961 additions (10,252 by immersion) and 7,473 separations — a loss of 58%. This compared with a loss of 46% calculated by Tickle for the decade 1875-85 in his paper. Both writers explained the loss largely in terms of inadequate pastoral care and teaching in the local church, coupled with the usual temptations, especially drink. Both writers also stressed the importance of marrying within the church fellowship. They recognized, though they did not explore, the problems created by migration in search of employment, including emigration overseas. Ellis did not suppose that all those separated were 'lost to the Lord', but he argued that this showed 'the necessity of doing all we can to plant churches in those districts where at present there are none'.

In fact, with the exception of South Wales, there was relatively little expansion into completely new areas. East Anglia, the south west and most of southern England remained areas where there was no Church of Christ at all. The distribution of the total membership was very similar in 1917 to that in 1892. Nearly half continued to live in the Midland and the Lancashire and Cheshire divisions, but the dominance of the Midland division was rather more marked in 1917 with 28% of the membership as compared with 24% in 1892. The North Western division, which contained Carlisle and a string of churches along the Cumberland coast, had declined from 6% to 2% with a net decline in the number of churches too. The percentage living in Scotland had also declined from 20% in 1892 to 18% in 1917. The newcomer on the scene was the South Wales division, consisting of seven churches in 1917 with 3% of the total membership. The distribution of the Christian Association churches which joined the Cooperation in 1917 meant that the Southern, North Wales, and Lancashire and Cheshire divisions gained in their proportions of the total membership at the expense of the Midland: nevertheless in 1920 the Midland division still contained a quarter of the total membership.

Under the impetus of the 'Forward Movement' the General Evangelist Committee was responsible for several of the new churches formed in this period: but some of these were quite short-lived; for example, Hawick, formed in 1891, ceased to exist in 1897. Generally speaking, new churches depended as much on the support which came from other churches in the district as on the evangelistic help which the G.E.C. could give. The most obvious exceptions to this are the Potteries and South Wales. In the Potteries Bartley Ellis began the church at Burslem in 1890, and then founded churches at Newcastle-under-Lyme in 1893 and Tunstall in 1895. In South Wales the leading figure was William Webley, a Welsh-speaking evangelist, who had formerly been a Baptist minister. He had been won over to the position of Churches of Christ by James Grinstead shortly after he began the new work in Bristol in 1890. Having indicated his willingness to work with the G.E.C. Webley went first to Cricceith in 1891. Then in 1892 he went south to Griffithstown and in the next twenty years founded six churches. It was under his influence that four others from South Wales became evangelists: John and Urbane Nicholls, David Morgan and William Probert.[51]

The enthusiasm of those who campaigned for the Forward Movement was not matched by the giving of the churches. As early as 1892 the G.E.C. had a deficit and during the year 1893-94 it passed the £500 mark, causing the bank to take notice. This led to the appointment of a special committee on Funds in 1895 which reported the following year. A scheme was proposed for clearing the deficit, and it was also agreed that it would be wise for the G.E.C. not to appeal for funds to churches which were already involved in divisional or district cooperation for evangelization.[52] This was the nemesis of the policy of making the opening up of new areas the special work of the G.E.C., thereby leaving ordinary work to the divisions and districts; and the results were disastrous. Though the deficit was cleared, giving to the G.E.C. dropped further, creating a fresh deficit in 1897. In 1898 another special committee was appointed to review the relationships between the G.E.C. and the divisions. A proposal that G.E.C. and divisional funds should be combined was rejected by the committee, but it was agreed to give the G.E.C. access to all the churches again. The committee's proposal that the G.E.C. should be enlarged to include representatives from each of the divisions was adopted in 1900.[53] These differences of opinion over organization were to some extent overcome by the campaign launched in 1898, on the initiative of G.Y. Tickle the younger, to win ten thousand souls for Christ before the end of the century. Unfortunately this was a resounding failure, prompting a good deal of soul-searching at the Conference of 1900 — R.W. Black thought that there should have been an appeal for money as well as souls! T.J. Ainsworth, one of the supporters of the Forward Movement, suggested that more emphasis on solid teaching was needed, thereby providing yet another example of the persistent tendency among Churches of Christ to emphasize dogmatic rather than experimental religion, a tendency which goes back to Campbell himself and also to the Scotch Baptists.[54]

Organizational solutions were again tried. Ainsworth suggested a paid secretary to the Cooperation in his Chairman's address in 1902, and a resolution of Conference authorized the G.E.C. to make an appointment. (Interestingly, this was supported by R.W. Black, but opposed by his elder brother, Sydney.)[55] Probably the retirement of John Crook in 1900 made this need more obvious. But it was easier to state the need than to find the man. A.J. Elwes was appointed in 1903 but had to give up after six months. George Collin was appointed in 1904 'as far as he might find it practicable'. Then in 1908 James Flisher of Manchester, who had already been appointed first organizing secretary to the General Sunday School Committee in 1907, took over as salaried secretary to the G.E.C. as well, an office he held until his death in 1925. From 1904 until 1910 there was also a Finance Committee whose job it was to stimulate systematic giving in the churches. The last attempt to bring some stability to the income of the G.E.C. was the establishment of the Evangelization Endowment Fund in 1915. The aim was to raise a capital sum, which would provide a guaranteed annual income, and the initial contribution came from the legatees of David King who made a gift of £1,350. By the end of the war the capital was more than £3,000. However, the Fund was also controversial, partly because some objected to the movement away from the voluntary principle in church finance, and partly because the necessity for a trust deed meant involvement with the law.[56]

Despite the various changes in the organization the practice of local evangelization remained very much the same. An evangelist like T.K. Thompson, though settled in Leicester from 1900 until his enforced retirement in 1912, would still spend several months in the year away from home helping with special efforts with churches or districts, including visits to the East Coast towns in the autumn to provide services for the herring fishermen and their womenfolk as they came down from Scotland to Great Yarmouth or Lowestoft. Bartley Ellis, another evangelist of the same generation, was in regular demand for the starting of new churches and for special efforts in connection with the opening of new chapels. Reference has already been made to his work in the Potteries in the 1890s. In 1909 he was involved with the opening of the church at Evington Road, Leicester; 1910 saw him in Bolton; in 1911 he was working with the new church at Broomhill Road, Bulwell; and in 1912 he was working with the new church at Chorley. In the same year the G.E.C. took a new step forward with the employment of the first Home Missions Sister, Mrs Ethel B. Cranfield. She was a trained nurse and began work with the churches in Glasgow in district visiting, nursing, Bible reading and women's meetings.[57] The money for her work was raised by the Sisters' Committee, and in 1913 she was joined by two others, Sister Hunt and Sister Hoyes.

Whilst the patterns of local church life were relatively slow to change, the discussions over finance and organization of the General Evangelist Committee are a reminder that the corporate life of the Churches was becoming more complex with the growing membership. The first standing orders of the Annual Meeting were adopted in 1890. In 1892 a new system for making nominations to committees was introduced and although it was abolished in 1895 as being too cumbersome, it was reintroduced in 1900, together with voting by ballot. From 1907 committee members were elected for three years, with a rota for retirement.[58] These changes were an acknowledgement of the fact that the growing size of the Annual Meeting made more formal procedures necessary: the new voting procedures also made committees more representative of the country as a whole and marked the end of the practice of basing a committee in a single area, which had obviously made meetings easier to arrange and kept costs down. On the other hand these changes did limit the number of people who had the time to serve, and there is an increase in the frequency of the accusation that the Annual Meeting was dominated by a more affluent class of people.

To combat this, an increasing number of people began to urge that a system of delegate voting be introduced. A letter from J.A. (? Joseph Adam) in the *Bible Advocate* for 1890 first proposed this, and the committee on nominations which reported in 1892 also had this question as an item on its agenda. No action was taken then, but another committee was appointed to look at the matter in 1905. It proposed that a system of delegate voting, with churches represented in accordance with their membership, be tried for the years 1907-9, but action was delayed in 1906 and in the following year the proposal was thrown out.[59] Always the argument against it was that such a system was the first step towards giving the Annual Meeting power to take decisions for the churches.

The work of the Cooperation continued to expand. In 1903 a central book depot for the Churches was opened at 100, John Bright Street, Birmingham. This brought together the distribution work of three committees, the Publishing Committee, the Magazine Committee and the Sunday School Committee, and also enabled the Churches to sell other literature as an ordinary bookseller. In 1905 the responsibility for the magazine was transferred to the Publishing Committee, whose terms of reference were enlarged. They soon published their first full-length books: Lancelot Oliver's *New Testament Christianity* (1911) and James Anderson's *Outline of my Life* (1912). Previously they had only published tracts, and reprints of American books. But the most important publishing venture of this period was a new hymn book. Previous Churches of Christ hymn books had been the work of individuals, beginning with James Wallis's collection of 1841, which was twice enlarged. In 1888 David King and G.Y. Tickle had produced a further enlarged edition, and in 1893 King made over the rights in this edition to the Publishing Committee. During the 1890s the Committee were at work on the production of a Gospel Hymnal, which was published in 1899, but suggestions were already being made for a new general hymn book. In 1903 a special sub-committee began work, and the new book was published in 1908, containing 1,036 hymns. The main editorial work was done by Lancelot Oliver and James Nimmo.[60]

The work of the Training Committee also gradually expanded, after a short period (1893-1895) when responsibility for it was returned to the G.E.C. In 1896 Lancelot Oliver was given the assistance of John M'Cartney for the Correspondence Classes, and the training work continued in their hands until the foundation of Overdale College.*

There was still considerable resistance, however, to too wide an expansion of the scope of the Annual Meeting. The Temperance Conference remained a separate entity until almost the end of this period, despite an intensifying interest in the drink question and an increasing tendency to see its solution as the key to solving all Britain's social problems. W.B. Ainsworth urged that the Temperance Committee be officially recognized by the conferenc in his Chairman's address for 1915, and in 1916, in response to a suggestion that churches indicate their support of such a change on the annual schedule to Conference, 72 churches said they would approve this step. It was therefore agreed that two Conference papers, one in favour and one against, should be read at the 1917 Conference. As a result the G.E.C. was instructed to prepare a plan for a Temperance and Social Questions Sub-Committee, reporting to Conference through the G.E.C., and this plan was approved in 1918. In 1919, however, it was decided that the existing Temperance Committee should continue and report directly to Conference, which it did for the first time in 1920. One of the items in its report was the appointment of the first organizing secretary to the committee, R.H. Parker. The change still produced a protest from William Chapman, that this was a breach of the rule that the Cooperation was for 'evangelization only'.[61]

Another area of difficulty was chapel building. In 1902 a

---

* Although the discussions which led to this step took place in this period, they will be considered in chapter 5 for the sake of continuity.

proposal from the church at Ballymacarrett that the Annual Meeting should establish a Chapel Building Committee was referred to the General Evangelist Committee, with the suggestion that it should negotiate with the Christian Chapel Building Committee. The report of the sub-committee appointed was referred back to the G.E.C. in 1905 with the request that further information should be obtained on the possibility of churches holding property without trust deeds. One persistent objection to trust deeds was that they involved a doctrinal statement which was tantamount to a creed. But a more subtle objection was made by Samuel Wolfenden in his Conference paper that year on 'Evangelistic Cooperation considered in relation to the Independence of Individual Churches'. Wolfenden did not accept the view that the doctrinal clause of a trust deed constituted a creed, but he did believe that, if the Conference began to hold church property, it was laying itself open to the possibility of being drawn into the internal affairs of churches, particularly if there was division in a church. Furthermore on trust deeds in general he said:

> Every Trust Deed does, and must, contemplate as the means of its enforcement in difficulties an appeal to an earthly court of justice, and the use of the forces of compulsion which belong to world powers. Such an appeal is forbidden to the Christian as a mode of settlement between him and his brethren.[62]

The whole question was, of course, a topical one, because the minority of the Free Church of Scotland which stayed out of the union with the United Presbyterian Church in 1900 had recently won its claim in the House of Lords to all the property of the Free Church, on the grounds that the union constituted a breach of trust. It was Wolfenden's argument which was later deployed against the Evangelization Endowment Fund.

Nevertheless the question of creeds proved more emotive. After a further reference back in 1906, it was reported in 1907 that there was no alternative to doctrinal clauses in a trust deed, and it was resolved (with a minuted dissent) that a committee should be appointed to arrange for the Annual Meeting to take over the assets of the Christian Chapel Building Fund. However, in 1908 it was decided not to proceed with this course of action and instead the G.E.C. was given power to nominate three of the five members of the C.C.B.F. committee.[63] There the matter rested until after the war.

In these and other ways it was becoming clear before 1914 that the range of opinions within Churches of Christ about the nature and purpose of the movement was widening. In 1906 it was formally recognized that the movement in the U.S.A. was divided when the conservative, non-instrumental churches were separately listed in the U.S. Census as Churches of Christ, the more liberal group being listed as Disciples of Christ. This division did not begin in 1906: arguably it can be traced as far back as the Civil War.[64] The British Churches had many personal links with the more conservative American group, and American support for the Christian Association churches tended to reinforce British determination to steer a middle, if not a clearly conservative, course. But the First World War had a polarizing effect on the British Churches in a way comparable to the effects of the Civil War in America. 'It would be difficult to exaggerate the strain which has been put upon the Churches in this Cooperation since the beginning of the war,' wrote Lancelot Oliver in 1918,[65] and he more than anyone else had to bear them as editor of the *Bible Advocate*.

He had to some extent been prepared for this by the Boer War, from 1899 to 1902. Traditionally, like the rest of English nonconformity, Churches of Christ had been opposed to war — a position which it was relatively easy for a nineteenth-century Englishman to hold, since with the exception of the Crimean War Britain was not involved in any European wars between 1815 and 1914. Nonconformist Liberals were also generally opposed to imperial ambitions (which were identified with the Conservative party), until the party split over Irish Home Rule in 1886. Thereafter party loyalties became less clear-cut, and the 1890s saw the emergence of a nonconformist Unionist group which moved towards the Conservatives. Thus Henry Tickle's criticisms of government policy in the Transvaal in the 'News and Views' column of the *Bible Advocate* in 1899 led to protests from some brethren. Lancelot Oliver's wish to avoid unnecessary controversy led to Tickle's resignation in January 1900 — an action which itself provoked a number of letters supporting his line in the weeks which followed.[66] Nevertheless the Annual Meeting felt no difficulty in adopting a resolution recording 'our solemn protest against the military spirit now so prevalent in British society generally', and expressing 'our deep grief and regret that this spirit so largely permeates many sections of the churches professing to be Christian'.[67]

In 1901 Henry Tickle read a Conference paper on the attitude of the Churches towards service in the army and navy, compulsory or voluntary, which was widely recognized as taking a balanced position. Whilst acknowledging without hesitation that Christianity did not sanction war in general and that its whole genius was antagonistic to the spirit of war, Tickle argued that Christianity did recognize that 'under given conditions, war becomes not only a possibility, but a dread inevitability'. Even so Tickle maintained that

> it seems to be today, as in the early days of the Church, the privilege and duty of the individual to decline all such (military) service, whether voluntary or compulsory, even if such a course should involve penalties in person or property.[68]

When war broke out in 1914, Tickle's paper was reprinted in the *Bible Advocate* for the guidance of members. But it soon become clear just how different the situation was. Whereas in 1899 support for government policy was confined to a minority in the churches, in 1914 the appeal that war was necessary to save Belgium enjoyed wide support. So there was a much greater response to the call for voluntary enlistment. The difference of opinion first became clear when William Mottershaw of Nottingham suggested that the *Bible Advocate* publish a list of the names and addresses of brethren in camp so that they could keep in touch with one another. After the first list had appeared, the evangelist T.E. Entwistle protested that publication seemed to encourage enlistment, and as a result he was given the job of keeping the list, presumably because he conducted the Temperance and Social Questions column in the *B.A.* As it became clear that Entwistle was totally opposed to the war, this arrangement could hardly work, and in May 1915 A.J. Elwes took over responsibility for correspondence with men in the armed forces.[69] By the beginning of 1916 his list included more than 600 names.

The outbreak of war coincided with the opening of the 1914 Annual Meeting, and a resolution was passed appealing to the government to remain neutral, copies of which were wired to the Prime Minister, the Foreign Secretary and Lloyd George (whose family were members of the church at Cricceith). Like the other main Free Churches, opinion slowly moved towards the view that war was a regrettable necessity, and the 1915 Annual Meeting passed no resolution on the war at all. The hope was, as Lancelot Oliver recalled in October 1915, that mutual respect for different convictions would prevail. The threat, and subsequent introduction, of conscription destroyed this possibility. The pacifists hoped that the Churches might be persuaded to oppose conscription, even if they would not oppose the war.

The hope was not unreasonable. Members of Churches of Christ had played a significant part in the anti-vaccination campaign in the late nineteenth century, which provided the precedent for 'conscientious objection' to the Military Service Act; a number had been passive resisters in the campaign against the education rate after the Education Act of 1902. But feelings were running too high for their hope to be realized. The situation was made worse by the different attitudes taken on exemption by the local tribunals in different parts of the country. The story of official attitudes to conscientious objectors during the First World War is one of the shabbier sides of modern British history and Churches of Christ did not escape it. The atmosphere in a church like Crafton Street, Leicester, which included in the membership Jonathan North, mayor of the borough during the war, and George Hassall, a prominent leader of the pacifist group, can easily be imagined. So developed the situation described by Walter Crosthwaite as follows:

> Leaders urged our young men to enlist and fight for King and Country, and scant sympathy was given to those who stood for the old attitude. With the coming of conscription, we saw our young men turned down by tribunals of which leaders in their own Churches were chairmen. Brethren, some of whom were elders in the Churches, sat on magisterial benches and handed their own Brethren over to their persecutors.[70]

In April 1916 a group of pacifists from the Lancashire churches met at Platt Bridge and agreed to organize a national conference of those opposed to the war in June. Objection was taken by some church leaders to an advertisement of this conference appearing in the *Bible Advocate*. The conference was well-supported, and a second was held at Leicester during the Annual Meeting of 1917. Two more were held in Leicester and Birmingham during 1918. In the course of the war, 61 men were arrested as a result of resisting the Military Service Acts, and twelve of these spent more than a year in prison. Arthur Wilson, of Blackburn, died in Strangeways Prison, Manchester in December 1918 of influenza. Clifford Cartwright was sentenced to death in France, but the sentence was commuted to penal servitude. (It should be noted that conscientious objectors who were taken to France rendered themselves liable to death by firing squad if they continued to disobey orders, since they were then technically on active service. This tactic was used in an effort to break the resistance of the most stubborn.) Groups of Churches of Christ objectors in both Dartmoor and Wakefield prisons held regular services for the Breaking of Bread.[71]

The strongly committed pacifist group was very small — 125 indicated their willingness to resist military service at the first meeting at Wigan, and it is unlikely that the total number of men involved was more than 300. This contrasts with more than 600 men on Julian Elwes's list of brethren in the armed forces by 1916. But the bare figures tell little of mental turmoil over the principles, both within and between brethren. The path of those like Oliver who wanted to respect conscientious beliefs on both sides was difficult. At the 1916 Annual Meeting Julian Elwes organized a service 'in sympathetic remembrance of all our men . . . who have fallen, are serving, or are suffering in the war'. He had hoped that this would include everyone, but inevitably the emphasis fell on those who had lost their sons in battle. Thus when it was proposed to repeat it in 1917, it was opposed as glorifying war, and the idea was dropped.[72] The 1916 Annual Meeting passed a long resolution on the war which referred to both those fighting and those resisting, and a similar resolution was passed in 1917 and reaffirmed in 1918. To read the obituary column in the *Bible Advocate* in these years is to be reminded how many leaders in the churches did lose their sons on the Western Front.

The strain of 'holding the ring' took its toll of Lancelot Oliver. In 1917 he offered his resignation as editor, but it was not accepted. Instead R.K. Francis, who was one of those taking the pacifist position, was appointed Assistant Editor. Then in 1918 Oliver suffered a breakdown in health, from which he never really recovered. He died in 1920. In a tribute Henry Tickle referred directly to the strain of the war years upon him:

> At times the criticism was frank, and, it is feared, cut deep into a sensitive nature. This can be said, that under circumstances in which

> no one could have succeeded, Bro. Oliver did not fail, and possibly the brotherhood owes more than it knows to his moderating influence during those testing years.[73]

These words gain added weight when Tickle's own experience in the Boer War is remembered.

VII

As the Churches faced the return to peace in 1919, they had become aware of the extent to which they had changed since they began. One obvious sign of this was in social status. In 1905 Samuel Wolfenden had observed:

> The last half century has made a change in the worldly status of the brethren. Fifty years since, even elders and leaders might usually be found in the lower ranks of life, among the humble handicraftsmen — now they may often be looked for among the locally influential. The change is not wholly to be deplored, but such results are not gained except at corresponding loss.[74]

More acidly this was noted by Walter Crosthwaite in 1916 when he wrote, 'Most of our brethren, and especially those who attend A.M.'s, with the exception of evangelists, are making more money than ever they did'.[75]

The change was seen in a more cautious attitude to social and labour questions. As it happened, the industries which contained most Churches of Christ employers — textiles and footwear — were not those most subject to strikes: there were no Churches of Christ colliery owners, so it was safe to express sympathy for striking miners, as in 1898 — even here though, there was more caution in 1912. Perhaps part of the appeal of the Temperance question was that it posited a solution to social and economic problems which did not involve any criticism of the economic structure of society.

But there was also questioning of the 'position and plea', or at least of its implications. For the moment the full implications of biblical criticism were felt only by a few. But the beginnings of ecumenical involvement and the union with the Christian Association were raising sharper questions. The issue turned on the nature of the Cooperation and the independence of the local church. Only a few wanted to see more power vested in the Annual Meeting. But the conservatives who supported the independence of the local church were in a dilemma. They saw that this independence allowed churches to introduce organs if they wished: in 1920 the Annual Meeting said that it felt that it was 'beyond its power to interfere with the action of any individual church in this matter'.[76] They had seen the consequences of this view in the refusal of the Annual Meeting to take a definite stand on the war. They feared that this attitude would now allow ex-Christian Association churches excessive liberty in their communion practice. The way was therefore open for the accusation that an increasing number of churches were deserting the 'old paths'. One of the first battlegrounds was the new arrangements for ministerial training introduced in 1920.

5 PEACE AND WAR

I

Churches of Christ reached their maximum membership in Great Britain in 1930 when the churches reported a total of 16,596. This is much later than most of the other Free Churches in the country, which usually reached their peak before the First World War. Although it is clear now that the inter-war years marked a turning point, it is important to remember that this was not so obvious at the time. Four out of the ten divisions reached their peak membership after 1930, with the Midland division peak coming as late as 1936. In many ways therefore the inter-war years were the heyday of Churches of Christ. The atmosphere was generally one of confidence, despite the serious tensions which developed.

In general the distribution of church membership remained very much the same. Half the membership lived in the Midland and the Lancashire and Cheshire divisions in 1945, as had been the case for half a century. But the dominance of the Midland division had increased still further: 31% of the membership now lived here. The areas of sharpest decline were Yorkshire and Cumberland, both of which had their maximum membership during the First World War. Another area of sharp decline was the Southern division, but here a major factor was the withdrawal of the largest church in the Association, Twynholm, with a membership of 671 in 1931: that represented between a quarter and a third of the membership in the whole division. Apart from this, the gains and losses resulting from churches joining and leaving the Association roughly balanced out. In 1917 the Christian Association churches had increased the total membership by 1,341. Between 1913 and 1948 twenty-three 'Old Path' churches withdrew from the Association and their membership was 1,338 — though about half of these withdrew after 1945.

The overall statistics therefore give a reasonably accurate impression of the real state of the Churches in this period. The picture is one of very slow increase in the 1920s, and then gradually accelerating decline from 1930 to 1945. During the 1930s the total number of baptisms was 6,389 and the total additions (excluding gains by transfer) amounted to 7,722. Separations (including the membership of churches withdrawing from the Association) numbered 7,504. This means that the separation rate had risen to 97%, compared with 58% between 1901 and 1911. One interesting feature is that the loss from emigration in the 1930s was almost negligible: 94, or 9 a year. This compares with a loss by emigration of 2,551 between 1900 and 1930 — an average of 85 a year. The decade immediately before the outbreak of war in 1914 (when the total membership was still increasing) saw emigration running at a record level of 129 a year. This makes it clear that emigration was not a significant cause of decline in a direct sense: in the 1920s nearly half those emigrating came from Scotland, but the peak membership in Scotland was nearly 3,000 in 1928. Indirectly, however, the fact that emigrants tended to be younger probably had an effect on the age structure of the Churches. In general, therefore, it seems likely that the causes for declining membership in Churches of Christ are not unique, but are probably the same as those which produced decline among the other Free Churches. The fact that the sharpest decline came during the Second World War made it rational to hope that things would improve after 1945. Only slowly did people realize that this was not going to happen.

II

The most significant event for Churches of Christ in the inter-war years, and indeed the twentieth century as a whole, was the reoganization of the training work which led to the foundation of Overdale College in 1920. It was significant in two ways — in principle and in practice. The acceptance of the principle marked a turning away from David King's vigorous anti-college line and a desire for a longer period of training for those called to the ministry among the Churches. In practice, the calling of William Robinson to be the first Principal of Overdale created the opportunity for the development of his great personal influence on Churches of Christ in the present century. By his theological scholarship he provided a reinterpretation of the 'position and plea' appropriate to the conditions of the twentieth century, and through his office as Principal he shaped the thinking of a whole generation of ministers and leaders. This was to be seen particularly in the period after 1945.

The idea of a theological college may be traced back to Alexander Brown, who had started the correspondence classes in the 1880s. He had won the support of some of the leading brethren and was studying privately with a view to graduating at a Scottish university when illness overtook him in 1893. So the idea never became public at that time.[1] In 1912 John M'Cartney, who had conducted the correspondence classes since 1896, was President of the Annual Meeting; and in his presidential address he stressed the need for a training period of at least two years (rather than six months) and expressed the hope that the Annual Meeting would set up a special committee to prepare a suitable scheme. It was agreed that W.B. Ainsworth (brother of T.J. Ainsworth) should read a Conference paper on the subject. W.B. Ainsworth was a graduate of Birmingham University and a schoolmaster in the same city. He boldly proposed a three-year course, associated with a university arts degree; the paper was warmly received, and the matter referred to the Training Committee.[2]

In 1914 the committee reported that they had circularized the churches on the matter but without response. They also reported a different initiative. The legatees under David King's will approached the committee to see whether they would be prepared to use some of the legacy to assist suitable individuals to obtain university training, in addition to that provided by the committee; and the committee indicated their willingness to do so for a suitably qualified person. In 1916 H.E. Tickle, one of the legatees, moved the appointment of a special committee to review the arrangements for training. This committee presented a detailed scheme to the 1917 Annual Meeting, the keystone of which was the proposal for a minimum course of three years, to be taken in a place where there was the possibility of attending university classes. This was approved, and an enlarged committee went on to do the work connected with the purchase of property, preparation of a trust deed, and consideration of appointments.

In 1919 the committee were able to report the purchase of a house, 'Overdale', in Park Road, Moseley, Birmingham for £1,000, and the appointment of William Robinson as Principal.

By 1920 more than £6,000 had been raised, part of which was used for the purchase and alteration of the property and the remainder for the establishment of the Training College Trust to endow the work. Of the identifiable donors, James Marsden gave £600, and J.W. Black, R.W. Black, H. Wormleighton and Frank Coop each gave £450: £300 came from the legatees of David King and the executors of Thomson McLintock of Glasgow. The mention of Frank Coop's gift is a reminder of the keen interest taken in this project by the ex-Christian Association churches, which had always had a small Bible College: Leslie Morgan, Secretary of the Association, reported to the F.C.M.S. that the proposal for a college was one of the first practical results of the merger, and it is likely that Frank Coop was the anonymous brother who had promised to give 10% of the sum raised provided that it reached $30,000 (just under £6,200 at the pre-war parity).[3]

William Robinson came from the church at Askam-in-Furness. He was a graduate in Chemistry of Liverpool University and had served as an evangelist in Wigan from 1911 to 1912 before becoming a schoolmaster. During the war he served in the Army and was wounded in action on the Western Front. The rest of his army service was spent in training cadets at Oxford. Following demobilization in April 1919 he remained in Oxford to undertake theological study at Mansfield College. The Principal of Mansfield at that time was W.B. Selbie, and under his influence he came to know the work of Congregationalist scholars like A.M. Fairbairn and P.T. Forsyth. In Oxford too, he was exposed to the liberal Anglo-Catholicism of men like Bishop Gore, whom he met at the Preparatory Faith and Order Conference at Geneva in 1920. Both Gore and Forsyth, in different ways, had opposed the developing liberal theology of the early twentieth century and Robinson adopted a similar position, as may be seen from his attitude to the Anglican 'modernists' of the Modern Churchmen's Union in the 1920s. But there was no question about his acceptance of biblical criticism. C.H. Dodd was on the staff at Mansfield during his time there, and B.H. Streeter was the leading New Testament critic at Oxford. William Robinson's first theological book, *Essays on Christian Unity* (1923), displayed all these early influences very clearly [4]

Overdale College was opened on 11 September 1920 by the

chairman of the Training Committee, R.W. Black. Ten students, including one woman, entered into residence. John M'Cartney continued in the training work as a Lecturer at the College, and retained responsibility for the correspondence courses.[5] In 1921 Albert Brown, who had been editor of the *Christian Advocate* since January, became a part-time Tutor at the College, but he had to give this up in 1923 because of the pressure of the two jobs. John M'Cartney now began to concentrate entirely on the correspondence work, and Joseph Smith was appointed as a new full-time member of staff. It will be remembered that Jo Smith was one of the first public exponents of critical views of scripture among Churches of Christ. He now took over responsibility for lecturing on the Old and New Testaments and for language teaching.

In 1923 also controversy about the college first came to the surface at Annual Conference*. In their report the previous year the Training Committee had indicated that the college intended to affiliate to the Student Christian Movement. The Principal was keen on this, both as a way of getting Churches of Christ known in wider religious circles and also for the benefits that the students would gain from belonging to an inter-denominational movement. But the S.C.M. was already acquiring something of a reputation for publishing books with advanced views, and in 1923 Brighton and Griffithstown churches in their annual schedules proposed that the Training Committee should require the college's withdrawal from the S.C.M. On the recommendation of the Reference Committee, the Conference indicated its dissent from some of the views published in S.C.M. books, but held that the educational benefits of affiliation outweighed this.

Next year 35 schedules referred to this matter (one church having taken the initiative in circularizing others) and this was linked to other vague charges about the teaching given by the Principal and staff. The resolution of 1923 was reaffirmed by 201 votes to 61. The agitation nevertheless continued, resulting in a major row at the 1925 Conference. The opposition had urged

*In the 1920s the term 'Annual Conference' gradually replaced 'Annual Meeting' in popular usage. The word 'Conference' is first used in the heading of the Minutes in 1905, in the text of the Minutes in 1913 and in the title of the Year Book in 1924. Up to 1917 the Annual Conference is said to be 'of delegates and other members of Churches of Christ . . .' From 1918 it is described as the 'Annual Conference of Churches of Christ . . .'

churches to withhold funds until affiliation was discontinued. R.W. Black, defending the Training Committee's action, pointed out that they were aware that the real hostility was to the college itself, but that no evidence had been offered for the charges levelled against the college staff. The Conference, by a majority of 216 to 28, declined to recommend disaffiliation and deplored the action of those who were trying to damage the work of the college and the various committees. The three-year rule, whereby any matter that has been voted on by Conference cannot be reopened for three years, was also introduced.[6] This seemed to settle the matter and when the Training Committee's report was discussed at the 1926 Conference the Principal said how pleased he was to be able to speak in such a favourable atmosphere.

This calm, however, was short-lived. At the 1926 Conference several schedules were received from churches, complaining of some of the teaching given at Overdale. Criticism centred on Joseph Smith, and two pieces he had written for the *Christian Advocate*. One was a leading article published on 28 August 1925, entitled 'The Prophet for Today?', in which he explored the question of how someone could speak the word of the Lord afresh to his own generation. He illustrated his point by referring to Jeremiah, and particularly his affirmation 'that *animal sacrifices are an unauthorised addition to the original Covenant with the Fathers of Israel*' (Jer. vii.23).[7] The other was a series of leading articles in January and February 1926 on the sacraments. Here he pointed out that the origin of the sacraments was a more complex matter than was often believed, but that their meaning could only be understood in the light of their origins.[8] In each case the correspondence columns were filled for several weeks afterwards because on the one hand Smith had challenged the harmony of Scripture, and on the other he had exposed the spiritual inadequacy of treating the sacraments simply as commands of Jesus. The experience of the S.C.M. controversy had convinced R.W. Black as chairman of the Training Committee that Overdale could only make progress if its staff adopted a conciliatory policy in relation to the conservative views of many in the churches. He regarded Smith's articles as unnecessarily provocative, and decided to resign as chairman. Unfortunately he was ill at the time of the 1926 Conference, and found himself re-elected chairman in his absence. When his wish to resign became known, the Principal indicated that he would also feel compelled to resign since the chairman's resignation would imply a loss of confidence in the college.

At a meeting of the Training Committee on 23 September 1926 R.W. Black agreed to withdraw his resignation, if Jo Smith was dismissed from the college staff, and the committee accordingly resolved to terminate his engagement 'believing Bro. Smith's continuance at the College is a barrier to the progress of the work'. When this became known, there was an outcry, both over the action and the manner in which it had been undertaken. The Principal publicly protested and said he regarded his departure as 'a great disaster'. The fact that Smith had not been formally invited to defend himself before the committee, together with the fact that there was no significant difference between the views of Smith and the Principal on the matters in question, made the committee's action seem very arbitrary. So, at a specially convened meeting on 20 October the matter was reconsidered and the decision to dismiss Smith was reversed. R.W. Black, J.W. Black and his wife thereupon resigned from the committee. They also withdrew their joint guarantee to the bank to meet an overdraft of up to £1,000. This would have meant that the October bills could not be paid, had it not been for prompt action by a group in Birmingham which took over the guarantee. C.R. Batten resigned as organizing secretary for the college, and Will Mander resigned as treasurer, though not from the committee. Both were associated with the Twynholm church, to which R.W. Black belonged, one as a member, the other as minister.[9]

With classic understatement the Training Committee reported to the 1927 Conference that 'the year has not been without its serious difficulties and anxieties'. The question of the teaching at Overdale was fully debated, and a special committee was appointed to confer with the Blacks, the Principal and Jo Smith, and the Training Committee about the difficulties which had arisen. This committee reported that various misunderstandings had now been resolved, though differences of view about the college remained. Jo Smith agreed to write to the *C.A.* repudiating any belief in transubstantiation or consubstantiation.[10] There the matter rested. The academic freedom of Overdale had been vindicated.

Jo Smith died suddenly at the age of 66 in May 1931, leaving an overwhelming sense of loss. William Robinson described him as 'the greatest scholar the Churches of Christ have ever produced on this side of the Atlantic' and spoke of the way in which 'from long before he came on the Staff of the College, I had leaned on him and been inspired by him'. In the sermon at the Memorial Service in Overdale College chapel, James Gray, one of the first Overdale students, said:

> Joseph Smith was a fearless teacher and preacher, not shrinking from declaring unto us anything that was profitable, however hard and unpleasing it might seem . . . He taught not because his job was teaching, but because he was aflame with the light of a great vision, and other minds must be kindled . . . he gave himself without reserve, and it was characteristic of him that straight from preaching he took to the bed from which he never rose.[11]

It was fitting that he should be commemorated in the Churches by the endowment of a lecture on preaching, which was first given by Dr J.S. Whale, sometime President of Cheshunt College, Cambridge, on 11 October 1947.

Jo Smith's place as Lecturer was filled by James Gray, who was released from his work as Sunday School organizer by the General Sunday School Committee. In 1931 also the college was moved from Moseley to Selly Oak, where it became a member of the Selly Oak group of Colleges. This move offered further opportunities for contact with teachers and students of other traditions. In 1933 Churches of Christ became givers as well as receivers when William Robinson was appointed Lecturer in the Philosophy of Religion and Christian Doctrine in the Selly Oak Colleges, a position he held until 1951: it was made a Professorship in 1940.

III

The other major controversy of the 1920s was not over a new issue, but an old one — the Communion question. As indicated in the last chapter the terms of agreement with the Christian Association churches in 1917 had envisaged movement towards a common practice in relation to admission to communion: what was not so clear was how rapid that movement should be. Different interpretations of the agreement were put forward, and in 1920 several churches expressed their disquiet over the situation. This led to the appointment of a special committee to ascertain whether a more satisfactory agreement could be arrived at. On the recommendation of this committee, the Annual

Conference of 1921 passed the following resolution:

> That this Conference recognises with satisfaction that some of the Churches of the late Christian Association have loyally carried out the agreement entered into in 1917, and are today in line with the general body of the co-operating Churches. In view, however, of the fact that four years have elapsed since the agreement was made, and of the misunderstanding that has arisen, the Conference now reaffirms its adherence to the New Testament teaching of immersion into Christ, upon a confession of faith in Jesus Christ as the Son of the Living God and of repentance towards God unto the remission of sins and membership in the body of Christ, and, in harmony with its long practice, resolves to have co-operation solely with those Churches which decline to permit, knowingly, any but immersed believers to break bread with them at the Lord's table.

Thirteen voted against this resolution, which was keenly resented by some of the ex-Christian Association leaders.[12] Frank Coop wrote several letters to the *C.A.*, to which J.W. Black responded, and the church at Mornington Road, Southport, where he was a member, withdrew from the Association at the 1922 Conference. Most of the other churches concerned had given the necessary assurances, and it was hoped that the matter was settled. Nevertheless Southport did not change its mind and in 1923 Potter Street, Liverpool also withdrew.[13]

The sensitivity of the whole area, however, was illustrated by another matter, which at first sight seems a quite separate issue — the evangelistic policy of the G.E.C. In 1917 J.W. Black succeeded James Marsden as chairman of the G.E.C. Like his elder brother Sydney, John Wycliffe always believed in the value of the special mission and in various ways during the next twenty years he sought to promote this method of evangelism through the work of the G.E.C. What was more controversial was the faith he placed in evangelists from Australia and the U.S.A. to carry out this policy. An early illustration of this was the controversy which arose over the appointment of F.D. Pollard as organizing secretary to the brotherhood in 1919. Pollard came from Western Australia and was a specialist in personal evangelism. In the first six months of 1919 he toured the churches in the midlands, the north and Scotland. At the 1919 Conference he was appointed organizing secretary for three years from the spring of 1921. But the resolution was only passed by a majority, and when the G.E.C. announced a few weeks after Conference that, owing to a change in his circumstances, they had made the appointment with immediate effect, there were letters of protest in the *Bible Advocate*. It had already been revealed at Conference that the G.E.C. were not unanimous on the matter, and whilst Pollard was acceptable as an evangelist, there was suspicion of the post of organizing secretary, notwithstanding the resolution passed by the 1902 Conference. The suspicion that the G.E.C. was trying to achieve on its own what it could not achieve through Conference was unfounded — Pollard's marriage, which made him decide not to return to Australia immediately, could not have been arranged — but the readiness of some to suspect ulterior motives is significant. Most of Pollard's time until his resignation at the Annual Conference of 1921 was given to special missions, though he did urge the adoption of systematic giving through the envelope system as a way of improving church finance. In the winter of 1920-21 there was a 'Win One' campaign to add 1,441 members to the Churches, but less than 500 additions were made.[14] Although Pollard returned to Australia in the autumn of 1921, the G.E.C. remained interested in the possibility of receiving help from overseas.

In 1926 the issue surfaced again with the visit of Jesse Bader, Secretary for Evangelism of the United Christian Missionary Society in the U.S.A. He came in the wake of a series of successful missions conducted by Dr Jesse Kellems, and brought greetings from the U.C.M.S. The Conference resolved to send a representative to the International Convention of Disciples of Christ in the U.S.A. and Canada at Memphis, Tennessee in November 1926, if a suitable person could be found to go. It also resolved to support the idea of holding a world gathering of Disciples of Christ. J.W. Black was able to visit Memphis, but he also went with the authorization of the G.E.C. Executive to make arrangements for the sending of American evangelists like Bader and Kellems to Britain, partly supported by American funds, with the aim of initiating a major evangelistic enterprise. He returned with promises of cooperation and the G.E.C. authorized him to visit various centres to lay the proposals before the Churches. This he did, and the proposals were supported in many places. But in Wigan and Birmingham they were rejected, in the latter case overwhelmingly, on the grounds that such an initiative would threaten once again to divide the Churches on the Communion question.

John M'Cartney published a pamphlet in June 1927 recounting

the history of the Communion question since 1866, and he urged churches to oppose the proposals on their schedules and ask for a reaffirmation of the 1921 resolution. Albert Brown resigned as editor of the *C.A.* because of his opposition to the proposals. W. Mander defended the proposals in another pamphlet. He pointed out that the current prosperity of the Australian Churches of Christ could be traced back to the work of American-trained evangelists fifteen years earlier: he argued that the position of the British Churches on communion would be respected by the visitors, but added that an increasing number of British brethren wished to see a more relaxed approach: and he asked how the British Churches could seriously work for Christian Union if they were not even prepared to cooperate with their American brethren. The correspondence columns of the *C.A.* were also filled with discussion.[15]

Of the 99 churches which referred to the matter on their schedules, 81 opposed the proposals, and there was a long debate at Conference. Eventually an amendment to the G.E.C. resolution adopting the proposals was carried by 210 votes to 138, the effect of which was to delay the reply until after the Conference of 1928. Julian Elwes was the Fraternal Delegate to the International Convention at Columbus, Ohio in April 1928, and the offer of assistance was renewed in the form of one evangelist for the period September 1929-June 1930. This proposal was adopted by the 1928 Conference by 208 to 104, the number of churches protesting having fallen to 41. The same Conference agreed to support the proposals for the celebration of the 1900th anniversary of Pentecost in 1930 and to send a large delegation to the first World Convention of Churches of Christ in Washington, D.C. in October 1930. In the end it proved impossible to arrange for a suitable evangelist to visit in 1929-30, but in the circumstances this may have been a blessing in disguise.[16]

Meanwhile two other ex-Christian Association churches had withdrawn because of disagreement with the Communion policy — Woolston in 1927 and Lancaster in 1928. The question of Christian union now became the context in which the discussion was continued. In 1927 the First World Conference on Faith and Order met in Lausanne, and Churches of Christ were represented by William Robinson. The Union Committee, which had become a standing committee in 1926, spent much of the year considering the findings of the Lausanne Conference, and Robinson's own report. In its report to the 1928 Conference it urged the Churches to take a more active part in the work for reunion. 'Is it not possible,' it asked, 'that we have lost something of our former vision of unity, and isolated ourselves in a way which makes it impossible for our witness to tell?'[17] One member of the committee, William Mander, minister at Twynholm, published an article in the Twynholm magazine, *Joyful Tidings*, which was reprinted in the *C.A.* At the heart of his survey of contemporary movements towards Christian unity lay this question, 'Ought not the next movement towards Christian union in this land be to embrace the Churches which practise Believers' Baptism?' The article provoked a series of responses from leading men, but the general attitude was cautious, to say the least.[18]

The Twynholm church asked the 1928 Conference to set up 'a large and representative committee to consider and formulate the essential points which make our existence as a separate community necessary'. This was dealt with by appointing a group to work with the Union Committee on the replies to the Lausanne Report, to be submitted to the 1929 Conference for approval. A full reply was therefore drawn up, and meanwhile discussion continued in the columns of the *C.A.* on the Communion question, provoked in part by an adaptation by Charles Greig of 1 Corinthians 8 which substituted communing with the unimmersed for eating meat sacrificed to idols. The proposed reply to Lausanne adhered firmly to the closed communion position, but on the eve of Conference a letter appeared in the *C.A.* over the signatures of W.B. Ainsworth, C.W. Black, A.J. Elwes, W. Mander, T.J. Webley and C.R. Batten, suggesting an additional footnote to the word 'Baptism' which would permit, on the principle of 'economy', the occasional admission to communion of members of other Churches who had not received believer's baptism. Ainsworth was chairman of the Union Committee and Mander was a member: the other four were members of the group appointed to work with the Committee in 1928. This suggestion — which anticipated the recommendation on 'Guest Communion' adopted in 1956 — was not taken up, and the Conference approved the Suggested Reply with only a few minor amendments, all of which had been agreed beforehand.[19]

The Communion question had, however, been raised directly for the 1929 Conference by seventeen churches asking for a reaffirmation of the 1921 resolution and two asking for it to be rescinded. The Reference Committee proposed as an amendment the reaffirmation of the two clauses of the agreement with the Christian Association in 1917 which referred to admission to the Church and the Lord's Supper, together with a third clause allowing participation by non-baptized persons in exceptional circumstances. After a long debate in which several amendments were lost, the Reference Committee's proposal was defeated by 116 votes to 105. On the following day a revised amendment was submitted by the Reference Committee and approved by a large majority as follows:

> That we reaffirm Resolution no 21 of the Annual Meeting of 1921 with the understanding that participation by non-baptized persons under exceptional circumstances shall not be regarded as inconsistent with this resolution, providing that the position of the Churches in regard to the Lord's Supper is made clear to the participant at the earliest possible opportunity, and that such participation is not to be of a recurring nature.

Whilst this satisfied the centre, it failed to satisfy everyone. The 1930 Conference received notice of withdrawal from nine 'old path' churches for whom this resolution was too liberal and from Twynholm for whom this resolution was too restrictive. The Reference Committee therefore proposed to rescind both the resolution passed in 1929 and resolution 21 of 1921 as going beyond the nature and limits of the Cooperation set out in 1861, leaving the position on communion as stated in the Reply to Lausanne. The proposal was welcomed, but an amendment going one stage further was moved by T.E. Entwistle, one of the evangelists clearly identified with the 'old path' position. He proposed that all resolutions on the Communion question since 1861 should be deleted, and this was carried unanimously. Only two of the 'old path' churches persisted in their intention to withdraw at the 1931 Conference, but Twynholm joined the Baptist Union in March 1931.[20]

In trying to understand this rather complex web of events, it is important to realize that there were at least three sides. Firstly, there was a conservative group which maintained the traditional position exemplified by David King, with the same kind of biblical literalism: the core of this group consisted of those identified with the 'old paths'. Then, there was a liberal group, which was the heir to Sydney Black's 'forward movement', placing great emphasis on evangelism and being prepared to accept some compromise on the Communion question for the sake of evangelism and unity: the heart of this was the Twynholm church and R.W. Black. But there was also a third group, which adhered to a closed communion position on 'catholic' rather than biblical literalist grounds and which held that unity would be hindered rather than helped by too great a readiness to ignore theology for the sake of evangelism: this was centred on Overdale. Jo Smith, William Robinson and Albert Brown all took this line and the first two were largely responsible for the reply to Lausanne. All three were critical of the theological shallowness which was so common in the Free Churches at this time, whilst being unable to accept the alternative of conservative evangelicalism. The 1930 resolution, therefore, was not simply an 'old paths' resolution, as one speaker in the debate suggested: the support of the theological leadership was vital. Moreover by returning to the 1861 position, the churches were in fact given considerable individual freedom and there was certainly no setback to the kind of 'progressive' opinion represented by the proviso to the 1929 resolution.

It may therefore be wondered why Twynholm persisted in withdrawal. The answer is provided by R.W. Black's biographer: 'Mr Black had become persuaded that the separate existence of the Churches of Christ as a denomination was no longer necessary'.[21] The individual nature of that conviction is emphasized by the fact that Will Mander left Twynholm for Evington Road, Leicester at the beginning of 1929, that George Hammond, who was serving Twynholm's daughter church at Boston Road, moved to Liverpool when that church joined the Baptist Union, and that Julian Elwes, who was minister at Twynholm when it joined the Baptist Union, returned to his home church at South Wigston in 1933. Those who shared R.W. Black's general views on unity matters did not all feel the same urge to become Baptists. It is likely also that his views were affected by his attitude to Overdale: not only was the closed communion position defended there, but also his belief, that the teaching given would not produce the kind of evangelists he was looking for, can hardly have altered. Both he and his brother retained their faith in the methods of the 1890s, epitomized by Sydney Black, until their deaths in 1951.

IV

The Communion question also appeared in another way at the 1930 Conference, in the accusation that Ernest Gray was teaching open communion on the Nyasaland mission field. The accusation was firmly rebutted, but the background to it is important. From 23 January to 4 February 1915 there was a native uprising in Nyasaland led by John Chilembwe. Some members of the Churches of Christ mission at Namiwawa were implicated in this rising, and as a result all the missionaries were interned. G.H. Hollis, who had begun the work, was known to have pacifist views and also to favour giving responsibility to Africans: he was deported. Mary Bannister and the Philpotts were allowed to return to Namiwawa provided that they did no teaching and held no meetings. These conditions remained until the report of the Committee of Inquiry into the Rising was published in 1916. The Colonial Secretary then refused to permit the missionaries to resume their work in Nyasaland during the war or to guarantee that permission would be given afterwards. The Philpotts moved to India in December 1916, and Mary Bannister went to the mission in Bulawayo, after spending some time with her friends, the Smiths, at the Baptist Industrial Mission at Gowa. She eventually returned to England in July 1919.[22]

There was little evidence of complicity in the uprising on the part of any members of the mission, and certainly not of the missionaries: Frederick Nkhonde, the head teacher at Mlanje, was accused of having fore knowledge of the rising and not reporting it to the authorities, but there was no question of his having taken part in it. Some African sympathizers with Chilembwe did have a Churches of Christ background, but they had already left the mission and formed independent churches. However, the presence of the mission was resented by the Church of Scotland missionaries, and there also seems to have been some feeling among white settlers that it encouraged too much independence of mind among the natives. It is therefore not surprising that the colonial administration should have taken advantage of this opportunity to suppress the mission, particularly in the wartime atmosphere. The Colonial Office did not agree to allow the missionaries to return until 1927, despite frequent requests from the Missionary Committee.

Meanwhile Mary Bannister remained in the employment of the Missionary Committee and did deputation work in the churches. She also corresponded with the African leaders and collected money and supplies to assist them, though obviously none of this money went through the Missionary Committee accounts. Negotiations for a return to Nyasaland were begun again in 1927 and in May 1928 Mary Bannister returned to the Baptist Industrial Mission at Gowa. In the following year it was agreed to accept the Smiths' invitation to tek over the work at Gowa, and an appeal was made for people to offer themselves as missionaries. Ernest and Louise Gray and Wilfred and Elsie Georgeson responded to this call. It was probably inevitable that there should have been some tensions between the new white missionaries and the native leaders who had been in charge for ten years. Frederick Nkhonde, whose salary was paid from Canada, had by the mid-1920s become the acknowledged leader in the native church. Soon after Ernest Gray arrived at Gowa, he was visited by Frederick and other leaders who asked both for an increase in the teachers' salaries and for a statement of his views on the Communion question. The first request had to be refused through lack of sufficient funds. Gray's statement on communion was either misunderstood or misrepresented, and it was alleged in a letter to W.E. Kempster of the *Bible Advocate* (the 'old paths' magazine, not to be confused with the official magazine) that he had advocated open communion. These charges were repeated in a schedule to the 1930 Conference, demanding his recall to England. The Missionary Committee rebutted the charges, and Conference passed a resolution of confidence in Ernest Gray and the committee by a large majority.[23]

The root of the problem lay in the conditions imposed by the Government when the resumption of missionary work was allowed. It was stipulated that the mission should be acceptable to and agree to join the Federation of Protestant Missions in Nyasaland. One of the conditions of membership was an agreement to respect each other's membership and discipline, and an agreement not to proselytize or enter each other's areas. One of Ernest Gray's first tasks was to see whether membership was possible for a mission with a closed communion practice. He discovered that it was not, and therefore had to seek permission from the Chief Secretary at Zomba for this condition to be waived. It was, and the mission did not join the Federation. The position was further complicated by the fact that the practice at Gowa always had been to admit Christians from other missions to communion, whether they had been immersed or not. The delicacy of the new missionaries' position, particularly with language problems as well, can easily be imagined.

In February 1931 the Grays moved to Namiwawa, leaving Gowa in the charge of the Georgesons. Tensions at Namiwawa continued with the result that in 1932 Frederick and others withdrew from the mission. This was due to disagreements over the policy of having catechumen classes, and in particular to Frederick's insistence on baptizing two members of the Church of Scotland mission who were under discipline, despite Gray's refusal to allow it. The Missionary Committee sent one of its members, Harry Langton, to Nyasaland to investigate the whole situation. Attempts at mediation failed, and in 1933 it was reported that Frederick and the others had formed 'the African Church of Christ'. Accordingly the committee announced that this body was 'excommunicate from our fellowship', and reported this to the government. The majority remained loyal to the mission, and the work continued to advance. Frederick's group were supported by the 'old paths' churches, who used the episode in their arguments against the general policy of the Association. Frederick died in 1935, but the group continued its separate existence.[24]

Mary Bannister retired in 1935 because of increasing deafness. She died in 1940 after a lifetime of service to Nyasaland. She has been called the 'Mary Slessor of our American mission.' 'When all seemed lost, and the labour of early years in Namiwawa was in ruins, *she* never gave up,' wrote Henry Philpott, secretary of the Missionary Committee at the time of her death and her colleague in Nyasaland during the wartime troubles. Harry Langton said that 'we are in Africa today, only because of the faith, courage and persistency of Mary Bannister'.[25]

Work continued on the other two mission-fields during the inter-war period. Robert Halliday withdrew from Siam and returned to Burma with the American Baptists in 1922 to resume his work among the Mons. Esther Halliday, his daughter, remained in Siam, where the work continued under the leadership of Percy and Mary Clark. Robert Halliday died in 1933, having been honoured by the award of the Kaiser-i-Hind medal by the Indian Government and also by the award of the honorary degree of Doctor of Letters by the University of Rangoon for his work on the Talaing language. Percy Clark was on several occasions Chairman of the Christian Council of Siam, but the Churches of Christ mission felt obliged to remain outside the United Church of Christ in Siam, when its formation was being discussed in 1934-35, because of an unwillingness to accept infant baptism.[26]

India was the main area of expansion. In 1914 the former L.M.S. mission at Dudhi in Mirzapur, United Provinces, was taken over and G.P. Pittman and his wife moved there from Daltonganj, where A.C. Watters and his wife took over. When the Philpotts arrived in India from Nyasaland in December 1916, it was decided that they should go to Dudhi to allow the Pittmans to go home on furlough. They were unable to visit Britain because of the war, and thus returned to India from Australia in 1917 and began a new work at Latehar, 40 miles east of Daltonganj. In the early 1920s three women missionaries went out: Elsie Francis, Bessie Melville and Anne Piggot. Elsie Francis was a teacher, and married Penry Pryce, Principal of a Boys' High School, run by the Society of Friends: he subsequently joined the Churches of Christ mission and took over the work at Dudhi. Bessie Melville took charge of the Orphanage at Daltonganj and Anne Piggot worked with the Bible Women there. Others who served in India were Stephen Brown and his wife, who died there in 1935, and J.C. Christie and his wife. In the mid-1930s another new area was opened up around Bhandaria, when Lyle and Connie Burdett joined the missionary staff. In 1935 Paul Singh, the pioneer evangelist on the Indian field, died at the age of 73. The inter-war period was, of course, a time of increasing tension in India as the movement for independence developed, and there are frequent references to the problems this caused.[27] The expansion of the work had been marked by the necessity to form the Foreign Missions Property Society Ltd in 1926 to hold the property on the various mission stations: it also acquired a house in Selly Oak for use by missionaries on furlough in 1937. By the time of the jubilee year of missionary work in 1942-43 a considerable achievement in three countries could be reported.

The inter-war period saw a number of changes in the organization of the work of the various committees and in their relationship to each other and the Conference. One of the striking characteristics of the 1920s was the concern to organize national events for young people. In 1923 the Temperance and Social Questions Committee, at the suggestion of its organizer, R.H. Parker, held the first of its summer camps for young men at Morecambe, which came to be known as the Livingstone Camps. They were held in various coastal places and were generally well supported. But the inspiration behind them was very much the personality of R.H. Parker and when he ceased to be able to lead them in the mid-1930s they were discontinued. Also in 1923 a suggestion was made to Conference that a Convention for Young Men should be held. This was referred to the G.E.C. which appointed a sub-committee under W.B. Ainsworth to prepare a scheme. The first Young Men's Convention was held at Stratford-on-Avon at Easter 1924 with a full programme of lectures: 78 attended. It was so successful that it rapidly became an annual event, providing a forum for open discussion in an informal atmosphere that had hitherto been lacking. The eager participation of the Overdale staff also meant that it became in some ways a piece of extra-mural work by the college, though it was always much more than that. Parallel to these developments was the beginning of holiday camps for girls in 1923 and of the Young Women's Convention in 1927, both being organized through the Sisters' Committee. Finally in 1929 came the foundation of what was later to become the Fellowship of Youth, but which began as 'The Bright Young People'. This started as a gathering of young people at Conference, and held its first business meeting in 1930: James Gray was the first president and Rene Hicken (later Mrs Alistair Robertson) was the first secretary. From this spread the idea of local youth groups in districts and churches.[28]

These developments were additions to a fairly traditional framework. In the 1930s more substantial changes began to take place. Reference has already been made to J.W. Black's enthusiasm for special missions. When his proposals to seek American help were shelved by the 1927 Conference, he was prepared to bridge the gap himself. From 1928, when he held a mission at Rodney Street, Wigan, he regularly conducted special missions in selected places. In 1930 the G.E.C. decided to launch a forward movement in evangelism, and the 1931 Conference authorized the committee to plan a programme of intensive missions. E.C. Hinrichsen of Australia was to be asked whether he would superintend such work in Britain. It was not until J.W. Black visited the Australian Federal Conference in Launceston in October 1933 that he was able to persuade Hinrichsen to come. Hinrichsen and V.B. Morris, who led the singing, arrived in February 1935 and conducted missions in Leicester, Chester and Manchester before Conference, resulting in 288 additions. Conference approved of the G.E.C.'s decision to invite Hinrichsen to become organizer of evangelism from 1 January 1936. Morris had to return to Australia in February 1936, and was replaced as song leader by J.A. Kay from the U.S.A. Hinrichsen himself had to return to Australia in October 1936 because of his father's illness. During his time in Britain over 1,000 had been added to the Churches. In the spring of 1939 he returned for a further period of service, which lasted until the outbreak of war. It should not be supposed that he was the only one to conduct missions in these years, but his impact was the most striking.[29] A more modest experiment was the 'Gospel Van' purchased in 1929, which Walter Lister used to good effect for several years.[30]

In some ways the prominence of special missions in this period reflects the fact that they were becoming exceptional. The old pattern of working by evangelists was gradually giving way to a more settled ministry. In 1929 the G.E.C. changed the arrangement whereby it engaged evangelists on a yearly basis, and adopted instead a system of permanent engagement with three months' notice on either side.[31] Archie Watters was one of those who urged the need for more full-time evangelists staying longer in a church. In an address to the Liverpool Conference of 1931 he noted the fact that the G.E.C. in Britain had been largely composed of business men throughout its history, and suggested that this might have something to do with the small number of evangelists employed in Britain by comparison with the U.S.A., where the full-time ministry had been more highly respected. He also criticized the peripatetic policy:

> Sometimes they have been allowed to stay long enough in one place to see the beginnings of a strong cause, then they would be summoned to save the situation in some other place, and the prospects in the first

place gradually dwindled. *We have never had enough evangelists to consolidate our new cause and to press on to new work.* The older men, and more especially their wives and families, paid a tremendous price, the servants of an inefficient policy. Time and time again, if they had been left to their own judgment, they would have stayed on where they were reaping success, but loyalty to committees and the rival claims of other congregations caused them to move on.[32]

He returned to the same theme in 1936 in a Conference paper on increasing the whole-time ministry. In it he noted that the number of whole-time preachers and pastors had risen from 18 in 1914 to 31 in 1936. He continued:

> What is equally significant, if not more so, not one of the 18 evangelists in 1914 spent the whole of that year with one church, whereas of the 31 workers in 1936, 21 have been attached to one church for a year or more. Very definitely a change of policy has been taking place amongst us . . .[33]

Watters also argued that such a development need not threaten the mutual ministry, which he thought was stultified as much by over-emphasis on the independence of each congregation as by a full-time ministry: he wanted to see much greater cooperation within a district.

One limitation on expansion was painfully obvious for much of this period — finance. The two major committees — the G.E.C. and the Missionary Committee — had overdrafts for most of the inter-war years, and they were not alone. The G.E.C. overdraft was generally in the region of £400, but it was more than £1,000 in 1926 and 1937. The Missionary Committee overdraft was generally more than £1,000, but in 1930 it reached a horrifying £3,694. In 1925 Conference suggested that the chairmen and treasurers of the standing spending committees meet together to review the financial resources of the brotherhood. The 1926 Conference urged the churches to adopt the principle of systematic giving, and appointed a Finance Committee to prepare such a scheme. Not a great deal resulted from this. In 1935 William Robinson, as President of Conference, launched a campaign to clear the overdrafts of all standing committees within two years. A gift of £2,100 had been offered if this was achieved, which meant that £4,636 2s 4d needed to be raised. During the next two years the Principal toured the country, and received some 1,600 gifts, ranging from 3d to £1,000. Because the overdrafts continued to mount during his campaign he had in the end to raise more than £5,300, which was achieved on 17 July 1937. At the Annual Conference that year he handed over cheques for the required amounts to the committee treasurers concerned. It is noteworthy that more than half the total raised came from the Leicester district. Nevertheless the Missionary Committee's overdraft was more than £2,000 again by 1939 and they needed a jubilee offering in 1942-43 to clear it.[34]

Clearly the 1930s were a difficult time economically, and Churches of Christ were not the only denomination to suffer. In certain parts of the country the membership of the churches was particularly exposed to economic distress. Between 1929 and 1939 just over £700 was raised by the Social Questions Committee for the Miners' Distress Fund, most of which was distributed in the South Wales and Notts. districts, with contributions also to the north east, Yorkshire and Wigan. But it is likely that the persistence of overdrafts indicated a deeper problem, namely the inability of the churches either to provide, or to organize, the kind of giving necessary to achieve their increasingly ambitious objects. When it is remembered that a significant proportion of the money given for national work came from a relatively small number of wealthy people, it becomes clear that in some ways Churches of Christ were sheltered from, rather than exposed to, the economic realities of the period: even more so in view of the relatively low salaries paid to those in full-time service.

Arising out of the financial problems there was a developing concern for some coordination in the work of committees. Again Archie Watters referred to this. In his Presidential address in 1929 he suggested the appointment of a special committee to consider the Churches' organization, and this was done by a special resolution later in the Conference. As a result of this the Conference of 1930 decided to set up a Central Council, on which representatives of all the main committees were to sit. Any new proposals from committees involving large expenditure were in future to be submitted to this Council so that the Council could report on them to the Conference. The Council was also to have the task of interesting churches, districts and divisions in the work of the various national committees and of making recommendations for increasing their income.

In its first few years the Central Council concentrated on organizing conferences in churches and districts to publicize the work of committees, but by the mid-1930s it had begun to consider more important matters. In 1935 it reported that it had been considering advice to be given to missionaries on their relationships with other religious bodies. In 1936 it made two major recommendations: the appointment of a commission to consider the ordination of evangelists, and the appointment of a financial secretary and an organizing secretary to the Churches. Both recommendations were acted upon: the Commission on Ordination was also asked to consider the ordination of elders and deacons; and a commision was appointed to consider the duties of a financial and organizing secretary, with power to make an appointment if possible.

In 1937 it was reported that A.C. Watters had been appointed General Secretary on a part-time basis, though the commission hoped to move to a full-time appointment. Unfortunately Watters was not able to accept the full-time appointment, and after a year's part-time service, in which a great deal was achieved, he resigned. A full-time appointment was not to be made until after the war.[35]

The Annual Conference was changing too. In the inter-war years the regular attendance rose to several hundred. It remained a non-delegate conference, despite continued discussion of delegate voting. Two Conference papers were devoted to this subject in 1928. A long-standing issue was resolved in 1923 when the assets of the Christian Chapel Building Fund were handed over to a Chapel Building Committee, appointed by the Conference. The C.C.B.F. had requested this again in 1921 and a committee was appointed to investigate the matter. A model trust deed was approved by the 1923 Conference, and although its doctrinal clauses were criticized, a motion to delay the matter for a year was lost. New Rules and Regulations for the Association were adopted in 1925.[36]

Perhaps the change which people felt most came in 1939 when the Conference programme was extended to four days instead of three. This involved the abolition of the separate Sisters' Conference and Temperance and Social Questions Conference, which had hitherto met on the Monday of Conference week. The Sisters' Committee became a full standing committee at the same time.[37] Ironically the changes made were almost immediately upset by the war. There was no Conference in 1940, and the Conferences of 1941 to 1944 were shortened to three days. The war also ended the tradition of the Missionary Breakfast, begun in 1910; henceforward it became a Missionary Tea.

VI

In theology the inter-war period was one of transition. The foundation of Overdale and the controversy over the critical approach to scripture adopted there have already been mentioned. But it was due to Overdale, and to William Robinson and Joseph Smith in particular, that Churches of Christ were provided with a credible reinterpretation of their position and plea for the twentieth century. Here it was recognized that, whilst historical criticism had made a traditional understanding of the plea for the restoration of New Testament Christianity untenable, the new emphasis on the Bible which had resulted, and the greater attention paid to the history of the Church, could be turned to the advantage of Churches of Christ in a different way. This opportunity could only be seized if the Churches were prepared to adopt a more positive attitude to the other Churches around them. In his first words in the *Bible Advocate* after being appointed Principal, William Robinson wrote:

> As a people we have fought valiantly for the completion of the great reforming work of the sixteenth century, arrested in its onward march by the legalism of the seventeenth century; and for a century have contended earnestly for a return to Apostolic Christianity. The fight has been hard, especially in this country where traditionalism is enshrined not only in the law of the land but in the hearts of men; but we will be the first to confess that our armour has often been faulty, our weapons blunted, our vision dimmed and our ideals narrowed by a want of that charity which is of the very essence of the religion we seek to glorify . . .

He went on to point out that Churches of Christ were virtually unknown in the religious world and had scarcely any literature which reached a wider circle than their own churches; and he suggested that by neglect of training and a positive cultivation of the uneducated, Churches of Christ in Britain had lost touch with the pioneers.[38] These words explain his policy as Principal of Overdale: they also show the way in which he sought to set the movement in a historical context, even if his historical characterization was sometimes too simple.

Robinson's own theological work was an attempt to present

150

the best insights of the Restoration movement in an ecumenical context, and it is significant that his first theological book was entitled *Essays on Christian Unity*. It was not intended primarily for a domestic readership, and was published by James Clarke. His new departing point was clearly indicated in his Preface:

> Too often those who have pleaded for 'New Testament Christianity' have pleaded for the 'feeding-bottle type'. The New Testament has been regarded as a law-book, written specially to provide us with details of worship, belief and conduct. Today the New Testament has come to be in very truth a new book, more valuable than ever, because freed from artificial theories about its origin. The days of textual theology are gone. The historic method of interpretation has come to stay. The New Testament, like the Church, is freed from the dogma of indefectibility; but this does not mean that it loses its supreme place as the norm by which to test all future Christianity. This it will never lose. But it does mean that the New Testament is seen in its proper relation — historically — to the Church; and that in effecting Christian Unity we must make our appeal to *Scripture, history* and *reason*.[39]

Thus Alexander Campbell's method was preserved, but in a very different theological context.

Robinson also had some trenchant words to say about those who claimed to have no creed but the Bible:

> The cry for the New Testament as the sole creed has not resulted in unity, but in disunity . . . What those usually mean who say that the New Testament is their only creed, is not the New Testament, but *their interpretation of the New Testament*. Moreover, is it not true that they have a creed — though unwritten — which is ten times more stringent than any written creed?

And he quoted Jo Smith with approval:

> 'As an unwritten creed is often more exclusive and more divisive in its tendency than a written one, the latter seems to be preferable. As to the tendency of a written creed to bring about division, may it not be that by its instrumentality divisions that already exist are made manifest?'[40]

The distance from David King here is obvious.

It was also significant that the main footnote reference to Churches of Christ came not in the chapter on Baptism, but in that on Conversion. This was in line with the argument he later advanced in *What Churches of Christ Stand For* (1926) that the great theological contribution of the Restoration movement, in its advocacy of believer's baptism, was its doctrine of conversion.

This is an important shift of emphasis: the point is not that infant baptism is unscriptural (though this is argued) and believer's baptism has to be restored because it is the New Testament practice; it is rather that believer's baptism should be restored because that is consistent with New Testament doctrine in a way that infant baptism is not. The case rests on the theological understanding of baptism, not on the copying of primitive practice for its own sake.

What Churches of Christ Stand For was written at the request of the Publishing Committee to meet the need for a succinct explanation of the 'position and plea'. In this it succeeded admirably. In a hundred pages it crystallized the self-understanding of the British Churches of Christ, and was reprinted many times. Characteristically it was set in a historical framework: herein lay its strength and also its main weakness, for in his anxiety to warn against 'creating a past which never was a present' in looking at the New Testament, Robinson perhaps overlooked the same danger in writing the history of Churches of Christ.

Some of William Robinson's best writing was done for the Faith and Order movement. Joseph Smith did the main work on the replies to the Lausanne Conference, but Robinson's voice can also be heard. After Smith's death he shouldered the burden alone. He was heavily involved in the preparations for the Edinburgh Faith and Order Conference in 1937, and contributed an article on the Disciple position to the volume *Ministry and the Sacraments*. This statement is a model of brevity, containing some reworking of his earlier material but with updated references. After the Edinburgh Conference came work on the replies, again falling mainly to Robinson who was secretary of the Union Committee from 1926 until 1950.

Much of this material had a very restricted circulation as far as the ordinary church member, or even the regular Conference attender, was concerned. This was shown by the failure to establish a viable circulation for the theological magazine, the *Christian Quarterly* (1934-39). Even Robinson's Presidential address in 1935 was more concerned with questions of policy than with theological reinterpretation. His two 'domestic' books, *What Churches of Christ Stand For* and *The Shattered Cross* (1945) had a wide circulation and a great influence: but it is a striking fact that he was never invited to read a Conference paper. Perhaps that is why the bluntness of his friend and colleague from Furness, W.J. Clague, created rather more of a stir. James Clague read two papers in successive years (1937 and 1938) on the subject, 'The Principles of Church Organization in Primitive Christianity and their application to present-day Church Life'. Nothing in them should have surprised anyone who was in touch with current scholarship, and their author did not claim any originality. But when he said, 'It is impossible to reproduce the primitive Church order in our age, nor is it necessary: it would be an anachronism' and 'The modern scientific historical method of research applied to the study of the New Testament documents . . . has shown our position on Church order and ministry to be untenable', he posed the theological dilemma facing Churches of Christ with stark clarity.[41]

Another way in which the theological influence of Overdale affected the churches in these years was in worship. Robinson's little manual, *Holy Ordinances* (first published in 1925, with five subsequent editions to 1952) was a simple explanation of baptism and communion, with devotional meditations. This made it rather different in style from J.B. Rotherham's *Let Us Keep The Feast* (c 1906), which was in any case only concerned with communion. *Holy Ordinances* was frequently given to new church members, and contained a certificate of baptism. The publication of *The Christian Hymnary* in 1938 also bore the stamp of Overdale upon it. A committee had been appointed to prepare a new hymn book by the Conference of 1932. The secretarial duties of the committee were shared by James Gray, F.S. Herne, Frank Allen and William Robinson. Some 480 hymns were retained from the 1908 book, which meant that nearly half the hymns were new. Apart from the more recent hymns which had been added, the main additions came in the form of translations from the Reformation period and earlier. Characteristically the sections on Baptism and the Lord's Supper were much longer than in most other books, certainly among the Free Churches.[42]

The greater willingness of Churches of Christ to work with other Churches was also demonstrated in the 1930s. Participation in the first World Convention of Churches of Christ in 1930 represented the desire for fellowship with Churches of Christ around the world. The second World Convention was held in

Leicester in 1935, when J.W. Black was the President; this was a memorable occasion for those who went. In 1938 Annual Conference agreed to join the proposed World Council of Churches, though its formal inauguration was delayed until after the war. The accident of the late timing of the Annual Conference meant that Churches of Christ were the first denomination in Britain to take this decision. Then in 1939 Conference requested Central Council to consider the question of joining the united body which would result from the amalgamation of the National Free Church Council and the Federal Council of Free Churches. The amalgamation to form the Free Church Federal Council took place in 1940, but there was no Conference that year. In 1941 Conference resolved to apply for affiliation to the F.C.F.C., with one dissentient. Then in 1942 Conference agreed to join the newly formed British Council of Churches.[43] These institutional affiliations were to transform the relations of Churches of Christ with other Churches, but in practical terms the change was illustrated by the broadening group of those who brought greetings to Annual Conference. Traditionally greetings had been received from those who had emigrated overseas and were visiting the old country for a short while, or from missionaries. In 1927 the practice of receiving fraternal delegates from the International Convention of Disciples of Christ in the United States and Canada began. In 1938 Annual Conference in Manchester was welcomed by the President of the local Free Church Council, and the following year in Birmingham Conference was welcomed not only by the Free Church Council but also by the Archdeacon of Aston, representing the Bishop of Birmingham.[44] Since then welcomes from representatives of other Churches have become customary.

VII

The outbreak of war in 1939 plunged Churches of Christ into another period of uncertainty. But unlike 1914, war was widely expected. It was not any more welcome. If anything, pacifist feeling in the Churches had strengthened in the inter-war years. At the Temperance and Social Questions Conference in 1929 William Robinson delivered a lecture on 'The Christian Attitude to War', which became the basis of his book, *Christianity is Pacifism*, published in 1933. The book gained power from the fact that its author had served in the First World War, but, as might be expected from Robinson, its real strength lay in the way he removed the issue from the arena of Old or New Testament law and placed it firmly in the theologial question of the nature of God and his revelation in Christ. The Temperance and Social Questions Conference of 1933 returned to the subject when James Gray was the speaker, again outlining a Christian pacifist position. There were Conference resolutions on disarmament every year from 1931 to 1934, and in 1935 it was agreed to establish an organization which would provide church members with 'the opportunity of individually pledging themselves to refuse service in any of the fighting forces'. This led to the formation of the Pacifist Fellowship, under the auspices of the Temperance and Social Questions Committee, in 1936. A year later the results of a 'pacifist poll' were published in the *C.A.* Over 500 replies were received, and the editor noted that the results revealed some inconsistency, for example, in supporting military sanctions by the League of Nations even though they were not prepared to fight themselves in any circumstances. But the majority against bearing arms was something like 5 to 1 overall, and overwhelming among those of military age. More than half the respondents also said they would rather go to prison than engage in work of national importance in a war.[45]

As the likelihood of war increased, however, it was recognized that if war came there would be the same division of opinion as had occurred in the First World War. A resolution of the 1939 Conference therefore, directly addressed itself to this problem. It recognized that all were agreed that war was 'contrary to the spirit, teaching and purpose' of Christ, as the 1938 Conference had affirmed, but that this did not resolve the question of the military service. The resolution continued:

> We, therefore, desire to place on record our conviction that loyalty to our Lord Jesus Christ and our unity in Him is deeper and more abiding than any divergence in our attitude to military service. We urge upon all who will have to make the difficult decisions, to do so with humility and with charity and with understanding towards those who differ from them, remembering that all are sharers in the guilt of the world, which is partly the heritage of the past and partly the result of our present sin and folly.
>
> We pledge ourselves to support with our love and sympathy and with what action it may be necessary to take, both those who feel it their duty to resist military service and those who feel it their duty to

accept, praying earnestly that that unity which we have in Christ and which is declared and sealed in our worship at our Lord's Table, and manifested in the life of fellowship which we share, will not be broken, and that it will be the ambition of all who bear the name of Christ to strive for peace, and if need be, to suffer for it.[46]

Soon after the outbreak of war, the Pacifist Fellowship published advice for conscientious objectors going before local tribunals, and comments in the early part of 1940 suggested that the tribunals were behaving more sensitively than they had done in the First World War, though obviously there were exceptions. The Pacifist Fellowship affiliated to the Fellowship of Reconciliation in 1941 and joined the Central Board for Conscientious Objectors.[47] By contrast with 1914 therefore, the Churches were much readier to lend official support to conscientious objectors, so much so that some wondered whether partiality was running in the other direction. In October 1939 W.B. Ainsworth suggested that the Social Questions Committee ought also to establish a 'United Services Fellowship' to maintain links with those serving in the armed forces. Six months later he wrote again to the *C.A.* regretting that nothing had been done, and offering his own services in organizing such a Fellowship. At that very moment the S.Q.C. were writing to ask him to undertake such a task, which he agreed to do. In 1941 the work was taken over by W.F. Aiton and his wife, who remained in charge for the rest of the war.[48] As in 1914-18 more church members served in the forces than became conscientious objectors. Complete figures are not available, but in 1943 there were 433 members of the Pacifist Fellowship and 750 men and 150 women in the United Services Fellowship.[49] It is also clear that the deep antagonisms of the First War were avoided. This was partly due to the different circumstances of the Second World War. Not only were the tribunals better organized and more consistent in their decisions, but the lack of any equivalent to the Western Front for most of the war and the much greater exposure of civilians to enemy attack meant that military casualties were fewer, and it was not possible to argue that people were sitting safely at home while the soldiers were fighting. The Churches were, moreover, much better prepared for the problems which arose, and the fact that prominent and respected leaders took a pacifist position made the kind of polarization experienced in the First World War much less likely.

It is difficult to gauge the effect of the war on church life. In the first two years there was much comment on the disruption caused, and the Sunday School Committee referred to the difficulties in their work for most of the war years. But the general impression gained from reading the *C.A.* is that life was much more normal than might have been expected. The 1940 Annual Conference was cancelled, but despite some protests Conferences were held for the remaining years of the war. They were held away from major centres of population — Ulverston, Kirkcaldy, Mansfield and Stockport — but even this had compensating advantages. The Centenary Conference in 1942 could not be held in Edinburgh, as had been planned, but Fife was more than glad to receive it, and the Historical Committee arranged an appropriate programme. During the war Overdale virtually ceased to function as a college: the Principal acted without salary, depending on his stipend from Selly Oak, and James Gray became a leader at Weoley Castle Boys' and Girls' Club. The Home Missions Committee (as the General Evangelist Committee had become in 1938) continued its work as usual, with relatively few financial problems. The Missionary Committee, on the other hand, had a desperate financial crisis in 1940, which was only overcome by their jubilee offering. By 1944 they had a substantial balance in hand, but this was largely due to the fact that remittances to Siam became impossible after the Japanese invastion and furloughs were impossible during the war. The Clarks and Esther Halliday were interned in Siam in December 1941.

Perhaps, however, the real effects of the war were not felt for some time afterwards. Writing in the *C.A.* for 18 May 1945 at the end of the war in Europe, the editor, William Robinson, referred to the shadow of a great sorrow that lay across the gratitude and rejoicing:

> We remember those of our number whom we shall see no more, who have not lived to see the fruit of their labour, their heroism and their sacrifice. We of Churches of Christ think especially of those young men and women whom we had hoped to see return to us, sharing with us the joys of peace and the burden of the new day. Who can count our loss?[50]

That loss was indeed incalculable. And as Conference assembled in Leicester in August 1945, another shadow appeared. The opening day, 6 August, was the day when the first atomic bomb was dropped on Hiroshima, a fact reflected in a resolution later in the Conference.

VIII

There remains to be considered one other aspect of the inter-war period: the 'old paths' question. This was the developing division within the British Churches of Christ that finally became formal at the end of the war. But, in fact, the parting of the ways had come earlier: by the mid-1930s a *de facto* separation existed. Most of the causes have already been touched upon, so that all that is required here is to draw the threads together.

The origins go back to the First World War, to the battles over pacifism and the Christian Association churches in 1916-17. The opposition to war, and union with the Christian Association found ready support in a monthly magazine called *The Interpreter*, founded in 1908 and edited by Ivie Campbell of Glasgow, with the assistance of John Scouller and J.H. Odd. Campbell was opposed to instrumental music and Conference committees, and had much in common with the conservative group of Churches of Christ in America. In June 1916 H.E. Tickle wrote a letter to the *Bible Advocate* criticizing the tone of articles in *The Interpreter*, especially on the war. He also criticized their advocacy of support for independent missionaries in India. His letter provoked several responses, including one from the evangelist, Walter Crosthwaite, who summed up the matter thus:

> As to *The Interpreter*, apart altogether from the war, it stands for simple New Testament Christianity, and serves to remind us of those principles our fathers sacrificed so much for, but which are so lightly esteemed today.[51]

In 1916 the title of the magazine was changed to *The Apostolic Messenger*, and when Campbell fell ill, the editorship passed to W.M. Kempster. After the *Bible Advocate* became the *Christian Advocate* in 1921, the old name was taken over by the *Apostolic Messenger*. In 1934 a further change took place when Walter Crosthwaite became editor and the name was changed to *Scripture Standard*. This rival magazine became the focus for all criticism of the leadership of the Annual Conference. The war and the Communion question, as it was affected by the union of

1917, have already been mentioned. In the early 1920s opposition to Overdale and the campaign for disaffiliation from the S.C.M. were led by those who published the paper. When Frederick Nkhonde complained about Ernest Gray, it was to Kempster that he wrote. The significance of this emerging group lay not just in their opposition, but in the policy they advocated. There were other individuals who who held conservative views on several of these questions — R.K. Francis is a notable example — but they did not advocate a policy of separation. Walter Crosthwaite, however, became (in the words of Walter Barker of Heanor, who published the magazine) 'an apostle of dissolution, urging on brethren and churches of like mind to separate themselves to follow the "old paths" '.[52]

In 1924 the first conference of 'old paths' churches was held, and these gradually became a twice-yearly occasion. By the time of the dicussions over communion in 1929-30, some of the 'old paths' churches were ready to withdraw, but in the end only four did: Blackridge and Crofthead in 1931 and Kilbirnie and Slamannan in 1934. In practice, the division had already come to exist. The 'old paths' Conference had its own Evangelistic Committee, and it also supported the seceding group on the Nyasaland mission.

The developments in the later 1930s added fuel to the flames. The creation of the Central Council was seen as a sinister infringement on the independence of local congregations. Affiliation to the World Council of Churches, the Free Church Federal Council and the British Council of Churches was seen as a fatal compromise of distinctive principles. At the heart of the whole matter lay the attitude to scripture. The 'old paths' brethren claimed that the Association supported those who 'no longer regard the Bible as an all-sufficient rule of faith and practice, and who undermine faith in the Scriptures'. In 1943 Annual Conference appointed a committee of five to see if it was possible to resolve the differences between the two groups. It soon became clear that there was no wish on the 'old paths' side to resolve them. Their representatives simply challenged the Conference committee to demonstrate where the 'old paths' brethren had departed from the 'position and plea', and in effect to admit that the cooperating churches were in error. The Conference committee were also questioned in detail about their personal beliefs. They concluded that no useful purpose would be served by prolonging the discussions. Conference in 1946 repudiated the charge made about their attitude to the Bible, but by then the exercise was becoming increasingly pointless. Crosthwaite's report of the 1946 Conference in the *Scripture Standard* was headed 'The Cooperation versus the Loyal Brethren'. Between 1943 and 1947 nineteen 'old paths' churches withdrew from the Association, and there have been several further withdrawals since. Usually this depended on waiting for the deaths of particular members so that the move would not split the church.[53]

It is impossible to avoid a feeling of sadness that such a division should have taken place. It is also clear that the division removed much of the spirit of contention from the proceedings of Annual Conference. The parting of the ways pinpointed the dilemma facing Churches of Christ as they approached the second half of the twentieth century. Were they to maintain their witness by remaining as a separate body, or were they to play a greater part in the ecumenical movement? By the end of the Second World War it had become clear that the leadership of the Association of Churches was committed to the latter course.

6 THE ECUMENICAL AGE

I

The end of the second world war in a single generation found Churches of Christ in a more sober mood than in 1919. Reading a Conference paper in 1946 on 'The Churches — Present Position and Future Prospects', Leslie Colver noted that the casualties in the war had been relatively light and that more men and women would be returning to their homes. He continued:

> It is speculative, however, as to whether they will come back to the Church any more than they did after the last war. Personally, I feel we shall lose many. . . . The enthusiasm and thrill of the Welcome Home Social soon passes — or so it seems. . . . Even as the men and women return, it is doubtful if they can stand our pedantic ways, unenterprising techniques and traditional thought-forms. . . . The *habit* of church-going has been broken, and there seems little effort to revive it.[1]

Statistically, the period since 1945 has been one of continuous decline. Perhaps as important has been the mood of the Churches. This is, of course, much more difficult to judge, but there does seem to have been a change within the period. In the earlier part, until the late 1950s, there was an underlying gloom about the future as church leaders and members came to terms with the situation. Since 1960 there has been a greater readiness to see signs of hope, particularly in closer relationships with other Churches.

The decline in church membership has not been at a steady rate. Between 1939 and 1945 the net decline in membership was 21%, and in the next five years it was 19%. The 1950s (which witnessed a mini-religious revival in the country as a whole) saw a slackening in the rate of decline, being 11% in each of the periods 1950-55 and 1955-60. In the 1960s the decline accelerated again and was nearly 22% in each of the periods 1965-70 and 1970-75. Between 1975 and 1979 the decline was 11%.

This decline in membership was unevenly distributed in space as well as through time. South Wales and Yorkshire have been the areas most seriously affected: in South Wales there were 8 churches in 1945, 3 in 1970 and 2 in 1979; in Yorkshire 10 in 1945, 6 in 1970 and 4 in 1979. The dominance of the midlands and Scotland has become even more marked, and the importance of Lancashire and Cheshire has declined. In 1945 31% of the membership lived in the Midland division; in 1979 36% did: the comparable figures for Scotland are 18% in 1945 and 20% in 1979. In the same period the proportion living in the Lancashire and Cheshire division dropped from 17% to 14%.

The explanation for these trends is not necessarily unique to Churches of Christ: indeed it has been observed that there is a striking correlation between the trend lines of religious statistics for all denominations in Britain since 1900, and this is particularly true of the main Free Churches.[2] Since the First World War these Churches have been characterized by an above-average proportion of women in their membership, particularly single women; by an age-structure which is higher than that of the population as a whole; and by lower fertility than the population as a whole. In a situation where recruitment to church membership has been increasingly from within the families of church members, these characteristics lead inexorably to decline. The deaths suffered in two world wars have certainly played their part in this, but wider social changes are also involved. The increasing freedom felt by church members to marry members of other denominations, or none, has weakened family loyalty to a particular denomination at the parental level, whilst the increasing problem of retaining the loyalty of the children of church members gives a further savage twist to the spiral of decline. The latter problem was a point for comment in the correspondence columns of the *C.A.* during the war. The failure to make a significant impact on outsiders was sharply demonstrated by a personal survey undertaken by Leslie Colver in preparation for his Conference paper of 1946. He discovered that the total number of non-members present at 140 Sunday evening gospel services was 590, giving an average of four per church. He also noted that half of those services were attended by less than 20 people each, with only eleven having a congregation of more than 50.[3] All this suggests that the roots of the decline which became so apparent in the post-war years have to be traced back much earlier.

Separations, which were attracting attention in the late nineteenth century, continued to be a topic of discussion. William Robinson in an editorial before the 1946 Conference noted that there had been no less than 11,330 separations in the period since 1930. He attributed this partly to lack of pastoral oversight, but also to what he called 'indiscriminate baptism': this he felt to be a charge as equally applicable to the practice of many believer-baptist congregations as to the infant-baptist Churches which had traditionally been accused of it. His suggested remedy was better preparation for baptism. In 1949 he returned to the subject with another suggestion, namely that many church rolls had been more vigorously pruned in the years since the war as a result of the voluntary levies made by Central Council and some district committees on the basis of membership figures.[4] Undoubtedly there was an element of truth in this, but it had also become equally clear that 'separations' was a label for the problem, rather than an explanation.

Economic and social changes were also affecting church life. The post-war decline in the numbers employed in coal-mining, particularly in South Wales, and to a lesser extent in north Nottinghamshire and Northumberland, had a depressing effect on the churches in those areas. Leslie Colver's perceptive eye saw the significance of the social context of the early Churches of Christ. In his Presidential address in 1956 he compared the Churches with some of the other small Free Churches and noted their democratic spirit and the opportunities open to laymen.

> Indeed (he continued), *I claim that the appeal of our mutual ministry was just as effective as our sacramental position.* We could make a place for men, and, in addition on a *platform* — this simple piece of furniture gave a touch of 'authority' we have lost sight of today.[5]

Nevertheless by the end of the first half of the twentieth century these denominations, including Churches of Christ, had become middle-class movements. 'We have settled down to being respectable Christians with respectable incomes and respectable views,' he had said in 1946.[6]

There were more subtle changes taking place as well. An analysis of the leaders of the Churches, particularly on Conference committees, but also in local congregations, before the Second World War, would show that they were dominated by business men, though they could be in business in quite a small way. Since the war, leadership has increasingly passed into the hands of men (and women) in professional or executive positions, including the full-time ministers of the Churches. There has also been an increasing proportion of graduates. It is true, as Leslie Colver observed in 1956, that professions such as medicine and the law have not been well represented in the membership of the Churches,[7] but this should not obscure the broader social change. Its significance is twofold: on the one hand, it is a reflection of the increasing equality of opportunity in modern Britain, which has enabled such people to secure jobs not open to their parents; on the other, such people have risen on the basis of intellectual merit through the educational system, rather than through business enterprise and the accumulation of capital, and this shows itself in different values and attitudes. A symbol of the change can be seen in 1928 when Frank Hepworth, a university graduate and a schoolmaster, succeeded R.W. Black, a self-made estate agent, as chairman of the Reference Committee. It is unlikely that this kind of social change has contributed in any significant way to the decline of the Churches, but it is worth noting that it is relatively unusual nowadays for church members to be employed by other members of the church. In former times this was more common, and for such people church membership provided economic as well as spiritual security.

Quite apart from these external influences on the life of the churches, there was also a change in their self-understanding. It had long been recognized that, in principe at any rate, joining Churches of Christ involved the acceptance of a theological position on church order as well as the acceptance of Jesus Christ as Saviour, and for this reason the Churches were unlikely ever to have a mass appeal. In practice, the evangelistic missions run from the time of Sydney Black to E.C. Hinrichsen were much more evangelical in atmosphere, save, of course, for the requirement of believer's baptism. But as sensitivity to the position of other Churches increased, this earlier policy began to be questioned. At the Home Missions Rally of the 1946 Conference, W.J. Clague declared:

> that the days of insular denominational evangelism in this country were coming to an end. We must think in terms of the *ecumenical movement.*[8]

This observation had significant implications.

There was also another problem. Unlike the Church of England the Free Churches do not have parishes. There is therefore no clearly defined community to which the local congregation can appeal. In practice, such congregations tended to appeal to their immediate neighbourhood, but in a small town it was feasible to hire a central hall and appeal with pamphlet publicity to the whole community. By the end of the Second World War urban development had made this increasingly difficult. A number of churches were becoming 'downtown' churches, drawing their congregation from a distance. In some cases the residential community in the immediate neighbourhood disappeared: where it remained, its social character often changed adversely for the church. This was accentuated with the rise in immigration from the Commonwealth which came in the later 1950s and the 1960s. West Indians found it difficult to adjust to the different style of worship, and Asians from a Muslim background had little interest in the church anyway. Historically very few Churches of Christ had been 'neighbourhood' churches: they therefore faced considerable problems.

As in the other Free Churches, there was a sharp drop in the number of new churches founded after the First World War. Between the wars sixteen new Churches of Christ were formed, just under 10% of the total on the list in 1939: by 1965 seven survived, and by 1979 four — a much higher closure rate than in the Churches as a whole. Since 1944 six new churches have been formed, two of them as a result of divisions in a congregation. These statistics illustrate the difficulties which Churches of Christ have had in church extension. They do not tell the whole story about new housing areas, because there are older churches which have moved out into new areas: but the great advantage which such churches had was a congregation of loyal members and a sense of tradition, and this put them in a different position from the really new churches.

II

The response of Churches of Christ to the problems of the post-war world took three main forms: one was a shift in the general policy over evangelism and church extension, particularly as reflected in the policy of the H.M.C. over ministerial placings; the second was a series of changes in the central organization of the Churches, particularly in finance; the third was a theological change, particularly in ecumenical policy. The boundary lines between these responses, especially the first and second, are not clear-cut, but they do define the main areas for discussion.

One change at the beginning of the period, which had implications both for policy and organization, was the appointment of Leslie Colver as the first full-time General Secretary of the Churches from 1 January 1948. This was, of course, the fulfilment of a policy agreed in principle in 1937. A.C. Watters had done the job on a part-time basis, and Arthur Brown had performed the duties of General Conference Secretary and secretary to Central Council and the H.M.C. in addition to his ministry at Burnage for the previous seven years, but at last a full-time appointment had been made. One great advantage which Leslie Colver brought to his new job was the intimate knowledge of the churches gained during his previous period of service as Sunday School organizer (1933-47). The significance of the post had also been increased by reorganization of the Central Council in 1942. The functions of the Reference Committee, the Emergency Committee and the Central Council had been combined, with appropriate alterations in the Council's membership, so as to create a body in which general policy for the work of the Association could be discussed, and which had an existence between Annual Conferences.[9]

In the section of his Conference paper for 1946 on 'Future Prospects' the new General Secretary had already isolated the two main areas for attention: the position and use of evangelists and the work of the local ministry, within the local congregation and in the wider work of local preaching. The same emphasis occurred in the Central Council report on the state of the Churches, presented at the same Conference. To assist the development of the local ministry, the H.M.C. appointed W.J. Clague to tour the churches holding courses in local leadership, usually on the basis of a three months' stay with a church or group of churches. He continued this work until his retirement in 1952. A commission was appointed by the Conference of 1947 to study 'the work and status of the Ministry'. Its report, adopted in 1953, will be discussed below.[10]

In addition to this, plans were made for a crusade of revival and evangelism, modelled on the 'Crusade for a Christian World' organized by the Disciples of Christ in America. The 1948 Conference gave its approval to this scheme, which became known as the Crusade of Christian Witness and lasted from 1950 to 1953. The year 1949-50 was designated a year of 'Inner Mission' in which the churches were to be prepared for the 'Outer Mission' in the three years following. Conference papers were read on the Inner Mission by David Rudkin and W.F. Aiton in 1949 and the Inner Mission was launched in a devotional service led by the Vice-President, Arthur Brown. The Outer Mission was launched the following year with a target of 3,000 additions in the next three years. Again the subject was tackled in Conference papers, read on this occasion by Richard Lampard and Andrew Blacklock. W.F. Aiton, who had been appointed national Crusade Leader, conducted the inaugural service.

In the years 1950-51 and 1951-52 about twenty intensive missions per year were held in the Churches, whilst for the last year 1952-53 the planning was largely in the hands of local churches themselves. It had become apparent as early as 1951 that the number of non-members attending was small. Notwithstanding the original target of 3,000, the Central Council report suggested that 'the full results of these efforts cannot be measured solely by numbers'. In 1952 the Crusade committee reported an increased emphasis on evangelism in local church life, but not a significant increase in numbers.[11] When the Crusade closed in 1953, the Central Council report to Conference frankly acknowledged the lack of success:

> We end the Crusade with the targets still far ahead of our achievements and with the Churches standing very much where they did at the beginning. The increase in membership throughout the years of the Crusade has been no more than average.[12]

The Crusade Leader in his report to Conference said that 'some had spoken of the Crusade as a "flop"'. The year of Inner Mission had been the most effective feature, though intensive missions had produced some results.[13]

The early 1950s were a gloomy period in other ways. Concern over the lack of recruits for the ministry led James Gray to resign as Principal of Overdale in 1954; and in the same year the Women's Committee had to restrict the work of Home Missions Sisters because there was no call from the Churches for their services. This led the Executive of the Women's Committee to suggest to Central Council that a Committee of Five be appointed to investigate the state of the Churches, and a group consisting of J.L. Colver, Mrs M. Montgomery, W.F. Aiton, S.

Mason and J.W. Rutt was given this task. Questionnaires were sent to all the churches, and members of the committee visited every district, usually in pairs. Three reports were published, in 1955, 1956 and 1957, in which the committee set out very clearly the facts as it saw them. Four main conclusions emerged:

> (1) Some Churches are, humanly speaking, quite ineffective.
> (2) There are many Churches depending on one man, and not a few depending on two men. If anything happens to that one figure, the days of that church are as good as numbered . . .
> (3) All admit the need for training young men — and others — for the public ministry of the Church. On the whole, young men are left to find their feet by the method of trial and error.
> (4) The number of local preachers is growing less and less. In some areas, the danger point has been reached and some Churches are needing to call in preachers from other Denominations to help. This is not because of some increased tempo in ecumenical action but largely to 'fill in the plan'.[14]

They went on to fill out the implications of this survey, as they saw them. They drew attention to the necessity for adequate male leadership in each church, and the need for a Sunday School and youth activities which would enable young people to look on the church as a spiritual home. The need for more full-time ministers was well-known, but they observed that it would be very helpful to have one or two younger ministers who were willing for the sake of the churches to remain single for a time, so that they could exercise a 'mobile' ministry. The effects of church members living at a distance from the church were noted: 'in some instances, nearly the whole congregation arrives by bus or car, and departs likewise, and that's that . . .' They pointed out that churches isolated by long distance from other Churches of Christ would find it difficult to sustain interest in 'belonging' to a brotherhood of churches. But perhaps their most poignant observation was this:

> Unless congregations have more zeal for the task (and urgency) of evangelism, the failing flame will die out or be reduced to such a small glow that it will be ineffective. If a Church arrives at the point of 'carrying on' just to keep the doors open there may be reasonable pride, but that does not, in itself, guarantee survival. In the longing to keep 'the truth' alive, even the very will to live can be atrophied. Even small-group prestige and especially family connections may hold the cause together long after fossilization has been noted by nearly anybody else. They would never dream of 'joining anybody else' even if they had to give up, but in splendid isolation remain aloof with (to them) honour, integrity and the 'cause' unsullied.[15]

The twenty years since 1956 have provided abundant examples of the sad truth of this analysis.

Nevertheless the Committee of Five's final report in 1957 contained some signs of hope, several of which were the result of developments which had matured since the committee's appointment. One was a programme of assistance from the Disciples of Christ in America, which became known first as 'Fraternal Aid' and later as 'Joint Ministries'. This began as a result of the concern of Dr Loren E. Lair, Fraternal Delegate in 1952, at the after-effects of the war on the British Churches. This concern was shared with other Disciple leaders and with British leaders resident in the U.S.A. at that time, such as Dr Robinson and Dr Watters, and with James Gray whilst he was lecturing in the U.S.A. The main thrust of the programme was a series of three-year settled pastorates with American ministers in seven churches — Burnage, Manchester; Coplaw St, Glasgow; Falkirk; Wandsworth Bridge Rd, London; Moseley Rd, Birmingham; Kirkcaldy, and Bournemouth. These began in 1955 and continued until 1961, when the emphasis was changed. Support was then given to a project which lasted from 1962 to 1968, whereby W.F. Aiton was appointed regional secretary to the Lancashire, Cheshire and North Staffordshire division, exercising a general pastoral ministry to the churches in the division and especially those without full-time ministers. Provision was also made for three visiting professorships at Overdale College, and for other short-term projects, such as the visit of J.V. Reeve, Disciple Stewardship Secretary, in 1964 to advise the British Churches on stewardship methods. The Joint Ministries Committee (as it became in 1966) also supported the ministry of Derek Nuttall in Aberfan after the disaster which hit the village in October 1966 when the slipping of a coal tip destroyed the local school. This ministry, following a series of short-term ministries in 1966-67, began at Christmas 1967 and lasted until 1974. The assistance from America was very much appreciated and came at a crucial time. It has continued in different forms since the Joint Ministries Committee was officially wound up in 1974.[16]

A second sign of hope in 1957 was the erection of new church buildings and schoolrooms in a number of places. New schoolrooms in places like Derby, Riddings, Saffron Lane, Leicester and Humberstone reflected new opportunities for youth work which had resulted from new housing close to existing churches. Avery Hill, London and Braunstone, Leicester were examples of new churches built in new housing areas by old congregations — Laurie Hall, Deptford and Andrewes Street, Leicester respectively. The new church at Avery Hill was opened in June 1958, when Philip Morgan went there as their first full-time minister. The new Braunstone church building, replacing the temporary building used since 1950, was opened in December 1960. The new church building at Burnage, Manchester was opened in 1961. All are examples of some of the best in simple church architecture since the war.

More lavish in scale, and with a unique scale of problems, was the new church at East Kilbride, near Glasgow, begun in 1953. East Kilbride was one of the first of the Scottish new towns developed in the post-war period, and the Glasgow District Committee of Churches of Christ was given the opportunity of a site in one of the first parts of the town to be built. The H.M.C. allocated East Kilbride the services of Alan Robinson, who had formerly been a missionary in India, from 1 September 1953, and the members of the new church first met in his home in November. A temporary building was quickly erected, and opened in February 1954. By October it had been decided to begin work immediately on the main building at a cost of £5,000. In 1956 the foundation stone was laid and the church was assisted by a work camp from the U.S.A. But then the dream began to turn into a nightmare. It had been planned to complete the building in phases, but the Development Corporation demanded that the whole building be complete by 1961. This entailed the expenditure of another £9-10,000, just at a time when the Glasgow District Committee had decided not to put any more building work out to tender until 75% of the cost was already in hand. The District appealed to Central Council for help. This meant that the Church Extension Committee set up by Conference in 1958, following discussion in 1957, was almost immediately involved in a rescue operation. By 1961 a modified version of the original plan had been approved by the Committee and £12,000 had been raised (about £8,000 coming from individuals). With great relief the new church was opened in November 1962 and the Churches acquired one of their most impressive buildings.[17] The experience had, however, been a salutary one, and enthusiasm for bold church extension schemes became suspect. The new church begun at Oadby, Leicester in 1965 was more modest in scale.

A third hopeful development in the mid-1950s was the expanding programme of youth work. The formation of the Fellowship of Youth has already been described. Churches of Christ were one of the first denominations to organize national youth work, and when in 1939 the Government published a circular on a national youth movement the Churches of Christ were ready to cooperate: indeed the National Sunday School Union sought their help and advice in preparing their own pamphlet on programme planning. By 1950 there were 80 local F.O.Y. groups. In 1949 a group of American young people visited the British churches, and this visit was returned by a British group in 1954. As a result it was decided to run an annual youth camp with a programme and organization similar to those used in the U.S.A., the first being held at Hollowford, Castleton, Derbyshire in 1955. It was a great success and in 1956 two camps were planned — at Grendon Hall in Northamptonshire, and Kinross in Scotland. Thereafter the youth camps became a regular part of the annual programme: not only have they given many young people a wider vision of the life of the Church, they have also led several to offer themselves for the full-time ministry. In 1960 the Fellowship of Youth was formally integrated into the life of Conference, when the Sunday School and Youth Committee became the Christian Education Committee, with separate sections for children's and youth work. This was itself a reflection of the extent to which leaders in the F.O.Y. had become involved in the life of Conference and were assuming positions of leadership in the Churches generally. But a Conference-appointed committee did not prove an adequate substitute for the self-government of the old system: at the beginning of the 1970s another self-governing group, the Young People of Churches of Christ, had emerged alongside the Conference committee structure. This was not in any sense a rival group and there was full cooperation with the Christian Education Committee; but it did also reflect the changing culture and life-style of young people in the late 1960s and early 1970s.[18]

Similar expansion took place in women's work, which also encouraged the Committee of Five. In 1946 a Women's Fellowship was inaugurated to link the long-established Sisters'

Committee with the churches, by the provision of a study programme. Again American ideas were used and this was assisted by the visit of Jessie Trout from the U.C.M.S. in 1947. The Young Women's Convention, which had lapsed during the war, was revived as a Women's Convention, and rapidly became a well-attended occasion. In 1952 a separate Convention for Scotland was begun. Links with women's work in other Disciple Churches around the world were established, and in 1953 the World Christian Women's Fellowship was formed. In 1956 the name of the national committee, which had been changed from Sisters' Committee to Women's Committee in 1947, was further changed to Christian Women's Fellowship Committee. May Segain was appointed as the first organizing secretary of the British C.W.F.[19]

Finally, the post-war years saw a considerable expansion of the scope of the Social Questions Committee's work. In 1947 Sam Mason was appointed committee organizer and he brought a new dynamism to the area of the Churches' life. To the traditional topics of temperance and pacifism was added a concern for a new social order at home and overseas. Money was collected for famine relief in India: the Christian Fellowship Association was formed to help people in financial need at home. From this too developed the Churches of Christ Housing Society with its homes for old people. In these and other ways the Churches were looking beyond their own immediate fellowship.

III

In the later 1950s, therefore, a more hopeful mood began to spread through the Churches. The Committee of Five had noted that there was a greater spirit of cooperation between churches at district level: and some of the earlier tensions that had marred Conference discussions, particularly the arguments with 'old path' churches, disappeared. In two areas, however, progress remained slow: training for the ministry, and national committee finance and organization.

In 1945 Conference gave its support to the launching of a Silver Jubilee Fund by the Training Committee, with the dual purpose of increasing the endowment of Overdale College and providing permanent college premises. A target of £25,000 was set. By 1950 the half-way mark had been passed, but the Training Committee noted that only a very small proportion had been contributed by the Churches: most had come from individuals. In the early 1950s, however, the number of new students coming forward dropped sharply and by the beginning of the 1953-54 session there were only six ministerial students in training. In 1954 James Gray, who had succeeded William Robinson as Principal in 1949, felt compelled to resign because of the small numbers and the deteriorating financial situation. Arthur Brown continued on the staff as Tutor-in-charge, until in 1958 he was appointed Principal. The plans for a completely new college building were abandoned in 1956 and instead it was decided to use the Silver Jubilee Fund, which by then had a capital of £21,000, to purchase and remodel the existing building. The new Overdale was opened in January 1959. Arthur Brown was succeeded as Principal by Stanley Sewell, formerly a missionary in Thailand, in 1966, but he resigned for personal and financial reasons after a year in office.

In 1968 John Francis became Principal, and a new policy of 'Open Overdale' courses was initiated to make more use of the college as a training centre for all the members of the Churches. To this end a Golden Jubilee Fund was launched in 1969 which reached its target of £5,000, thus enabling (with other monies) the opening of a new wing in February 1970. The 1970s were a time of retrenchment in theological education generally, and Churches of Christ did not escape. By 1975 there were no ministerial students in training, and a change in the policy of the Selly Oak Colleges generally, in the direction of short courses for Christian students from overseas, had led to changes in the central teaching staff, which made Selly Oak a less suitable centre for ministerial theological training. In these circumstances it was decided to transfer ministerial training to the Manchester Congregational College, where John Francis became a part-time member of the college staff as Churches of Christ Ministerial Training Advisor. The sale of the Overdale building was completed in September 1977. It marked the end of an era: but it was also the beginning of a new one, and was an example of the growing cooperation with the United Reformed Church. By 1979 there were five students in training for ministry among Churches of Christ.[20]

One of the discouraging features of the 1945-55 period had been the number of men who left the full-time ministry, either to serve in other Churches or to take up secular employment. Some of the reasons given for this included low stipends and frequent movements. There was some improvement in stipend, though it was slow. The first formal scale was agreed in 1942 and published in 1945: this gave a basic stipend on appointment to the permanent staff, exclusive of marriage, children's and cost-of-living allowances, of £180 p.a. The minimum payment for a married man was £221 p.a. These figures represented only slight increases over those payable in the mid-1920s. By 1961 these figures had rather more than doubled. In 1975, after the structure of the scale had undergone two major changes, the starting stipend was £1,368 p.a. Although this was a reflection of the rising rate of inflation, it also represented a significant movement in the direction of paying ministers an appropriate stipend. Yet it remained true that it was often only where their wives could go out to work, that ministers had any chance of reaching the standard of living of many working members of their congregation. Joseph Smith's wife had written movingly in the 1930s of the way in which ministers' wives bore the strain of their husbands' low pay and insecure conditions: similar problems could still be found in the 1960s and 1970s, but progress had been made.[21]

In relation to the other complaint — frequency of movement — the situation had been transformed. Although the principle of a minimum pastorate length of three years did not become H.M.C. policy until 1963, in practice it had become established early in the post-war period. In 1961 nine of the fifteen ministers, who had also served as full-time ministers in the previous year, had been with their church for at least three years, and twelve had been with their previous church at least three years. In 1970 sixteen of the twenty-five ministers who had served as full-time ministers in the previous year, had been with their church for at least three years, and six had been there for at least five years. By the late 1970s it was not uncommon for ministers to have served a church for ten years.[22]

This marked a dramatic change in policy from the pre-war period. It was partly affected by the need to place ministers in churches or districts which could meet full salary without subsidy from the H.M.C. It was also a result of a decision in the 1970s not to make too many ministerial changes whilst discussions for union with the United Reformed Church were proceeding. But it was mainly due to a response to the long-made criticism that ministers in the past had never stayed long enough to consolidate their work. Moreover, although the H.M.C. remained willing to make ministers available to other churches for short periods of service, scarcely any wished to take advantage of this possibility. So far as can be judged, this change of policy has not had the results that its opponents always feared — the introduction of 'one-man ministry'. It is still rare for a full-time minister to preside and preach at the communion service, though it has been customary for many years for the preacher at the evening service to conduct the worship also. The full-time minister is a member of the elders' meeting, but he works as one of a team. This is not to say that there have been no examples of 'one-man ministry' within Churches of Christ: but where it has developed, this has not been primarily due to the length of pastorate but to the attitude of the congregation — and such instances were not unknown before 1945!

The reorganization of national committees and finance was also slow. The question had been raised periodically in the inter-war period but without much effect. Charles Green, in his Presidential address for 1946, urged a delegate Conference which would accept responsibility for planning the work of the Churches, with a budget committee to coordinate the raising of funds. The idea of a delegate Conference proved no more popular after the war than before, and in 1951 the proposal was rejected after the opinion of the Churches had been sought. Out of 78 replies received, 43 churches were against it and only 23 in favour. J.R. Francis also suggested a reorganization of the Churches' committee work, when he was President in 1948. Central Council set up sub-committees to examine the coordination of finance and the size of committees. One result was the allocation of a month to each of the main standing committees as the month for their appeal for funds. No progress was made on reducing the size of committees.

Pressure nevertheless continued, and in 1955 Charles Green was invited to read a Conference paper on organization and finance. He suggested a streamlining of committee structure and a unified finance committee which would raise and distribute the money for the total corporate work of the Churches. A Committee of Three was set up to bring forward proposals, and reports were submitted to Conference in 1956 and 1957. It was agreed to reduce the size of standing committees by about half overall, but the proposals for a scheme of unified finance based on an assessment of each church, though accepted by Conference, failed to gain the support of a sufficient number of churches for it to be implemented. Instead the 1959 Conference agreed to establish a voluntary system of Unified Finance, which came into operation in the year 1960-61. Though this was in some ways a contradiction in terms, it proved a sensible solution. In 1960-61 24 churches contributed to the national work through Unified Finance: by 1970 this number had risen to 45 and in 1979 it was 51. This was not only two-thirds of the total number of churches, but also included all those which contributed most generously.[23]

The impetus behind these changes was undoubtedly the financial crisis of the early 1950s. In 1952 the Missionary Committee's overdraft was more than £5,000 at a time when they estimated their annual expenditure at £9,000. The Training Committee had an overdraft of £1,700 and the Home Missions Committee had a debit balance of some £250. By 1960 the overdrafts of standing committees had mounted to the point where Paul Smith, as President of Conference, set out to repeat the work of William Robinson in 1935 by raising a fund to clear them. Some £6,300 was raised and distributed to the committees concerned in the year 1960-61. In 1965 it was decided to appoint a Stewardship Committee to improve giving in the Churches, and from 1969 there has been a part-time financial secretary to the Churches. The Carmichael-Montgomery Charitable Trust, set up by F.T. Carmichael in 1962 and enlarged by Arthur and Minnie Montgomery in 1965, has also given generous assistance to the churches in various ways.[24] All this has meant that in the 1970s the financial position has become easier, though it has to be remembered that the reduction in the number of missionaries overseas, as the missions have become independent Churches, removed one of the main causes of the problems of the earlier period.

Throughout the period since the war the Churches have benefited greatly from the leadership given by successive General Secretaries. Leslie Colver served with devotion and efficiency until 1961 when he returned to the pastoral ministry. He was followed by Walter Hendry, who had served as an evangelist in Leicester and Birmingham from 1931 to 1942 and then became a personnel manager in industry. A former chairman of the Social Questions Committee, he brought a concern for the total witness of the Church into his conception of the office; and it was largely due to his vision that Churches of Christ made such an immediate response to the Aberfan disaster of 1966. Walter Hendry's successor was Philip Morgan, himself the son of an evangelist, who had served in South Wales, London and Leicester before taking up the office of General Secretary in 1967. Forty years earlier David Morgan had written to the *C.A.* in the correspondence over help from the U.S.A. with these words:

> Let the G.E.C. secretary move on from being correspondent to become organising secretary. Let him go up and down the country to know the divisions, districts, Churches; come into contact with committees and oversights. Discuss plans of work, wise ways of getting money, advise, help, teach. Let him conduct a mission now and again, to try out his own counsel, to show that what he advocates he can do, and to keep living contact with actual work. Begin now, do not wait for the super-man; use the ordinary man until the better man comes. Give God a chance to show what he can do through ordinary brethren.[25]

The father's plea is the best description of his son's achievement.

IV

It will already have become apparent that the changes described so far would have been impossible without some serious theological rethinking of the nature of the witness of Churches of Christ. This became clear first in the understanding of the ministry. In 1936 a Commission on Ordination had been appointed by Conference, and its report was ready for the Conference of 1941. The Churches were given a year to consider the report, which was discussed by the Centenary Conference of 1942. The commission's understanding of the nature of ordination was expressed in their sentence, 'It is Christ Himself, *through the Church*, who appoints, ordains, and sends His Ministers forth'.[26] The commission noted that in the early period of the history of Churches of Christ it had been customary to ordain elders and deacons by prayer and the laying-on of hands, but that this became controversial later. It recommended that all churches set themselves in order by the election and ordination of elders and deacons, with the assistance of neighbouring churches if necessary. It also recommended that evangelists, whose ministry was to the wider Church and not only the local church, should be ordained at a solemn service during Annual Conference, and suggested that the service be conducted by the President of Conference, who would also lay on hands together with the Principal of the College and 'one Presbyter or other appointed representative from the candidate's home Church'.[27] One significant amendment which was carried in the Conference discussion was the deletion of the suggestion of a district eldership to act for all the churches in a single town. Two amendments, also moved by J.W. Black, were both rejected — one to substitute ordination in the local church for ordination at Conference, and one opposing the ordination of elders and deacons for life.[28] Following the adoption of the Report, twelve evangelists and one deaconess were ordained at the Conference of 1943, in a service which made a profound impression on those present.

In 1947 Conference appointed another special commission, this time to study 'the work and status' of the ministry. Its report, largely drafted by William Robinson, was discussed at the Conferences of 1951, 1952 and 1953. On the first occasion no resolutions were moved: in 1952 the first part, on 'Theological and Historical Considerations', was approved; and in 1953 the second part dealing with practical implications was approved. Whereas in the report of the Commission on Ordination great care had been taken to cite the writings of early Disciple and Churches of Christ leaders, the first part of the report of the Commission on the Ministry was given over entirely to an eirenic appraisal of the evidence of the New Testament and early Church, in the light of modern historical scholarship.

Two significant changes of emphasis occurred in this part of the report. The first concerned the understanding of the Church and its relation to the ministry:

> It is not the local communities in different places and different times which add up to the one Church. Rather the Church is one in all places and all times, the one Church finding its expression in the local community from place to place and from age to age. The Ministry must in some way express this unity and continuity of the one Church.[29]

This represented a significant modification of traditional conceptions of the independence of the local church. The second was the abandonment of the view that Churches of Christ possessed the only form of ministry which was consistent with New Testament practice:

> We also believe that the form of ministry claimed by Churches of Christ to be the form derived from the New Testament, is not the only

178

possible form in which the essential elements of structure can be embodied; for instance an Episcopal system, shorn of its mediaeval corruptions (such as the centralisation of the Papacy and the turning of Bishops into 'Prelates') or a Presbyterian system, may equally well express these essentials.[30]

An 'Additional Note on the Ministry of Women' concluded that

there is no barrier in theology and tradition to the extension of the ministry of Deaconessess, even if the question of the ordination of women to the Presbyterate has to be left open until a larger measure of agreement is reached.[31]

The practical implications contained in the second part of the report were inevitably more domestic in character. But the nettle of 'independency' was firmly grasped:

. . . the 'independence' of each congregation has been mistakenly regarded as an absolute principle. The form of Church organisation implied by the New Testament is more closely knit than that practised by Churches of Christ . . . We are, as a community, part of the whole Body, which unhappily is divided. As a contribution towards Christian unity, rather than as a mere completion of our own organisation, we should aim to set forth the unity which was a mark of the New Testament Church, and which must be a mark of the re-united Church. In working towards that aim we see the need for a much closer liaison between the Churches and the Annual Conference, and among the individual Churches themselves.[32]

It recommended that evangelists should in future be called ministers, and where it was necessary to distinguish them from ordained elders, deacons and deaconesses who were also ministers, the term 'full-time minister' might be used. As part of its concern to give full recognition to the leadership which full-time ministers could give to the Churches, it also recommended that there should be no restriction on the number of ministers who could be elected to standing committees; that ministers should be so placed that there was at least one in each district; and that district committees should be composed chiefly of the ordained ministers (including elders and deacons) of the churches in the district.[33]

Several of the Commission's recommendations were gradually adopted in the next few years, but it became clear during the ecumenical discussions of the 1960s and 1970s that the theological position assumed by the report had been slower to penetrate. One advance on the report was registered in 1973 when

Conference discussed the ministry of women and endorsed the following statement presented by the C.W.F. Committee:

> After careful study and believing that according to the teaching and example of Christ, men and women are spiritually equal, all being full citizens of the Kingdom and together forming His Body the Church, the Christian Women's Fellowship Committee see no reason why women when spiritually mature, having the necessary ability and being fully committed to the service of Christ, should not be equally considered for leadership in the ministry of the Church including admission to the full-time ministry.[34]

The statement went on to call the Churches to decide on their own future practice, particularly in the light of the fact that the United Reformed Church, with whom negotiations for union were proceeding, accepted the principle that all ministries were open to men and women. It was appropriate that such a resolution should have been passed under the chairmanship of the first woman to be President of Conference, Mrs Winifred Clark of London. Although several churches have ordained women elders and deacons, at the time of writing no woman has yet been ordained to the full-time ministry; one has nearly completed her training.

Although the reports of the Commissions on Ordination and the Ministry were clearly set in an ecumenical context, the impetus behind them came mainly from domestic considerations, rather than as a result of relations with other Churches. By contrast the rethinking which has taken place on the inter-related issues of baptism, communion and church union has been very largely the result of increasing involvement in the ecumenical movement. As previously noted, Churches of Christ joined the Free Church Federal Council in 1941 and the British Council of Churches in 1942. The Free Church Federal Council contained both those who saw the Council as a first step towards a united Free Church of England and those who saw it as a means to closer cooperation, which would make such a united Church unnecessary. It also contained those who saw it as a means for closer cooperation with the Church of England, and possibly Roman Catholics (though this was unusual in the 1940s); and it contained those who saw it as a means of providing a united Free Church witness against Anglican (or Roman Catholic) claims. There were similar tensions within the British Council of Churches, but perhaps the main consequence of the foundation of the B.C.C. for these tensions within the F.C.F.C. was to sharpen the dilemma for Free Church advocates of union. For such people there was no point in having two federal bodies, if the main purpose was cooperation. That could be more effectively pursued through the B.C.C. which had a wider constituency. Only if the F.C.F.C. could become something more like a united Free Church did it have a distinctive role. In the early 1940s and again in the early 1950s there were two attempts to move the F.C.F.C. in this direction: both failed. By the 1950s, therefore, advocates of church union turned their attention to bilateral or multilateral union conversations, leaving the two Councils of Churches with the more limited goal of cooperation.

Because of size, as well as tradition, Churches of Christ tended to be the 'odd man out' amidst these tensions; but the issues raised were none the less important in moulding their thinking. For at the heart of all discussions on union lay the questions of mutual recognition of membership and ministry. The question of membership was the sticking point for Churches of Christ because of their belief both in believer's baptism and in closed communion. They had been assured in 1941 that membership of the Free Church Federal Council was not incompatible with this position, and had joined on this understanding. The same understanding committed them to the belief that progress towards Christian unity was only possible if there was agreement on the doctrine of the Church, and that church union was to be seen as the goal of the ecumenical movement. This 'catholic' position distinguished them from some other Free Churchmen, and particularly from many in the denomination which was in other respects closest to them, the Baptists. It was clearly illustrated in William Robinson's book, *The Biblical Doctrine of the Church*, published in 1948, based on lectures given the year before at the School of Religion of Butler University, Indianapolis, U.S.A. (now Christian Theological Seminary).

Robinson was convinced that the Lausanne Faith and Order Conference had demonstrated that no progress could be made ecumenically until the doctrine of the Church was tackled. Although the Edinburgh Conference of 1937 dealt with Ministry and the Sacraments, the Church itself was not treated in depth. As a member of the theological commission appointed to prepare material for the Lund Conference of 1952, Robinson also contributed to the volume, *The Nature of the Church*, which was edited by R. Newton Flew. His lectures at Butler were an exercise in the 'biblical theology' which so influenced the formative phases of the modern ecumenical movement, and provided a historical treatment of the biblical material concerning the Church. The book was revised in 1955 after the Amsterdam and Evanston assemblies of the World Council of Churches, and thus provides, indirectly, a reappraisal of the Restoration movement in the light of modern ecumenical developments:

> Every church which is in the ecumenical conversation is in the sin of schism, even the most ancient churches, the well-established churches, as well as the most recent who may even claim to have restored the true church! How can we restore the true church without continuity in history, and with the major part of the church left outside?[35]

The view advanced here, that restoration of New Testament Christianity was impossible for any Church or group of Christians on their own, lies behind the developing commitment to organic union among Churches of Christ in the 1950s and 1960s. A similar catholicity in understanding the relation of local Churches of Christ to each other and to the Association of Churches was seen in the Statement on this subject adopted by the Annual Conference of 1959, with its crucial sentence, 'It would be most misleading to suggest that Churches of Christ have adopted, either in theory or in practice, a policy of "complete autonomy of the local Church"'.[36]

William Robinson died in 1963. His commitment to the Ecumenical Movement was demonstrated by a lifetime of service. He represented Churches of Christ at every major international ecumenical meeting from Geneva in 1920 to the Evanston Assembly of the W.C.C. in 1954 (with the exception of the Lund Faith and Order Conference in 1952). He was also their representative for many years on the B.C.C., and served for some years after 1949 as Chairman of the Faith and Order Department. He was invited to be Moderator of the F.C.F.C. in 1948-49 but had to decline because of ill-health. Although he brought new life into all aspects of the thinking of Churches of Christ, it was perhaps in the understanding of the Church that his greatest contribution lies. As Dr W.G. Baker wrote at the time of his death:

> If Churches of Christ are to continue in this living encounter (the ecumenical movement) *with something to give to the fulness of the Church*, it will be because they have learned of him and seek to express

freshly, as occasion demands, the valuable elements of their position and plea which William Robinson loved and taught.[37]

Nevertheless in the immediate post-war period the emphasis still lay very much upon baptism. It is important to remember that this was a period when theological opinion in general seemed to be turning against infant baptism. In 1946 Robinson provided a summary in the *C.A.* of Karl Barth's lecture on *The Teaching of the Church regarding Baptism* before it was translated into English, and commented as follows:

> Something new is happening. Leading theologians in paedo-baptist Churches are becoming uncomfortable about this matter of Infant Baptism. Our witness and that of the Baptists is beginning to tell. Let us hold fast to this witness. These scholars are all coming down on the side of Alexander Campbell, not only as to the subjects and the mode of Baptism, but as to the design or doctrine as well.[38]

In 1948 James Gray published a little book entitled *Towards True Baptism*, which outlined some of this disquiet as it expressed itself in movements for baptismal reform. Also in that year the representatives of Churches of Christ and the Baptist Union, who had been holding conversations, published a book, *Infant Baptism Today*, which covered similar ground. Similarly in 1951 and 1952 great interest was taken in the discussions of the Methodist Conference on infant baptism.[39] In the 1950s, however, the theological tide seemed to turn, especially with the reports of the Church of Scotland theological commission on baptism, which not only claimed the support of tradition for infant baptism, but argued strongly for its theological validity. Those reports were, and remain, an extreme statement of the other point of view, and they led to the publication in 1959 of *Studies on Baptism,* by members of the Union Committee under the editorial direction of James Gray.

They also served to provoke further consideration of a question first posed by Dean Bate, secretary of the Committee of Reference of the World Conference on Faith and Order, in his response to the Draft Report on the Lausanne Conference which was discussed at the Annual Conference of 1929. After commenting that it was the best piece of work done by any denomination, Dean Bate went on to refer to the section on Baptism which he described as 'a defence of Believers' Baptism' rather than 'an attack on the practice of Infant Baptism'. He wondered whether Churches of Christ were prepared to face the issue which lay beyond it, namely this:

> Infant Baptism being so very deeply rooted in the practice and tradition of many churches, great and small, it is in the last degree improbable that any general abandonment of this usage is within the furthest bounds of practical possibility; that being so . . . are there no terms of amity on which churches which follow your use could enter into close relations with churches which follow ours?[40]

After the New Delhi Assembly of the W.C.C. in 1961, this became the central ecumenical issue for Churches of Christ.

V

Until 1961, however, the main emphasis in relations with other Churches rested on closer cooperation with the Baptists. In the early 1940s discussions between Baptists and Churches of Christ were going on in the U.S.A., New Zealand and in Victoria, Australia. Early in 1942, R.W. Black, who was President of the Baptist Union for the year 1941-42, suggested that a group of five from Churches of Christ might meet with a similar number from the Baptist Union to discuss closer cooperation. The Union Committee consulted the Emergency Committee, and together they decided to appoint J.W. Black, W.J. Clague, W. Mander, W. Robinson and A.C. Watters to confer with a group consisting of R.W. Black, Dr Percy Evans, Dr Gilbert Laws, C.T. LeQuesne and Dr Wheeler Robinson. The first meeting was held on 27 March 1942. Apart from R.W. Black's personal interest in closer relationships between the two bodies, the conversations also need to be understood in the context of the hostile reaction of a number of Baptists to the proposals for Free Church union. The initiative was welcomed by Conference in 1942 and the five persons named by the Emergency Committee were appointed as official representatives.[41]

By 1944 it had been agreed to encourage local contacts between Baptists and Churches of Christ with a view to increasing mutual understanding, and also to exchange fraternal delegates with the Baptist Union assembly. However, the discussion of the understanding of baptism soon ran on to the familiar rocks of open membership in Baptist churches. This was indirectly apparent when the Central Council indicated to the F.C.F.C.

Commission on Closer Cooperation in 1945 that the practice of infant baptism was an obstacle to the proposal for freedom of transfer for those in full membership of one Church to any of the others. Because of the illness of several of the members there were scarcely any meetings of the two groups between 1944 and 1946. In 1947 the Union Committee reported that 'the practice of open membership in some Baptist Churches was a real barrier to any progress to organic union of the two bodies', but it had been agreed to continue to work together to present their common witness on infant baptism and to cooperate as far as possible in other ways. The publication of *Infant Baptism Today* in 1948 was the result of this cooperation.

Proposals for closer cooperation submitted in 1948 were approved by the Baptist Union Council, but the Churches of Christ Central Council asked for some amendment of the proposal to include the names of Churches of Christ in the *Baptist Handbook*, because of the opposition of J.W. Black. Eventually in 1950 a modified version was approved by Conference with only 18 dissentients. This envisaged an association between the Baptist Union and the Annual Conference of Churches of Christ in such a way that Churches of Christ would continue as a distinctly organized religious body, but with as much local and national contact as possible. A programme for such cooperation was prepared and approved in 1951, suggesting united meetings, joint discussion groups, occasional interchange of preachers and speakers, cooperation in publishing work, weekend youth conferences, and mutual commendation of members in areas where either communion was not represented.[42]

In fact, relatively little of lasting value was achieved. At first there were several attempts at local cooperation, but these gradually faded as it became clear that they were not leading any further. In 1955 Conference, acting on a schedule from the Burnage church, asked the Union Committee to consider whether conversations with the Baptists should be reopened, and suggested that the possibility of printing the list of Churches of Christ in the *Baptist Handbook* should be raised again. Informal discussions took place in 1956, but in April 1957 the Baptist Union Council rejected the project for closer cooperation without stating a reason.[43]

The main impetus for closer cooperation had really disappeared with the death of R.W. Black in 1951. Ironically his elder brother, who had been one of those on the Churches of Christ side who was most hesitant about the idea, died a few months earlier. Their passing removed the last two of a family of brothers who had exercised a powerful influence in bringing Churches of Christ out of their isolationist period.[44] J.W. Black ceased to be chairman of Home Missions Committee in 1940, though he remained on the Executive until his death, having been made a life member of the committee in 1942. Nevertheless he remained a powerful force in the Central Council and the Conference, and was not easily quelled. It would, however, be wrong to blame J.W. Black for the failure of the Churches of Christ-Baptist conversations. The disagreements of the two brothers did not help discussion, but the root of the problem lay in the Baptist practice of open membership, which meant that there could be no real uniting of the two denominations.

Meanwhile pressure was building up for a reconsideration of the 'closed communion' position within Churches of Christ. In 1949 Penry Pryce spoke strongly against the practice of closed communion on the Mission Field, in the discussion on the Union Committee's report, and said that this was why he had left India. The church in Daltonganj was the only town church on the Indian field, and visitors from other denominations were regularly refused communion. This led the Union Committee to consider the matter once more, and in 1951 a document entitled, 'Who shall be allowed to commune at the Lord's Table?', was prepared by the committee and submitted to the Central Council. The Council, having consulted the missionaries in Nyasaland and India, decided to make no recommendation to Conference on the matter, fearing controversy at home — an attitude whch was perhaps understandable in view of the scars left by the 'old paths' controversy.[45] The Council did, however, decide to ask the secretary of the Union Committee, R.N. Walters, to read a Conference paper on 'Intercommunion' in 1954.

The paper was a masterly one — simple and concise in language and style, yet penetrating in the theological challenge it presented. Norman Walters pointed out the need of the Church constantly to re-examine its understanding of the faith in a changing world, always remembering the key virtues of humility and love. The ecumenical movement had changed the context of

Churches of Christ witness since the days of the resolution of 1861:

> In fact the question which looms up before our churches at this juncture is in a sense simply this — whether we are finally going to decline into a narrow sectarian body, or whether we are going to adventure in faith, grasping the countless opportunities of the moment towards furthering the cause of Christian Unity.[46]

He went on to argue that, since the situation in which the Churches found themselves had no parallel in the New Testament, a way forward could not be found simply by the application of logic, but only by a prayerful concern to seek the guidance of the Holy Spirit.

Three alternative solutions were suggested: full open communion, whereby 'all who profess to love the Lord Jesus' might be invited; modified open communion, whereby all who had been baptized, whether by immersion or not, as infants or adults might be invited; and 'guest communion', whereby occasional visitors from other Churches not practising believer's baptism would be offered communion, it being understood that the Churches of Christ position would be explained to them tactfully and charitably afterwards. (The last was essentially the position of the 1929 resolution.) In concluding, he suggested that members of Churches of Christ should feel able to take part in communion on ecumenical occasions, even though they could not conscientiously press for the holding of such services: this issue had been a concern of the Sunday School and Youth Committee as a result of comments made by the young people attending the Bangor Youth Conference arranged by the B.C.C. in 1951.[47]

The paper was favourably received, and in 1956 Conference adopted the recommendation of the Union Committee that the third alternative, 'guest communion', should be approved by the Conference and commended to the churches, recognizing the right of each local church to decide upon its own practice. This resolution was carried without dissent, and gave official approval to a practice which several churches had already adopted.[48] It was significant not only for the step taken, but for the spirit and atmosphere in which it was taken, which marked a clear break with the acrimony of the 1920s.

A new urgency was beginning to enter the Churches about

unity. At the 1956 Conference which adopted the recommendation on guest communion, Leslie Colver in his Presidential address quoted some words of his predecessor, Sam Mason: 'We can rejoice how the ecumenical tide is flowing our way: we don't notice that it may be flowing past us.'[49] Yet it seemed impossible to take bold steps. In the next year, on the advice of the Union Committee, Conference rejected for the third time in forty years proposals for Free Church Union on the grounds that the suggestion of mutual transfer of members took no account of the differences in the theology of baptism.[50] In the same year, however, the Publishing Committee published *Notes on a Service of Thanksgiving for Childbirth and Dedication of Parents* by W.G. Baker, which gave substance to a suggestion originally made by William Robinson in 1948 to meet the fact that believer-baptist churches had tended to take no account of the special position of the children of Christian parents in the church. This order of service set out to provide a positive alternative to infant baptism.[51] Nevertheless in the book prepared by members of the Union Committee to mark the 1960 World Convention of Churches of Christ held in Edinburgh, *Towards Christian Union*, the editor, James Gray, still thought, albeit uneasily, that if a reunion scheme were devised which resolved satisfactorily all questions apart from baptism, Churches of Christ should stay outside on the sole ground that such a scheme would contain Churches practising infant baptism.[52]

The experience of the third assembly of the World Council of Churches at New Delhi in 1961 changed his mind. James Gray was the representative of Churches of Christ at that assembly, and at the 1962 Annual Conference in Nottingham he reported his impressions in a memorable address, which marked the turning point in the ecumenical position of the Churches in the post-war period. This was far more than a report of the assembly: it also contained a fresh challenge to face the implications of the ecumenical movement. Two points in particular were to be important. One was the question whether official approaches to some other Church or Churches with a view to closer union ought to be considered. Here he could make no immediate suggestions, but the position was to change in the mid-1960s. The second was the radical suggestion that Churches of Christ, particularly in new areas, might extend the practice of guest communion by admitting as 'guest members' members of paedo-baptist Churches who wished to join, whilst still preserving the practice of believer's baptism alone in the life of the congregation.[53] This suggestion was elaborated in two Conference papers given in 1964 in London by James Gray and J.E. Francis, the latter drawing particularly on the experience of the church at Burnage, Manchester, where he was minister. In his paper James Gray referred again to his experience at New Delhi in a crucial passage:

> At New Delhi I reached the painful conclusion that the Churches of the world are not going to abandon Infant Baptism. The battle of scholarship on the question of Baptism is not being won for 'our side'. Some of the greatest scholars and theological leaders of the world who have spoken most strongly against the present practice of Infant Baptism, and who believe that New Testament Baptism was solely for believers, are not yet prepared to abandon Infant Baptism today. Therefore, if we are to move closer to Infant Baptist Churches we must make up our minds to accommodate ourselves to this situation: it is the real situation and it is likely to remain so for the forseeable future.[54]

Thus Dean Bate's question of 1929 received an answer. As at Wigan ten years earlier the discussion of the papers was conducted in a good spirit.[55]

The suggestion of 'guest membership', or 'ecumenical membership' as it quickly became known, commended itself immediately to the new churches at East Kilbride and Oadby, Leicester. With the renewed ecumenical interest of the later 1960s older churches began to consider it as well. By the end of 1971 about 20% of the churches in the Association had adopted it. In 1972 the Union Committee published a statement commending the practice of ecumenical membership to the churches, which was adopted by the Annual Conference of that year with three dissentients. The resolution was framed in the same terms as that of 1956 on guest communion, and recognized the right of each local church to determine its own practice. (By 1972 over 80% of the churches practised guest communion.)[56] The basis for the policy of ecumenical membership was the recognition of those from other Christian traditions who were in good standing with their own Church, without passing judgement on the practice of the other Church. It was conceived in pastoral terms and clearly fulfilled a pastoral need. It was also accompanied by new moves towards union with other Churches.

In 1964 the British Council of Churches organized a British Faith and Order Conference at Nottingham, which was attended by six members of Churches of Christ. The Conference called upon the Churches represented to covenant together to unite by an agreed date, which, it was suggested in a separate resolution, might be Easter Day 1980.[57] As a result commissions on covenanting were set up in England, Scotland and Wales, and Churches of Christ representatives took an active part in the discussions in England and Scotland. In England the work of the commission was overshadowed by the bilateral negotiations proceeding between Anglicans and Methodists on the one hand, and Congregationalists and Presbyterians on the other, and little progress was made until those negotiations reached a conclusion. In Scotland a Multilateral Church Conversation was set up which has slowly proceeded to explore the possibilities of a united Church in that country, and a small but faithful band of Churches of Christ representatives, under the leadership of Dr W.G. Baker, has taken an active part in these discussions. The Union Committee also decided to explore the possibilities of open-ing negotiations for union with other Churches. Informal approaches were made to the Congregational-Presbyterian Joint Committee and the Baptist Union, and the 1966 Conference authorized the Union Committee to continue these. Another session of the same Conference was devoted to the consideration of current union schemes.[58]

The discussions with Baptist leaders, whilst being warm and friendly, also revealed that the Baptists had serious doubts about any commitment to the search for wider organic union. They were happy for Churches of Christ to join the Baptist Union as it was then constituted, but feared that any movement which involved significant change in the structure of the denomination would provoke division. The Congregational-Presbyterian Joint Committee was by contrast clearly committed to the goal of organic union, and had indeed expressed the hope that their union might be an 'open-ended' one. They readily invited Churches of Christ to send observers to their meetings, and this began in 1966. The observers rapidly discovered that their comments on the draft plant of union were very seriously considered.[59]

The Conference of 1968 approved a four-stage plan of 'Steps

towards Christian Unity' presented by the Central Council and Union Committee. The first stage was the visitation of every church in the Association by two representatives of Central Council to seek support for a covenant to work and pray for Christian union. The second stage would be a similar process to secure the approval of the Churches for the opening of negotiations with a particular Church or Churches. The third stage would be the negotiations themselves, and the fourth a further consultation with the Churches to seek their decision on the proposals arising from the negotiations. The first stage was completed by 1969 when 71 out of the 103 churches on the list (representing more than 85% of the total membership) approved the covenant.

Unexpected delays in the drafting of the Congregational-Presbyterian Basis of Union meant that it was not possible to begin the second stage until 1971, when Conference invited the Churches to agree to the opening of negotiations for union with the United Reformed Church when it was formed in 1972. By the Conference of 1972 a majority of the churches, representing more than 60% of the membership, had given their support, and this made it possible to invite the United Reformed Church at its inaugural assembly on 5 October 1972 to open negotiations — a decision that assembly took with acclamation. The final number of churches supporting the opening of negotiations was 72 out of 93, representing approximately 88% of the total membership. A Joint Committee consisting of seven representatives from each side was set up with the Revd Dr Norman Goodall as chairman and Dr D.M. Thompson as secretary. Its first report was discussed at Conference in 1974, and at the same Conference a welcome was given to the decision of the Scottish churches to negotiate with the Congregational Union of Scotland. A third opportunity for ecumenical discussion was taken when the Conference of 1974 agreed to support the establishment of the Churches' Unity Commission for England, which included eight denominations ranging from the Roman Catholics to the Baptists.[60]

Ecumenical involvement was not confined to talks at national level. During the whole of the post-war period ministers, elders and other local leaders in Churches of Christ took an active part in the work of local Free Church councils and Councils of Churches, and many held office in them. Churches of Christ were members of the Scottish Churches Ecumenical Committee from its beginning in 1950, and they became keen supporters of Scottish Churches' House at Dunblane, where the Northern Men's Convention held its annual meeting. Richard Murray and others were active in the 'Tell Scotland' movement in the 1950s, and young people from Churches of Christ have been well-represented in the Scottish Christian Youth Assembly. There was widespread participation in 'The People Next Door' programme of 1967, which was organized by the B.C.C. as a local follow-up to the Nottingham Faith and Order Conference. That Conference also suggested that the Churches might consider giving approval to local 'areas of ecumenical experiment', where different denominations would work together with some relaxation of the normal denominational rules concerning recognition of membership and ministry. At first such 'local ecumenical projects' (as they were soon renamed) were largely confined to new housing areas and areas of redevelopment, and the numbers grew slowly. But as inter-church talks at national level seemed to be getting nowhere after the failure of the Anglican-Methodist scheme in 1969, local initiatives began to flourish and were encouraged by the Sharing of Churches Act of 1969. Churches of Christ in Swindon, Moseley Road, Birmingham and Leeds have joned local ecumenical projects. Also in 1969 the Hornsey Church of Christ and Harringay Congregational Church united to form the Harringay United Church.

These developments took place during a period when Disciples of Christ in other parts of the world were also involved in a similar enterprise. The Union Committee maintained close contacts with the Churches of Christ in New Zealand, and were very much helped by some of the work done in the multilateral negotiations in that country. In the U.S.A. the Christian Church (Disciples of Christ) was a participant in the multilateral Consultation on Church Union from 1962. As the personal ties between the British Churches and those overseas through emigration weakened with the passage of time,* links were maintained through ministerial exchanges with the U.S.A., Australia and New Zealand. The decision of Pope John XXIII to invite observers from other Churches to the Second Vatican

---

*Between 1945 and 1970 the average number of emigrants per year was 15, compared with 85 in the first 30 years of the century. Statistics are not available after 1971.

Council enabled Dr W.G. Baker to attend the Second Session in 1963-64 as a representative of the World Convention of Churches of Christ, he being one of a group chosen by the Convention Executive Committee to represent Disciples from around the world.

Nevertheless it has also to be recorded that the post-war period saw a widening division among Disciples over attitudes to the ecumenical movement. In the U.S.A. a second division took place, between those churches which supported the United Christian Missionary Society and the International Convention, and those which were more attracted to direct-support missions and associated themselves with the North American Convention. This division was institutionalized as a result of the restructure of American Disciples in the 1950s and 1960s. Although it was concerned with domestic American issues, this further division did affect other countries as ministers trained in 'Independent' colleges moved to work in Australia, New Zealand and Britain. Their indifference or hostility to the 'conciliar ecumenism' represented by the World Council of Churches has served to weaken support for movements towards organic union. The official links of the British Churches of Christ remained with the International Convention and its successor body, the General Assembly of the Christian Church (Disciples of Christ) in the U.S.A., which held its first meeting in 1969.[61] Those Disciple Churches which supported the ecumenical movement found the World Convention, which represented all strands of the Restoration movement whether ecumenically-minded or not, increasingly unsuitable as an international forum to represent their ecumenical concern; and this led to the formation in 1977 of the Disciples' Ecumenical Consultative Council, which the British Churches joined.

The concern for unity at home also found expression on the mission field, where it was linked to the transfer of the mission churches to local control. In Thailand the U.C.M.S. took over responsibility for the mission work begun by the British Churches, when Dr and Mrs Clark and Miss Esther Halliday retired. The British link was maintained by an annual gift, and the service between 1955 and 1965 of Stanley and Iris Sewell. In December 1962 the mission work became a part of the Church of Christ in Thailand, after several years of increasing cooperation.[62]

The work in India was extended in the early 1950s to new territory around Surguja in the state of Madhya Pradesh. This aroused the hostility of the local Hindu leaders, and false charges were brought against some of the missionaries which led to considerable legal expense. Jack Christie actually spent some time in prison before his appeal was successful. Nevertheless the work met with success, and the obstacles were overcome. The 1950s were also the period when the control of the work passed increasingly to the local Churches' Representative Committee. The work at Latehar, Dudhi and Daltonganj was transferred to other missions, and Daltonganj became a union church in 1957. That year saw the retirement of the Christies after 27 years' service. The missionaries were also involved in the discussions for the formation of the Church of North India in this period, but this broke down over the problem of 'rebaptism'. Then in 1969 came breakthrough, and the Indian Churches voted unanimously to accept the revised plan of union. This was a fitting climax to the ministry of Lyle and Connie Burdett which ended with their retirement that year after 26 years' service overseas. When the Church of North India was inaugurated in 1971 George Sharpe, the remaining English missionary on the field, and four Indian leaders were accepted as Presbyters of the new Church.[63]

In Nyasaland an era ended in 1956 when Ernest and Louie Gray retired after 26 years' service, during which the Churches of Christ in the country had grown to 34 congregations and 4,190 members. Ernest Gray had been involved in the Nyasaland Christian Council since its formation and had laid the basis for friendly cooperation with the Anglican and Presbyterian missions. Nyasaland achieved its independence with the new name 'Malawi' in 1964, and at the same time the mission became officially the Churches of Christ in Malawi. With the retirement of Eddie Terry after 22 years' service in 1968 and the furlough of Victor and Nellie Smith in 1970, it was necessary to transfer the leadership of the churches completely to Africans, and this was done with great rejoicing. When the Smiths returned to Malawi in 1971 Victor was unanimously appointed by the Christian Council as the first full-time chaplain to the University of Malawi, where he served until his retirement from the mission field in 1977 after 27 years' service. For this work he was awarded the M.B.E. in 1978. During the 1960s and 1970s Churches of Christ in Malawi have participated in church union talks with the Anglicans and Presbyterians, but no scheme of union has been agreed.[64]

Since 1975 in India and 1977 in Malawi there have been no British missionaries working with the former Churches of Christ missions, and a new church-to-church relationship has been developing. This was assisted in 1978 when Conference confirmed the action of the Missionary Committee in joining the Council for World Mission, which includes Churches of the Congregational and Presbyterian traditions and United Churches in nineteen countries.[65]

VII

The Joint Committee for Negotiations between Churches of Christ and the United Reformed Church published its Proposals for the unification of the two communions in 1976. These proposals envisaged the acceptance by Churches of Christ of the conciliar structure of the U.R.C. with its four decision-making levels of local church, district council, provincial synod and general assembly. On the question of baptism a revision of the U.R.C. Basis of Union was proposed which recognized two patterns of initiation — believer's baptism upon profession of faith, and infant baptism followed by a later profession of faith; both forms of baptism were to be made available in the worshipping life of every congregation, and both convictions were to be honoured by the Church; provision was also made for those with conscientious objections to a particular form. On the question of ministry it was proposed to establish an auxiliary ministry for those in secular employment and it was envisaged that Churches of Christ elders would become some of the first auxiliary ministers.[66]

The Proposals were approved by the U.R.C. General Assembly in 1977 by an overwhelming majority, but they were not voted on a second time because by January 1978 it was known that the legally required majorities of two-thirds of the churches representing three-quarters of the membership of Churches of Christ had not been reached. The voting was as follows: 45 churches (58.5%), representing 69.9% of the total membership, voted in favour of the Proposals by majorities of 75% or more; 5 churches (6.5%), representing 4.8% of the membership, voted in favour by less than 75%; 27 churches (35%), representing 25.6% of the membership, voted against.[67]

Space forbids a detailed analysis of the reasons for this result, and the present writer was perhaps too closely involved in the negotiations to be completely objective. The figures themselves show that the churches voting against were mostly the smaller ones; several of them were isolated, and had not taken much part in the corporate life of the Churches for some time. Undoubtedly fears of being swallowed up in a larger body were involved, alongside understandable feelings that the Proposals were too high a price to pay for union in terms of traditional Churches of Christ principles. But there was also evidence that the observations of the Committee of Five in 1956 quoted earlier about the fossilization of some small congregations were very much to the point. In some quarters the negative vote reflected disillusionment with the ecumenical movement and schemes of union and a belief that a more vigorous policy of evangelism and renewal was a more appropriate response to the contemporary situation. Why a concern for evangelism and renewal should have led to a rejection of the Proposals has never been made clear.

Perhaps, however, the really remarkable feature of the voting was not the number who voted against, but the number who voted in favour. When the history even of the period since 1945 is recalled, the movement of opinion which is represented by the support for the Proposals is striking. It is true that this has to be set against a background of numerical decline; and it is also true that some churches left the Association in the 1960s and 1970s, either for the 'old paths' or for the Baptist Union, who were clearly opposed to the emerging ecumenical policy. Even so the relatively small degree of support for such a proposal as ecumenical membership in the early 1970s indicates the distance that had to be traversed. The high result in favour of the Proposals reflects the care taken to explain the policy within local churches by the members of Central Council, and the relationship of confidence in the national leadership which had been built up.

The Central Council realized that a period of prolonged uncertainty about the future would be very damaging for the morale of the Churches. A meeting of the Consultative Council, consisting of all members of standing committees, was held in April 1978 at which it became clear that a substantial majority favoured a policy of full cooperation with the U.R.C. until an alternative way into union could be found. The Conference of 1978, after a very full discussion, decided to ask the churches which had failed to support the Proposals in 1977 to reconsider their position: if there was no significant change, the Central Council was authorized to set in motion a procedure to dissolve the Association of Churches, so that each local church could follow the path it wished. The response from the churches to this resolution was not sufficient to make another approach to the U.R.C. possible. Consequently in the early part of 1979 the Churches voted on the question of dissolution, when 54 churches voted in favour of dissolution: 20 against; and one did not return a vote. The decision to dissolve the Association having been taken by the Churches, Conference in 1979 decided that the date of dissolution should be 31 March 1980 and took the other necessary decisions to bring this about.[68]

Steps have subsequently been taken on the initiative of the Glagow District to set up a Re-formed Association of Churches of Christ to seek union with the U.R.C. The livelier Scottish churches had been particularly frustrated by the ecumenical *impasse* that had developed in Scotland: the Multilateral Church Conversation was making snail-like progress and the negotiations between Churches of Christ in Scotland and the Congregational Union of Scotland had foundered because the latter were not prepared to make baptism a condition of church membership. Those Churches of Christ which did not wish to join the U.R.C. also took steps to form a new association, to be known as the Fellowship of Churches of Christ.

VIII

It is both sad and ironic that the British Churches of Christ should reproduce the tripartite division of the American Restoration movement — the British 'old paths' churches being roughly the equivalent of American Churches of Christ. But the heritage of Alexander Campbell and Barton Stone has been ambiguous from the beginning, and the tension between a concern for Christian unity and the restoration of the New Testament order has always existed. 'Names and sects and parties fall' has always been as much a prayer as a proclamation. Few members of Churches of Christ today would use the hymn as confidently as David King did to imply that Churches of Christ had the answer to the disunity of the Church. This history of the Churches shows how slowly and how painfully such a view has been abandoned. The tenacity of the view that Churches of Christ were not a denomination and the belief that the Churches could restore primitive Christianity on their own seems almost unbelievable today.

Yet it is important to understand why such beliefs could be so firmly held if the inner dynamics of the movement are to be appreciated. As late as 1938 a man like Laurie Grinstead, who had devoted much of his life to the work of the Churches particularly on the Missionary Committee, could write in these terms to the *C.A.:*

> After reading the current *Year Book*, where the President of the Conference seemed to be cancelled out by the writer of the Conference paper, I have wondered how much of the plea remains, and if what remains is worth maintaining a separate community for. . . . It seems to me that the only way forward is the way back. Back to the New Testament, with the Church's quiet waiting on God for power, with the challenging convictions of mighty truths, with the living faith that swept through the nations like a prairie fire, consuming all that opposed it, and its unfaltering courage which did not flinch before the Hitlerism of its day.[69]

The reference, of course, is to the Presidential address of J.W. Black, which was entirely traditional in character, and the Conference paper of W.J. Clague, which ran in a radically different direction. These words of Grinstead were repeatedly quoted by those in the 'old paths' churches as proof of the way the Association was going. Unfortunately the references to 'mighty truths' and 'living faith' do not answer the historical and theological problems under discussion. Albert Williamson, gave a vivid assessment of the situation in his Presidential address to the Conference of 1957:

> I feel that if we had been as assiduous in the past to keep the real spirit of the Christianity of the New Testament, as we have been to keep its form and doctrine, we might now be assuming the role we have always sought — that of bringing together the scattered and divided remnants of the Body of Christ. Unfortunately we have built a house for God but not made it His home; we have been satisfied with a hut for pygmies, when what we needed was a cathedral for giants.[70]

Awareness of this danger was not new. In his *Memoir of David King*, Joseph Collin wrote:

All reforms tend to become stereotyped into sectarianism. The 'plea' becomes a creed, and dogma becomes legalism. Every plea ought to be held in solution and tested, ever and anon, by the essence of truth; and so all foreign growths be precipitated and, in due time and order removed.[71]

This forms part of a passage which was quoted several times by James Gray in the 1960s as an example of the best kind of open-mindedness which had been found in Churches of Christ. It comes at the conclusion of a discussion of the question how far David King's life and work should influence those who followed him:

The answer is plain and simple: As far as he was under the direct and clear power of the 'Truth as it is in Jesus'. But *his* sign-manual is not to be accepted as proof. His earnestness, his devotion, his fearlessness and determination for the right, his loving kindness, his incorruptibi- lity — these are attributes we may take and copy without qualification. They are reflections from the Light of Life. Beyond these we must go — as he taught us — to the Fountainhead — Truth. That is his chief lesson to us. . . . No man's deductions are final for others. David King's are not, and cannot be. *He* must have grown beyond his first apprehension of the Truth; we may grow beyond his last. . . . If we are truly in Communion with the Infinite, and we 'will to do His will', there is no limit to our growth; no end to our knowledge of the only true God and Jesus Christ whom He has sent; and in this is Life Eternal. Nor must we despise any light, because of the vehicle by which it is brought to us. We want — we need — the sum of all. Test it, nevertheless, by the invariable and infallible standards.[72]

Those standards were the New Testament scriptures.

The change which took place was a revolution in the understanding of history. The Campbells inherited the intellec- tual approach of the eighteenth-century Enlightenment, which tended to see history in terms of 'decline and fall' — Gibbon's choice of title for his great history of the Roman Empire was significant. For men reared in such a world, restoration of the primitive was not only possible but essential if the purity of original truth was to be preserved. This view changed in the nineteenth century, and Darwin's theory of evolution was but the most striking illustration of the change. Wise men avoided swinging to the opposite extreme of assuming that the best lay in the future, particularly after the collapse of liberal optimism in the First World War. But it was increasingly realized that it is impossible to restore what happened in the past.

The achievement of the new form of critical reflection on the past, which shaped biblical criticism, was to free men to think creatively about the embodiment of New Testament principles in new situations, instead of confining them to the increasingly hopeless attempt to imitate New Testament practice in completely different circumstances. This was what William Robinson did for Churches of Christ in Britain: and it may be illustrated by these words from his pupil, James Gray, on whom so much of the burden of leadership fell in the 1960s and 1970s:

> If we learn to read the New Testament with fresh and unprejudiced eyes, and to see our own historic witness in the light of other Christian traditions, we shall be eager to embody the insights of our tradition more worthily and more persuasively; and we shall be more eager to consider the possibilities of union with other Christian bodies, because we realize the limitations of our own and can begin to understand how in the purpose of God the tradition in which we have been reared may fulfil His purpose in union with other Christian traditions: as it certainly cannot fulfil God's purpose in isolation from them.[73]

The proposal to dissolve the Association of Churches of Christ undoubtedly came as a great blow to many church members, and provoked them to wonder whether the movement had failed. Perhaps in a sense it had; but perhaps also by sharpening the sense of division, dissolution served to remind the Churches that their unity was in any case partial. To write the history of a denomination is to write only a part of the history of the Church. But the glory of the Christian belief in the incarnation is the associated belief that God reveals himself in particular events. So it is still possible to believe, with all humility, that God has revealed something of himself in the history of Churches of Christ.

Nor are there tidy beginnings and ends in history. 'Each venture is a new beginning,' wrote T.S. Eliot in *East Coker*, and one of the themes of his *Four Quartets* is the way men are both imprisoned by and yet also freed from their history. As the history of Churches of Christ is surveyed, it is worth reflecting on the fact that for each of those leaders who lived a full three-score years and ten, or even reached their nineties like William Webley and John M'Cartney, there are others who scarcely lived long enough to make their mark: John Frost of Nottingham, who died in 1846 at the age of 26 when the movement was scarcely launched, or Norman Walters, also of Nottingham, who died in 1967 at the age of 44 in the prime of life with so much still to give to the Churches. Yet all are part of a complex interaction of events, the key to which, in the Christian understanding, lies not just in the events themselves but in the action of God through and beyond them. To claim any significance for the history of Churches of Christ apart from the purpose of God for his whole Church would indeed be to take refuge in 'a hut for pygmies'.

Perhaps therefore it is appropriate to end with a quotation from a puritan poet with a strong belief in the over-ruling providence of God. In the closing lines of John Milton's *Samson Agonistes*, as he reflects on Samson's death, there are grounds for confidence even in the most puzzling events:

Nothing is here for tears, nothing to wail
Or knock the breasts, no weakness, no contempt,
Dispraise or blame; nothing but well and fair,
And what may quiet us in a death so noble. . . .
All is best, though we oft doubt,
What th' unsearchable dispose
Of highest wisdom brings about,
And ever best found in the close.
Oft he seems to hide his face,
But unexpectedly returns
And to his faithful champion hath in place
Bore witness gloriously; whence Gaza mourns
And all that band them to resist
His uncontrollable intent,
His servants he with new acquist
Of true experience from this great event
With peace and consolation hath dismiss'd,
And calm of mind all passion spent.

APPENDIX I

(This table is taken from the Year Book, *and no attempt has been made to recalculate the statistics.)*

CONFERENCES, PRESIDENTS AND STATISTICS

Date	Place of Meeting	President	Churches on List	Churches Reported	Membership of Churches
1842	Edinburgh	John Davies	50	42	1300
1847	Chester	A. Campbell	80		2300
1848	Glasgow	John Davies	87	77	2057
1849	Sunderland	Francis Hill	94	51	1029
1850	Nottingham	James Wallis	83	54	1816
1851	London	James Wallis	No statistics gathered		
1852	Buckingham	W.D. Harris	77	76	2081
1853	Wigan	J.K. Tener	81	66	1932
1854	Wrexham	T. Coop	79	67	1998
1855	Manchester	J.K. Tener	70	55	1823
1856	Manchester	J.K. Tener	80	69	2103
1857	London	James Wallis	85	67	2065
1858	Birmingham	J.K. Tener	83	65	2275
1859	Birmingham	G.Y. Tickle	86	74	2475
1860	Birmingham	G.Y. Tickle	87	72	2326
1861	Leicester	J.K. Tener	88	69	2528
1862	Liverpool	J.K. Tener	90	69	2782
1863	Huddersfield	T. Coop	100	74	3148
1864	Wigan	A. Paton	101	77	3400
1865	London	J.K. Tener	101	92	3869
1866	Nottingham	G.Y. Tickle	108	81	3616
1867	Birmingham	G.Y. Tickle	109	78	3971
1868	Manchester	J. Moffitt	108	78	4023
1869	Liverpool	W. Ludbrook	112	83	4040
1870	Newcastle	D. King	112	81	3988
1871	Huddersfield	G.Y. Tickle	109	78	3776
1872	Leicester	G.Y. Tickle	110	84	4053
1873	Wigan	R. Black	107	82	4115
1874	Carlisle	D. King	109	81	4394
1875	Glasgow	W. McLintock	125	93	4936
1876	Leeds	J. Marsden	126	89	4903
1877	Birmingham	A. Brown	124	105	5764

Date	Place of Meeting	President	Churches on List	Churches Reported	Membership of Churches
1878	Liverpool	D. King	120	108	6166
1879	Edinburgh	W. Linn	119	103	6003
1880	Huddersfield	G.Y. Tickle	122	102	5844
1881	Manchester	T.S. Wallis	125	108	6451
1882	Leicester	A. Ferguson	125	108	6632
1883	Wigan	J. Marsden	125	111	7112
1884	Newcastle	G. Collin	129	118	7327
1885	Wortley	W. McLintock	127	121	7654
1886	Nottingham	A. Brown	133	127	7872
1887	Glasgow	H.E. Tickle	135	127	8306
1888	London	B. Ellis	135	131	8608
1889	Leicester	J. Leavesley	146	139	9137
1890	Leominster	D.S. Collin	146	138	8985
1891	Wigan	G.Y. Tickle, Jr	156	150	9511
1892	Edinburgh	J. Nimmo	162	155	9954
1893	Birmingham	T. McLintock	168	157	9944
1894	Bristol	G. Collin	173	168	10249
1895	Leicester	W. Richardson	175	161	10559
1896	Huddersfield	W. Chapman	180	164	10834
1897	Glasgow	S. Black	173	166	10932
1898	London	J. Marsden	175	163	11124
1899	Newcastle	L. Oliver	176	162	11117
1900	Liverpool	D. Drummond	173	165	11789
1901	Nottingham	J. Flisher	176	171	12224
1902	Edinburgh	T.J. Ainsworth	182	166	12537
1903	Birmingham	H.E. Tickle	183	171	12841
1904	Wigan	J. Anderson	183	176	13063
1905	Leeds	J.W. Black	183	179	13958
1906	Leicester	R.K. Francis	188	188	14265
1907	Glasgow	R.W. Black	188	188	14326
1908	Manchester	J. Crockatt	192	186	14500
1909	London	A. Brown	191	184	14440
1910	Liverpool	G. Nicol	194	190	14822
1911	Leicester	C.W. Batten	200	197	14725
1912	Edinburgh	J. M'Cartney	201	196	14778
1913	Birmingham	S. Wolfenden	202	191	15256
1914	Wigan	H.J. Johnson	200	191	15228
1915	Leeds	W.B. Ainsworth	198	188	15182
1916	Nottingham	T.E. Bambury	198	187	15191
1917	Leicester	A.J. Elwes	198	186	15101
1918	Birmingham	N.F. Bambury	208	194	16437
1919	Glasgow	J.C. Drummond	205	193	16243
1920	Liverpool	J. Smith	206	196	16011
1921	Newcastle	T.H. Fraser	205	191	16068
1922	London	L. Grinstead	201	191	16306
1923	Nottingham	W. Mander	201	191	16465
1924	Edinburgh	W. Webley	196	181	16382

Date	Place of Meeting	President	Churches on List	Churches Reported	Membership of Churches
1925	Manchester	T. Birkett	194	176	16349
1926	Birmingham	J. Speirs	194	181	16283
1927	Glasgow	F. Hepworth	191	182	16447
1928	Leicester	H. Langton	186	179	16576
1929	Wigan	A.C. Watters	183	174	16595
1930	Leeds	T.W. Nelson	184	174	16596
1931	Liverpool	W.C. Crockatt	181	162	15991
1932	Nottingham	E. Bell	181	151	16126
1933	Barrow	F.W. White	181	161	16018
1934	Edinburgh	T.M. Selbie	180	163	15527
1935	Leicester	W. Robinson	176	166	15327
1936	London	Alfred Brown	176	167	15838
1937	Glasgow	H. Philpott	175	161	15823
1938	Manchester	J.W. Black	175	153	15482
1939	Birmingham	A.W. Kuypers	176	155	15229
1940	No Conference		174	139	14948
1941	Ulverston	E. Green	168	150	14303
1942	Kirkcaldy	W.J. Clague	165	146	13511
1943	Mansfield	W. Lister	163	148	13107
1944	Stockport	G.E. Barr	161	141	12764
1945	Leicester	J. Gray	156	142	12101
1946	Birmingham	C.K. Green	155	139	11660
1947	Glasgow	J. Garner	141	141	10628
1948	Chester	J.R. Francis	142	142	10359
1949	Nottingham	W.W. Hendry	140	140	10001
1950	Liverpool	A.L. Brown	138	134	9811
1951	Barrow	F.S. King	135	135	9598
1952	Edinburgh	G.J. Hammond	135	135	9511
1953	London	J.W. Rutt	133	133	9334
1954	Wigan	A.W. Scott	133	133	8950
1955	Leicester	S. Mason	129	129	8761
1956	Manchester	J.L. Colver	127	127	8741
1957	Glasgow	A. Williamson	126	126	8462
1958	Birmingham	W. Arthur	123	123	8239
1959	Chester	J.R. Jenkins	119	119	7854
1960	Edinburgh	P.A.W. Smith	119	119	7821
1961	Liverpool	E. Gray	119	119	7617
1962	Nottingham	D. Black	119	119	7529
1963	Wigan	W. Georgeson	119	108	7257
1964	London	R.N. Walters	114	112	6823
1965	Swanwick	R. Hallows	114	109	6585
1966	Leicester	S. Oakden	113	101	6398
1967	Glasgow	W.G. Baker	112	102	6091
1968	Swanwick	J.E. Francis	109	99	5615
1969	Birmingham	W.F. Aiton	106	99	5369
1970	Chester	J. Gray	98	89	5148
1971	Swanwick	K.C. Burdett	95	88	4884

Date	Place of Meeting	President	Churches on List	Churches Reported	Membership of Churches
1972	Edinburgh	R. Murray	93	80	4638
1973	Birmingham	Mrs W. Clark	93	81	4449
1974	Swanwick	A.L. Brown	82	76	4180
1975	Birmingham	G.B. Waterton	80	72	4028
1976	Swanwick	A.B. Webster	80	75	3884
1977	Glasgow	P.D. Arthur	78	77	3703
1978	Swanwick	G. Sharpe	75	71	3613
1979	Swindon	D.M. Thompson	75	69	3586

APPENDIX II
CONFERENCE PAPERS

Date	Subject	Writers
1872	The Causes, Consequences, and Prevention of Divisions	G.Y. Tickle
1873	Our Co-operation for Evangelization	D. King
1874	The Standard of Holiness: How to attain it	J. Strang
1875	Our Relation to the Religious Associations around us	J. Aitken
1876	Evangelization	D. King
1877	Evangelization	D. King
1878	The Evangelist's Position in relation to the Church	A. Brown
1879	The Eldership	G. Greenwell
1880	The Qualifications and Work of Pastors, etc.	G.Y. Tickle
1881	The Duty of Churches in Relation to the Drinking Customs of our Land	G.Y. Tickle, Jnr.
1882	Have we a Mission to the Masses of the People?	D.S. Collin
1883	The Work of the Holy Spirit in the Church	D. King
1884	Were the Apostles authorized by the Lord to organize a Visible Church? and if 'Yes', what are its essential features?	G.Y. Tickle
1885	The Region of Expediency in relation to the Worship and Service of the Lord	A. Brown
1886	Some of the Chief Causes of Defection from the Churches of Christ	H.E. Tickle
1887	Christianity in its Aggressive Character, etc.	B. Ellis
1888	Special Training of Young Converts in Holiness and Service to the Lord	J. Marsden
1889	The Position and Work of Sisters in evangelization	S. Black
1891	Foreign Missions and our relation thereto	J. Crook
1892	Fifty Years' Work and the Lessons it suggests	D. King
1894	What is Spiritual Life, and how to deepen it?	G. Collin
1895	Our Strength and our Weakness as Churches of Christ pleading for a complete return to Christianity as taught by Christ and His Apostles	J. Grinstead
1896	How best to secure a Scriptural and efficient Eldership in every church	J. Straiton
1897	The Christian's Duty, Responsibility, and Privilege as taught in the Scriptures, of giving of his Substance to the Lord's Work	W. Crockatt
1898	The Doctrine of the Laying on of Hands	L. Oliver
1899	Work for Young Converts	R.W. Black

Date	Subject	Writers
1900	The Lord's Supper and its Scriptural Observance	J. M'Cartney
1901	What should be the Attitude of the Churches of Christ towards service in the Army or Navy, compulsory or voluntary?	H.E. Tickle
1902	Our Opportunities and Possibilities for Work among the Young in the Twentieth Century	R.K. Francis
1903	The Scriptural Basis of Christian Unity	J. Anderson
1904	The Relation of Christianity to the Social Questions of the Day	T.J. Ainsworth
1905	Evangelistic Co-operation considered in relation to the Independence of the Individual Churches	S. Wolfenden
1908	The Relations of Churches to the Co-operation, with a special view to the elucidation of the grounds upon which the minority may expect the majority to give way	C.W. Batten
1909	Is Instrumental Music in Public Worship and Service Scriptural and expedient, considered in relation to our Plea for the Restoration of Apostolic Christianity and our Co-operation as Churches for Evangelization?	J. Marsden J. M'Cartney
1910	In what form, and with emphasis on what aspects, ought the Gospel to be preached today, so as to stay the alienation of the masses from the Church and to win them to Jesus Christ?	J. Smith
1911	A Review of the Work of the Higher Criticism and its Bearing on New Testament Christianity	C. Greig
1912	Some Main Causes of Separations, and suggestions for staying this serious drainage from our numbers	B. Ellis
1913	Suggestions as to the best means to be adopted for improving the Fitness of Brethren for Public Service in the Lord's Work	W.B. Ainsworth
1914	What Churches of Christ might do to promote unity among Baptized Believers	L. Oliver
1916	What opportunities are likely to arise and what claims are likely to be made on us as Churches when the men return from the War?	F. Hepworth W. Marshall
1917	What shall be the Relationship between the Work of the Temperance Committee and the Annual Conference of Churches of Christ co-operating for Evangelistic Purposes?	R.K. Francis U. Nicholls
1918	The Formularies prepared for presentation to the proposed World Congress on Faith and Order	H.E. Tickle
1919	The Place of Women in the Ministry of the Church	A. Brown
1920	The Work of the Holy Spirit in the Church and in the Individual, not only in New Testament times, but today	R.K. Francis
1921	What Truths of Belief, Practices, and Organization does the New Testament make essential to Christian Union?	J. Smith

Date	Subject	Writers
1922	Does the New Testament contain a Permanent Organization for the Church of Christ? If so, what is its Character?	W. Mander
1923	The Christian's attitude towards Recreation and Amusements	F. Hepworth
1924	The Origin, Development and Recognition of the New Testament Canon of Scripture	J. Smith
1927	Worship in the Church	A. Brown
1928	Delegate Voting	C.W. Black
		W.C. Crockatt
1936	How may we increase Whole-time Ministry, and at the same time preserve Mutual Ministry in our Churches?	A.C. Watters
1937	The Principles of Church Organization in Primitive Christianity and their Application to Present-day Church life	W.J. Clague
1938	(do)	W.J. Clague
1939	A Policy for a more Progressive Method of Evangelization	A. Macmillan
1943	The Church and Youth Work	J. Gray
1944	The Expansion of the Church	A.L. Brown
1946	The Churches: Present Position and Future Prospects	J.L. Colver
1948	Evangelism and Personal Salvation in their Individual and Social Aspects	P.A.W. Smith
1949	Preparing for the Crusade:	
	Spiritual Preparation	D.J. Rudkin
	Method of Organization	W.F. Aiton
1950	Evangelism in the local church	R.D.C. Lampard
	Visitation Evangelism	A. Blacklock
1954	Inter-Communion	R.N. Walters
1955	Some Ruminations on Organization and Finance	C.K. Green
1961	Functions of Conference	J. Gray
1962	Worship and Work	R.N. Walters
1963	The Sunday Evening Service — should it be mended or ended?	J.L. Colver
		D.M. Thompson
1964	What is God requiring of us now?	J. Gray
	Pastoral Implications of Guest Membership	J.E. Francis
1967	The Authority of the New Testament in relation to Christian Union	J. Gray
1969	Christian Responsibility towards World Hunger	Muriel Garrow
		K.A. Forrest

ABBREVIATIONS

B.A.	*Bible Advocate*
B.H.	*British Harbinger*
B.M.H.	*British Millennial Harbinger*
C.A.	*Christian Advocate*
	(This is used both for the 19th and the 20th century series, the dates marking the difference.)
C.A.W.	*The Christian at Work*
C.B.	*Christian Baptist*
C.M.	*Christian Messenger* and *Christian Monthly*
	(Since the latter appeared in the 20th century and the former in the 19th, the dates mark the difference.)
C.M.F.M.	*Christian Messenger and Family Magazine*
E.O.	*Ecclesiastical Observer*
M.H.	*Millennial Harbinger*
S.S.	*Scripture Standard*
T.B.H.S.	*Transactions of the Baptist Historical Society*
Y.B.	*Churches of Christ Year Book*
Y.C.	*Young Christian*

NOTES

In these Notes references to periodicals are given using the abbreviations listed. Since the volumes are annual, with the exception of the early volumes of the *Christian Messenger*, only a reference to the year is given: full details are in the Bibliography. All books are referred to in abbreviated form, and the full title may be found in the Bibliography. Since 1886 the Minutes of the Annual Meeting or Conference have been published in the *Year Book*, and references to resolutions of Conference are given simply by listing the number of the resolution.

Chapter 1: Origins

1 *M.H.*, i 15-19; Jones, *Autobiography*, 122-25 (this mistakes the date of the visit).
2 What follows is based on Richardson, *Memoirs*, i.
3 *Declaration and Address* (ed. Robinson), 15.
4 Richardson, *Memoirs*, i 401.
5 *C.B.*, 270-72, 273-75, 281-82, 288-89, 296-97 (by T. Campbell), 301-2 cf. 374-77; Owen-Campbell *Debate.*
6 Richardson, *Memoirs*, ii; Garrison & DeGroot, *Disciples of Christ*, 201-30; McAllister & Tucker, *Journey in Faith*, 159-88.
7 Jones, *Memoir of McLean*, xx-xxii; Hornsby, *John Glas;* Mitchell, *Archibald McLean*; Watters, *History*, 8-14.
8 Jones, *Memoir of McLean*, liv, lxxvii-viii.
9 Davies, *T.B.H.S.*, vii 147-81; Douglas, *History of Baptist Churches*, 191-93, 249, 272, 276, 285.
10 Author of *Essays on Grace, Faith and Experience*, a controversial work, which was one of the marks of the breakdown among Baptists of older Calvinist beliefs about grace in conversion.
11 Jones, *Autobiography*, 1-77; Jones, *William Jones*, 1-6.
12 *M.H.*, i 1.
13 Jones, *Primitive Christianity*, 485-503, especially 487-88; cf. Jones, *Autobiography*, 125.
14 Jones, *Primitive Christianity*, 502-3.
15 Preface to Eng. ed. of Grew, *Tribute*, 3; *C.M.*, i 202. David King was in error in saying that Wallis received this in 1834, *B.H.*, 1868, 374.
16 Watters, *History*, 13-14.
17 Grew, *Tribute*, 22-24, 75-83.
18 Copy in the possession of the author. The full title is given in the Bibliography.
19 *C.M.*, vi 101-3; Mottershaw, *History of the Long Hedge Lane Church*, 4-5; *B.H.*, 1868 374.
20 *C.B.*, 621-22; Richardson, *Memoirs*, i 25, ii 292-95; *B.H.*, 1868 337; *E.O.*, 1882 303; Watters, *History*, 28-29; *B.M.H.*, 1857 596-97, 1858 415-16; *C.M.*, i 323-24 (the initials should be J.D.).
21 *B.M.H.*, 1865 247-48.

22 Wallis to Campbell, 21 Feb 1837, *C.M.*, i 204.
23 *C.M.*, i 1-2, 202-3.
24 List on title pages of *C.M.*, i & ii; *C.M.*, iv 430.
25 *C.M.*, i 325-31, ii 26-33, 164-71. (The *Strictures* was the appendix to Jones, *Primitive Christianity*.)
26 *C.M.*, i 328; ii 35, 422-26, 428; iii 5-12; iv 125, 146; vi 268-73, 389.
27 Scott, *Discourse*, (Eng. ed.), note on p 2; cf. *C.M.*, v 141-42.
28 *C.M.*, vi 343-49.
29 *C.M.*, v 141, 316-17.
30 *C.M.*, iv 430; v 33, 214.
31 *C.M.*, i 323-24; cf. J. Davies to W. Clarke, 10 Oct 1837 (Davies Correspondence).
32 *C.M.*, i 324, 357-58; ii 72; vi 416-21.
33 *C.M.*, i 252; ii 322; iii 177, 213, 242-47, 280-83; v 73, 289, 354, 355-56, 392.
34 *C.M.*, ii 34-35, 179; cf. iv 398.
35 *C.M.*, iii 25-26, 324.
36 *C.M.*, i 321-23.
37 *C.M.*, v 311; vi 70-71, 109, 286.
38 *C.A.*, 1874 17-20, 75-78, 112-17, 168-70, 239-41; 1875 10-16, 349-55, 376-81; 1876 55-59, 116-23.
39 *C.M.*, ii 69.
40 *C.M.*, ii 68-70, 159-64; v 156-59.
41 *C.M.*, iv 37-38, 145, 240-42; *G.C. Reid*, 3-13.
42 *C.M.*, iv 38.
43 *G.C. Reid*, 12-13.
44 *C.M.*, v 357-62.
45 *C.M.*, vi 55-70.
46 *C.M.*, vi 105-8, 142-46, 176-78.
47 *C.M.*. vi 157-62, 183-88.
48 The figure printed was 1,305.
49 *C.M.*, vi 247-49, 279-84.
50 *C.M.*, vi 310-17, 396-97.

Chapter 2: Early Cooperation
1 *C.M.*, iv 145; vi 325, 397.
2 *Y.B.*, 1892 65.
3 Shaw to Davies, 15 Aug 1842 (Davies Correspondence).
4 *C.M.*, vi 197.
5 *B.M.H.*, 1848 95; *C.M.*, iv 208; vi 358, 394.
6 *C.M.*, vii 102.
7 *C.M.*, vii 383-85, 414-19.
8 *G.C. Reid*, 23-24.
9 *C.M.*, ix 410-11.
10 *C.M.F.M.*, 1845 143-45, 243, 336.
11 *C.M.F.M.*, 1845 40-41 (italics original).
12 *C.M.F.M.*, 1845 334-35; 1846 86-88.
13 Harrell, *Quest for a Christian America*, 40-41; Billington, 'Churches of Christ', 24-25; see also *C.M.F.M.*, 1846 366-68; 1847 135-37 for Adventist speakers in Nottingham.
14 *C.M.F.M.*, 1846 183-84, 219-20, which though not publishing the resolutions makes it clear that they were those cited.
15 *C.M.F.M.*, 1846 46-49, 184-85; cf. 1845 203-11.

16 *C.M.F.M.*, 1846 220-22 (italics original).
17 *C.M.F.M.*, 1846 239-40.
18 *C.M.F.M.*, 1846 479-80.
19 *C.M.F.M.*, 1847 234-39.
20 *C.M.F.M.*, 1847 326-31, 367-71, 382-84, 414-29, 453-66; *B.M.H.*, 1848
    36-41, 367-71; 1849 524-25; Chalmers, *Alexander Campbell's Tour.*
21 *C.M.F.M.*, 1847 494-500.
22 *C.M.F.M.* 1847 501-2; *B.M.H.*, 1849 536.
23 *C.M.F.M.*, 1847 519; *B.M.H.*, 1848 244-45.
24 For Thomas generally, see R. Roberts, *Dr Thomas*; and also *B.M.H.*, 1848
    529-31; 1851 94.
25 *B.M.H.*, 1848 511-12; *Gospel Banner*, i 306-7, 322-25, 329-31.
26 *B.M.H.*, 1851 371. Reports of the Annual Meetings, 1849-54, are to be
    found as follows: *B.M.H.*, 1849 318-26; 1850 281-88; 1851 369-75; 1852
    377-84; 1853 415-23; 1854 419-29.
27 *B.M.H.*, 1853 235; *Gospel Banner*, iv 143-46.
28 *B.M.H.*, 1854 421.
29 Rotherham, *Reminiscences*, 14-34.
30 King, *Memoir of King*, 1-8; *B.M.H.*, 1854 326-27.
31 *B.M.H.*, 1854 576.
32 *B.M.H.*, 1855 359, 410-12, 452-57.
33 *B.H.*, 1866 274-79; *B.M.H.*, 1861 257-58; Yuille, *History of Baptists in
    Scotland*, 78, 130, 236; Milner, *Messiah's Ministry*. x-xi.
34 *B.M.H.*, 1861 469.
35 King, *Memoir of King*, 239-41. J.N. Darby, one of the early leaders of the
    Brethren did not believe that a congregation was entitled to choose its
    presidents or pastors: Rowdon, *Origins of the Brethren*, 210.
36 *B.M.H.*, 1858 257, 361; 1859 618-19; 1860 517.
37 *B.M.H.*, 1861 463-64.
38 *B.H.*, 1867 221.
39 *B.H.*, 1867 226.

Chapter 3: Towards the Jubilee
 1 Yuille, *History of Baptists in Scotland*, 214-15; *C.A.*, 1859 219-20; *B.A.*,
    1900 243-44; *B.H.*, 1870 285-86.
 2 Anderson, *Outline of my Life*, 56.
 3 Robinson, 'History of Churches of Christ in Furness', *C.M.*, 1920 3-4,
    21-22, 41-42.
 4 *B.M.H.*, 1850 331, 427-28; 1856 255; Moore, *Life of Coop*, 52, 188-92.
 5 *E.O.*, 1874 325.
 6 *Y.B.*, 1886 7.
 7 *E.O.*, 1871 310.
 8 *B.H.*, 1866 320; *C.A.*, 1877 321; *E.O.*, 1878 218; *C.A.*, 1880 379-80;
    Resolution 39 of 1888
 9 *B.M.H.*, 1862 218.
10 *B.M.H.*, 1862 248-49.
11 *B.M.H.*, 1863 318.
12 *B.H.*, 1869 309, 394-95.
13 *B.M.H.*, 1864 321; *B.H.*, 1866 74-75, 137-39, 290; 1868 179; 1869 395;
    E.O., 1872 172; 1873 315, 317; 1874 312; 1875 304; 1877 219-20; 1880
    25-26, 35-36, 107-9.
14 *B.M.H.*, 1864 318, 325; *B.H.*, 1866 318-20.

15 *E.O.*, 1872 316-17; 1874 315.
16 *E.O.*, 1875 244-46.
17 *E.O.*, 1875 304-5; 1876 251; *B.H.*, 1870 311.
18 *C.A.*, 1863 203-5; 1864 159-60; 1865 153, 158-60.
19 *B.M.H.*, 1865 223-25; *B.H.*, 1866 286-89; 1868 36-37.
20 *B.H.*, 1868 37.
21 *E.O.*, 1871 315, 347-50, 415-18; 1872 14-18, 63-67.
22 *E.O.*, 1871 105-6; 1875 147-52.
23 *E.O.*, 1874 315; 1875 305; 1876 250-51, 281-83.
24 *E.O.*, 1879 237; 1880 213-14; *C.A.*, 1880 374-75; 1882 395; 1883 364-65, 367.
25 *E.O.*, 1883 227; 1884 132; 1885 134; *Y.B.*, 1887 60.
26 *B.M.H.*, 1865 431.
27 *B.H.*, 1870 2.
28 *B.H.*, 1871 132; *E.O.*, 1872 318; 1873 318; 1874 319; 1876 253; *Y.B.* 1887 71, 79, 86-87; 1888 66.
29 *C.A.*, 1880 376, 381-83.
30 *C.A.*, 1881 394-97.
31 *Y.B.*, 1889 33.
32 *C.A.*, 1889 372-74; *E.O.*, 1889 140.
33 *B.M.H.*, 1863 68-70, 109, 178-80.
34 *B.H.*, 1868 320; 1869 309-10; 1871 315; *E.O.*, 1873 317; 1876 251; 1878 218; 1879 217; 1880 214-15; *C.A.*, 1880 380-81; 1881 397.
35 *C.A.*, 1881 397; *E.O.*, 1884 33-34, 58-60.
36 *C.A.*, 1888 373-78, 384-85; 1889 378-80; *E.O.*, 1888 115-16.
37 *B.M.H.*, 1860 451-52, cf. 1859 462.
38 Payne, *Baptist Union*, 88-89; *B.M.H.*, 1858 517. (Kinghorn, whom Greenwell supported, had been a Baptist minister in Norwich who opposed Robert Hall's position.)
39 *B.M.H.*, 1861 464; 1864 218-19; *B.H.*, 1869 317-20, 347-52; 1870 163-66.
40 *C.A.*, 1864 175-76.
41 *B.M.H.*, 1865 314; *B.H.*, 1866 314-15.
42 *B.H.*, 1866 320.
43 Moore, *Life of Coop*, 247, 266: cf. Lancelot Oliver's review in *C.A.*, 1889 244-47, 278-88, which demonstrates the unreliability of Moore as a source for this episode.
44 Harrell, *Social Sources*, 17 and chapter 1 generally: cf. Harrell, *Quest for a Christian America*, ch 5 and ch 8.
45 *B.H.*, 1867 72.
46 *B.H.*, 1868 236-47.
47 *B.H.*, 1869 13-17: the quotation is from p 14.
48 *B.H.*, 1870 90-92: the quotation is from p 92.
49 *B.H.*, 1868 320.
50 *E.O.*, 1872 315-17.
51 *E.O.*, 1872 325-36: the quotations are from p 328 and p 329.
52 McLean, *History of the F.C.M.S.*, 51-52.
53 *E.O.*, 1876 13, 77, 265; *C.A.*, 1876 394.
54 *C.A.*, 1877 142-43, 249-50, 320; *E.O.*, 1877 220, 231-37.
55 *E.O.*, 1878 209-10, 218, 327; Moore, *Life of Coop*, 325-33.
56 McLean, *History of the F.C.M.S.*, 57-58, 136-38; post-card in the possession of the author.

57   *C.A.*, 1881 413-25, 447-50.
58   *E.O.*, 1879 223-28: the quotation is from p 227.
59   *E.O.*, 1879 243-46, 258-59, 272-73: the quotation is from p 259.
60   *E.O.*, 1880 205-8, 210; 1882 96-97, 108-9.
61   Ainsworth, *Sydney Black*, 38-43; *E.O.*, 1885 112; *Y.B.*, 1887 15-42; *B.A.*, 1890 233-34, 236.
62   *Y.B.*, 1892 72.
63   *Y.C.*, 1891 2.

Chapter 4: Widening Horizons

1   *B.A.*, 1891 169.
2   *B.A.*, 1891 247, 275.
3   *B.A.*, 1890 254-55, 305-7.
4   *C.A.*, 1888 33-35, 114-16.
5   *Y.C.*, 1891 2-4.
6   *C.A.W.*, 1894 171.
7   *B.A.*, 1894 261-75: the quotation from T.K. Thompson is on pp 274-75.
8   *C.A.W.*, 1894 181.
9   Ainsworth, *Sydney Black, passim.*
10 *E.O.*, 1876 2.
11 *C.A.*, 1886 116.
12 Resolution of 1886; *Y.B.*, 1887 37-39; resolutions 40-41 of 1890.
13 *Y.B.*, 1891 18-31; *B.A.*, 1891 233, 243-47; *Y.C.*, 1891 142-44: the quotation is from *B.A.*, 1891 247.
14 *Y.B.*, 1892 88-97; resolution 35 of 1892; *B.A.*, 1892 307-9; *Y.C.*, 1892 200-1.
15 These paragraphs are based on the reports of the Foreign Missions Committee from 1892 to 1914.
16 *Y.B.*, 1895 17.
17 *C.A.W.*, 1894 180.
18 Rotherham, *Reminiscences,* 53-60, 86-93.
19 *Ibid.,* 80-81 (italics original).
20 *Ibid.,* 82-83; cf. *B.A.*, 1905 654.
21 *Y.C.*, 1892 194.
22 *C.A.*, 1931 322.
23 *Y.B.*, 1910 25-40: the quotations are from p 32 and p 36.
24 *B.A.*, 1910 501.
25 *Y.B.*, 1911 28-46: the quotation is from p 45.
26 *B.A.*, 1911 518.
27 *B.A.*, 1892 346.
28 *Y.C.*, 1892 220.
29 *Y.B.*, 1897 10-34: the quotations are from p 11 and p 33 (italics original).
30 *B.A.*, 1903 729.
31 Moore, *Life of Coop,* 346-47 (italics original).
32 *B.A.*, 1902 241-48; *Y.B.*, 1905 144-66.
33 *Y.B.*, 1912 16-19: the quotation is from p 18.
34 *Y.B.*, 19-33: the quotations are from p 30 and p 31.
35 *Y.B.*, 1917 61-69 (the quotations are from p 61, p 62 and p 63); *C.M.*, 1917 136-37.
36 *C.M.*, 1917 121-22; *B.A.*, 1917 387.
37 *C.M.*, 1917 144.
38 *C.M.*, 1917 171; *Missionary Intelligencer*, 1911 478-79.

39   *Missionary Intelligencer,* 1917 534.
40   Resolution 31 of 1912.
41   Resolution 26 of 1916.
42   *B.A.,* 1917 387.
43   *B.A.,* 1916 640.
44   *B.A.,* 1919 73-75.
45   *C.M.,* 1920 123.
46   *B.A.,* 1918 268-69. The paper was not printed, but it formed the basis of articles in *B.A.,* 1920 397-98, 409-10. The Formularies themselves are reprinted in Gray, *Towards Christian Union,* 68-73.
47   *B.A.,* 1920 422-23, 447, 471-72, 496-97, 509, 518; *C.M.,* 1920 160; *C.A.,* 1921 99-100.
48   *C.A.,* 1921 207-8.
49   *Y.B.,* 1912 26-41.
50   *Y.B.,* 1886 14-29.
51   *B.A.,* 1891 80-81; *C.A.,* 1949 89.
52   *Y.B.,* 1896 32-34; resolutions 19, 23-26 of 1896.
53   *Y.B.,* 1899 88-91.
54   *B.A.,* 1898 513, 701-2; 1900 654, 670.
55   *Y.B.,* 1902 20; *B.A.,* 1902 516-17.
56   *B.A.,* 1915 473, 489-90, 505-6, 658; 1917 97, 117, 129, 140, 153.
57   *B.A.,* 1912 228-29, 371-72.
58   Resolution 14 of 1890; resolution 37 of 1892; resolution 3 of 1895; *B.A.,* 1895 302-3; resolution 51 of 1899; resolution 53 of 1900; resolution 32 of 1907.
59   *B.A.,* 1890 223; resolution 38 of 1891; resolution 55 of 1905; *Y.B.,* 1906 99-101; resolution 29 of 1906; *B.A.,* 1907 526-27.
60   *Hymns for Churches of Christ,* iii-v; *Y.B.,* 1893 46; *B.A.,* 1898 504; *Y.B.,* 1899 71; *B.A.,* 1903 539; resolution 40 of 1903; *B.A.,* 1908 532-34.
61   *Y.B.,* 1915 39-41; *B.A.,* 1916 514; resolution 35 of 1916; resolution 25 of 1917; resolution 12 of 1918; resolution 13 of 1919; *Y.B.,* 1920 133; *B.A.,* 1920 45.
62   *Y.B.,* 1905 42.
63   Resolution 47 of 1902; resolution 54 of 1905; *Y.B.,* 1905 26-44; resolution 35 of 1906; resolutions 21-22 of 1907; *Y.B.,* 1907 105-7; *B.A.,* 1907 527; resolutions 39-40 of 1908.
64   Harrell, *Quest for a Christian America,* ch 5, especially 170-74.
65   *B.A.,* 1918 129.
66   *B.A.,* 1900 40, 55, 74, 93.
67   Resolution 55 of 1900.
68   *Y.B.,* 1901 46-47.
69   *B.A.,* 1914 645, 669-70, 681, 715; 1915 188, 189, 245.
70   *For His Name's Sake,* 9.
71   *Ibid.,* 25, 65-76, 99-101, 129-37.
72   *B.A.,* 1916 532.
73   *B.A.,* 1920 133.
74   *Y.B.,* 1905 35.
75   *B.A.,* 1916 236.
76   Resolution 53 of 1920.

Chapter 5:   Peace and War
 1   *C.A.,* 1928, 821.

2 *Y.B.*, 1912 24; 1913 26-41; resolution 44 of 1913.
3 *Y.B.*, 1914 108-9; *B.A.*, 1916 517; resolutions 18-19 of 1916; *Y.B.*, 1917 108-10; resolutions 23, 30 and 44 of 1917; *Y.B.*, 1918 96-98; resolutions 22-23 of 1918; *Y.B.*, 1919 125-27; *B.A.*, 1919 395; *Y.B.*, 1920 112-21; *Missionary Intelligencer*, 1917 574.
4 See also Gray, *W.R.*, 17-18, 62-63, 66-74, 124.
5 *B.A.*, 1920 458-64.
6 *C.A.*, 1923 524; 1924 524; 1925 519, 522; resolution 28 of 1923, resolutions 21-22 of 1924; resolutions 17 and 32 of 1925.
7 *C.A.*, 1925 552 (italics original).
8 *C.A.*, 1926 56-57, 63, 72-73, 76, 88-89, 92, 120-21, 123.
9 *C.A.*, 1926 646, 726-27, 735.
10 *Y.B.*, 1927 118; resolutions 17 and 35 of 1927; *C.A.*, 1927 502-3, 506.
11 *C.A.*, 1931 321, 324-25.
12 Resolution 52 of 1920; resolution 21 of 1921; *C.A.*, 1921 386.
13 *C.A.*, 1921 410-11, 435-36, 459; resolutions 24-25 of 1922; *C.A.*, 1922 538-39; resolution 4 of 1923.
14 Resolution 11 of 1919; *B.A.*, 1919 267, 311, 323, 338, 354-55, 370, 381.
15 Resolutions 53-55 of 1926; *Y.B.*, 1926 39; J. M'Cartney, *Can we cooperate . . .?*; W. Mander, *Can we cooperate . . .?*; *C.A.*, 1927 126, 135, 150, 182, 196, 223, 230, 246, 262, 268, 278, 294, 310, 326, 342, 358, 374, 390.
16 Resolution 9 of 1927; *C.A.*, 1927 501-2; 1928 487, 506; resolutions 11-12 of 1928; *C.A.*, 1929 514.
17 *Y.B.*, 1928 141.
18 *C.A.*, 1928 371-72, 403-5, 419-22, 437.
19 Resolution 41 of 1928; *C.A.*, 1928 534; *Y.B.*, 1929 129; *C.A.*, 1929 81, 484, 517; resolutions 30-31 of 1929.
20 *C.A.*, 1929 517-19; resolution 48 of 1929; *C.A.*, 1930 518-19, 612; resolution 17 of 1930; Townsend, *R. W. Black*, 70-71.
21 Townsend, *R.W. Black*, 71.
22 *Y.B.*, 1915 109-14; 1917 71-72; Shepperson & Price, *Independent African*, 341-55.
23 *Y.B.*, 1925 78-79; 1929 68-69, 85-87; resolution 22 of 1929; *Y.B.*, 1930 65, 82-83; resolution 35 of 1930; *C.A.*, 1930 530-31, 570; *Y.B.*, 1931 86-89.
24 *Y.B.*, 1932 63; *C.A.*, 1932 516-17; *Y.B.*, 1933 67-68; *C.A.*, 1933 519-21; 1935 558.
25 *C.A.*, 1940 481-83, 490.
26 *C.A.*, 1922 155; *Y.B.*, 1933 63; 1934 55-56, 62, 128; 1935 66-67.
27 *Y.B.*, 1915 88-89, 101-9; 1917 82-86; 1918 63-64, 71-73; 1921 75-76; 1922 i-iii; 1923 74-75; 1935 67; 1936 77, 88-89; 1938 91; *C.A.*, 1935 741.
28 *Y.B.*, 1923 133; *C.A.*, 1947 78; *C.A.*, 1923 531; *Y.B.*, 1924 61-62, 148; 1925 127; 1927 143; *C.A.*, 1936 421.
29 *Y.B.*, 1928 49; 1931 35-36; resolutions 12-13 of 1931; *Y.B.*, 1934 29-30; 1935 37; resolution 7 of 1935; *Y.B.*, 1936 50-51; 1937 72; 1939 52-53; 1940 23.
30 See, e.g. *C.A.*, 1930 691-92.
31 *Y.B.*, 1929 35.
32 *C.A.*, 1931 545-46 (italics original).
33 *Y.B.*, 1936 37.
34 Resolution 43 of 1925; resolutions 9-10 of 1926; *C.A.*, 1935 541; *Y.B.*, 1937 50-58; 1943 45.

35 Y.B., 1929 32-33; resolution 28 of 1929; resolution 19 of 1930; Y.B., 1935 35; 1936 48; resolutions 36 and 58 of 1936; Y.B., 1937 59-60; 1938 61-62.
36 C.A., 1921 314; resolution 35 of 1921; Y.B., 1923 141-48; resolution 10 of 1923; C.A., 1923 522; resolution 7 of 1925.
37 Resolution 37 of 1937; Y.B., 1937 48-49; resolutions 7, 17 and 18 of 1938.
38 B.A., 1919 230-31.
39 Robinson, Essays on Christian Unity, 10-11.
40 Ibid., 79, 81 (quoting C.A., 1921 230).
41 Y.B., 1938 51, 58.
42 Resolution 3 of 1932: Christian Hymnary, iii-vii.
43 Resolution 10 of 1938; resolution 57 of 1939; resolution 55 of 1941; resolution 15 of 1942.
44 C.A., 1938 483; 1939 498-99.
45 C.A., 1929 523; 1933 499-500; resolution 25 of 1935; Y.B., 1936 159; C.A., 1937 103.
46 Resolution 27 of 1939.
47 C.A., 1939 667; 1940 10-11, 22, 59; Y.B., 1941 113.
48 C.A., 1939 694; 1940 151, 167, 186-87, 263; Y.B., 1941 113-14.
49 Y.B., 1943 62.
50 C.A., 1945 154.
51 Watters, History, 105; B.A., 1916 413, 428-29, 444-45.
52 S.S., 1961 79-81.
53 S.S., 1946 90-91; 1970 123-26, 133-35; Report of Discussion of Differences (1945); resolution 21 of 1945; resolution 48 of 1946; C.A., 1946 290-91.

Chapter 6: The Ecumenical Age

1   Y.B., 1946 28-29 (italics original).
2   Currie, Gilbert & Horsley, Churches and Churchgoers, especially pp 17, 73.
3   C.A., 1940 590-91, 619, 650; Y.B., 1946 30-31.
4   C.A., 1946 249-50; 1949 289-90.
5   Y.B., 1956 44 (italics original).
6   Y.B., 1946 28.
7   Y.B., 1956 43.
8   C.A., 1946 277.
9   Resolution 24 of 1947; Y.B., 1947 25, 32; 1942 30; resolution 7 of 1942.
10 Y.B., 1946 33-37, 40-43, 46; resolution 37 of 1947.
11 Y.B., 1948 34; resolution 22 of 1948; C.A., 1948 364; Y.B., 1949 25-33, 121; 1950 25-36, 37-38; 1951 37-38; 1952 39-40.
12 Y.B., 1953 41.
13 C.A., 1953 266.
14 Y.B., 1956 177.
15 Y.B., 1956 178-79.
16 Y.B., 1961 69-70; resolution 51 of 1966; resolution 17 of 1974.
17 C.A., 1953 332, 384; 1954 7-8, 78-79, 138, 351; 1956 450; 1958 337-38; 1959 402-3; 1961 481-83; 1962 621-22, 633; resolution 18 of 1957; resolution 40 of 1958.
18 C.A., 1950 267; Y.B., 1956 47-48; 1954 96; 1955 98; 1956 95; resolution 35 of 1960.
19 C.A., 1950 277; Y.B., 1947 79; 1952 106; 1953 108; 1956 129; resolution 22 of 1947; resolution 13 of 1956.

20   Resolution 36 of 1945; *Y.B.*, 1950 84; 1954 109-10; resolution 15 of 1958;
     Y.B., 1956 111; 1959 97; 1966 126; 1967 154; 1969 138-39; 1970 126; 1975
     28-30.
21   *Y.B.*, 1942 39; 1945 35; 1961 61; 1975 12; *C.A.*, 1936 183.
22   *Y.B.*, 1963 82; 1961 64; 1970 78.
23   *Y.B.*, 1946 22-24; resolution 34 of 1951; *C.A.*, 1951 292; *Y.B.*, 1948 21;
     1955 43-52; 1956 181-83; 1957 55-58; resolutions 27-30 of 1957; *Y.B.*, 1959
     54-56; resolution 32 of 1959; *Y.B.*, 1960 52-55; 1961 56; 1970 66.
24   *Y.B.*, 1952 53, 69-71, 92; 1961 133-35; 1966 61; 1970 64; resolution 15 of
     1962; resolution 30 of 1965.
25   *C.A.*, 1927 335. For Walter Hendry's role in Aberfan, see J. Miller,
     Aberfan, 125-27.
26   *Y.B.*, 1942 134.
27   *Ibid.*, 136-40 — the quotation is from p 138. Conference amended the
     word 'presbyter' to 'elder' — resolution 24(a) of 1942.
28   *C.A.*, 1942 275.
29   *Report of the Commission on the Ministry*, 12-13.
30   *Ibid.*, 13-14.
31   *Ibid.*, 23.
32   *Ibid.*, 26.
33   *Ibid.*, 26-31.
34   Resolution 43 of 1973.
35   Robinson, *Biblical Doctrine*, 219.
36   *Y.B.*, 1959 109.
37   *C.A.*, 1963 535.
38   *C.A.*, 1946 281, cf. 283.
39   *C.A.*, 1951 188, 267; 1952 279.
40   *C.A.*, 1929 517.
41   *C.A.*, 1942 46, 52, 97-98, 128; *Y.B.*, 1942 113; resolution 16 of 1942;
     Townsend, *R.W. Black*, 103-14, 136-43.
42   *Y.B.*, 1944 73; 1945 25-26, 62-63; 1947 72; 1948 87-88; 1949 35, 86-87;
     1950 38-39; 1951 49; resolution 23 of 1950; *C.A.*, 1950 274; 1951 169-70;
     Payne, *Baptist Union*, 221.
43   *Y.B.*, 1952 43; 1953 43; resolution 38 of 1955; *Y.B.*, 1956 118; 1957 113.
44   *C.A.*, 1951 217-19, 234, 255, 411.
45   *C.A.*, 1949 274; *Y.B.*, 1950 90; 1951 39, 107; 1952 40, 97; 1953 41-42.
46   *Y.B.*, 1954 43.
47   *Y.B.*, 1954 39-50.
48   *Y.B.*, 1956 119-21; resolution 8 of 1956; *C.A.*, 1956 455-56.
49   *Y.B.*, 1956 40.
50   *Y.B.*, 1957 113-16.
51   *C.A.*, 1948 262; Baker, *Service of Thanksgiving*.
52   Gray, *Towards Christian Union*, 64.
53   Gray, *Implications of New Delhi*, 22-25.
54   *Y.B.*, 1964 61.
55   *C.A.*, 1964 443-44.
56   *Ecumenical Membership*, 1972; resolution 14 of 1972; Thompson,
     'Churches of Christ', 33.
57   Davies & Edwards, *Unity begins at Home*, 43-48, 77-78.
58   *Y.B.*, 1965 141; 1966 55-57, 142; resolutions 24 and 37 of 1966.
59   *Y.B.*, 1967 168; 1968 66-67; resolution 19 of 1967.

60   *Y.B.*, 1968 68; 1969 59-60; 65-70; 81-82; 1970 57-58, 73; 1971 69; resolution 8 of 1971; *Y.B.*, 1972 7-8; resolution 21 of 1972; resolution 41 of 1973 (N.B. the final report inaccurately states that 74 congregations voted in favour); resolutions 48-50 of 1974.

61   Corey, *Fifty Years*; McAllister & Tucker, *Journey in Faith*, 382-86, 435-51; *C.A.*, 1960, 428-29, 434-35, 447-48, 594-95.

62   *Y.B.*, 1952 56-59; 1963 95-96; *C.A.*, 1963 190.

63   *Y.B.*, 1949 52-53; 1951 67-70; 1957 78; 1969 97-100; 1971 78-79; resolution 28 of 1969.

64   *Y.B.*, 1956 84; resolution 24 of 1956; *Y.B.*, 1963 95-96; 1964 95; *C.A.*, 1964 466; resolution 29 of 1969; *Y.B.*, 1970 87-88; 1971 80-81; 1977 15-16; resolution 30 of 1977.

65   Resolution 32 of 1978.

66   *Proposals for Unification.*

67   *Y.B.*, 1978 31.

68   Resolution 45 of 1978; resolutions 6-16 of 1979.

69   *C.A.*, 1938 759.

70   *Y.B.*, 1957 37-38.

71   King, *Memoir of King*, 60.

72   *Ibid.*, 59.

73   *Y.B.*, 1967 78.

BIBLIOGRAPHY

1. Manuscript sources
Correspondence of John Davies (Churches of Christ Historical Society collection).

2. Unpublished dissertations
J.T. Hornsby, 'John Glas' (Edinburgh Ph.D., 1936).
R.D. Mitchell, 'Archibald McLean, 1733-1812: Baptist Pioneer in Scotland' (Edinburgh Ph.D., 1950).
A.C. Watters, 'History of the British Churches of Christ' (Edinburgh Ph.D., 1940).

3. Periodicals
The Millennial Harbinger and Voluntary Church Advocate, vols i-ii, London 1835-36.
The Christian Messenger and Reformer, vols i-ix, London 1837-45. (Vols i-vi contain twelve monthly numbers, beginning in March one year and ending in February the next; thus vol i is Mar 1837-Feb 1838. Vol vii is from Mar 1843 to Dec 1843; vol viii from Jan 1844 to Aug 1844; and vol ix from Sept 1844 to Apr 1845.)
The Christian Messenger and Family Magazine, vols i-iii, London 1845-47. (Vol i is from May 1845 to Dec 1845; vols ii and iii are for the calendar years 1846 and 1847.)
The British Millennial Harbinger and Family Magazine, devoted to the spread of primitive Christianity (Third series), vols i-xiv, London 1848-61.
The British Millennial Harbinger, devoted to the spread of Christianity as it was at the first and the defence and promotion of Biblical truth (Fourth series), vols xv-xviii, London 1862-65.
The British Harbinger, devoted to the propagation of Christianity as it was at the first and the defence and promotion of Biblical truth (Fifth series), vols xix-xxiii, London 1866-70.
The Ecclesiastical Observer, devoted to Christianity as it was at the beginning and the defence and promulgation of Biblical truth (Sixth series), vols xxiv-xxviii, London 1871-75.
(Seventh series), vols xxix-xlii, London 1876-89.
The Bible Advocate and Precursor of Unity, vol i, London 1847.
The Gospel Banner and Biblical Treasury, containing the writings of Alexander Campbell and his coadjutors in America and Great Britain, vols i-iv, London 1848-51.
The Christian Advocate: a monthly magazine to plead for an unqualified return to the faith once for all delivered to the Saints, vols i-vii, Edinburgh 1857-63: (Second series), vols i-ii, Edinburgh 1864-65.
The Christian Advocate: a monthly magazine to plead for an unqualified return

to primitive Christianity; the cultivation of personal piety; and loving service to Christ, (New series), vols i-v, Edinburgh 1873-77: (Third series), vols i-xi, Edinburgh 1879-89.

The Bible Advocate, pleading for a complete return to the faith and order of the Churches of Christ as perfected by the Apostles, vols i-xx, Birmingham 1890-1909.

The Bible Advocate, pleading for a complete return to the faith and practice of the Church of Christ as perfected by the Apostles, vols xxi-xxx, Birmingham 1910-19.

The Bible Advocate, pleading for a complete return to the faith and practice of the New Testament Church, vol xxxi, Birmingham 1920.

The Christian Advocate, vols i-lix, Birmingham 1921-79.

The Christian Baptist (edited by Alexander Campbell, revised by D.S. Burnet), vols i-vii, 1823-30: Stereotype edition in one volume, Cincinnati, 1835.

The Old Paths, vols viii-xlv, Birmingham 1873-1910.

The Young Christian, vols i-iii, Leeds 1890-93.

The Christian at Work, vol iv, Leeds 1894.

The Christian Quarterly and Missionary Gleaner,vols i-iv, Gloucester 1903-6.

The Christian Monthly, vols xv-xix, London 1917-21.

The Watchword, nos 1-28, Leeds 1917-19.

The Scripture Standard, pleading for a complete return to Christianity as it was at the beginning, vols x-xlvii, Nottingham 1944-79.

Annual Reports of the Foreign Christian Missionary Society, 1879-90.

The Missionary Intelligencer, F.C.M.S., 1894-1917.

Churches of Christ Year Book, 1886-1979.

The Christian Quarterly, vols i-vi, Birmingham 1934-39.

4. Published books and pamphlets
P. Ainslie, The Message of the Disciples for the Union of the Church, New York 1913.

T.J. Ainsworth, Sydney Black, London 1911.

J. Anderson, An Outline of my Life, Birmingham 1912.

W.G. Baker, Thanksgiving for childbirth and dedication of parents, Birmingham 1957.

G.E. Barr, Edwin Henry Spring, Gloucester 1935.

L. Billington, 'The Churches of Christ in Britain: a study in nineteenth-century sectarianism', Journal of Religious History, vol viii (1974-75).

A. Campbell, (Christianity Restored) A connected view of the principles and rules by which the Living Oracles may be intelligibly and certainly interpreted: of the foundation on which all Christians may form one communion: and of the capital positions sustained in the attempt to restore the original Gospel and order of things, Bethany, Va. 1835.

A. Campbell & R. Owen, Debate on the Evidences of Christianity, London 1839.

A. Campbell & N.L. Rice, A debate on the action, subject, design and administrator of Christian Baptism; also, on the character of spiritual influence in conversion and sanctification, and on the expediency and tendency of ecclesiastic creeds, as terms of union and communion, Lexington, Ky. 1844.

A. Campbell, The Christian System in reference to the union of Christians and restoration of primitive Christianity as pleaded by the current reformation, (1839), first English edition, Birmingham n.d. (c 1905).

T. Chalmers, Alexander Campbell's Tour in Scotland, Louisville, Ky. 1892.

The Christian Hymnary, for use of Churches of Christ, Birmingham 1938.

R. Coad, *A history of the Brethren movement*, Exeter 1968.

S.J. Corey, *Fifty years of attack and controversy*, St Louis, Miss. 1953.

R. Currie, A. Gilbert & L. Horsley, *Churches and Churchgoers*, Oxford 1977.

R.E. Davies & D.L. Edwards (eds), *Unity begins at home*, London 1964.

T. Witton Davies, 'The McLeanist (Scotch) and Campbellite Baptists of Wales', *Transaction of the Baptist Historical Society*, vol vii (1920-21).

D. Douglas, *History of the Baptist Churches in the north of England from 1648 to 1845*, London 1846.

R. Dunkerley (ed), *The Ministry and the Sacraments*, London 1937.

Ecumenical Membership, Churches of Christ Occasional Paper no 2, Birmingham 1972.

H. Escott, *A history of Scottish Congregationalism*, Glasgow 1960.

P.W. Evans, H. Townsend & W. Robinson, *Infant Baptism today*, London 1948.

R. Newton Flew (ed), *The nature of the Church*, London 1952.

For His Name's Sake, being a record of witness given by members of Churches of Christ in Great Britain against militarism during the European War, 1914-1918, Heanor 1921.

W.E. Garrison & A.T. DeGroot, *The Disciples of Christ*, (revised edition), St Louis, Miss. 1958.

J. Gray, *Towards True Baptism*, Birmingham 1948.

J. Gray (ed), *Studies on Baptism*, Birmingham 1959.

J. Gray (ed), *Towards Christian Union*, Birmingham 1960.

J. Gray, *Implications of New Delhi for Churches of Christ*, Birmingham 1962.

J. Gray (ed), *W.R. The man and his work*, Birmingham 1978.

H. Grew, *A tribute to the memory of the Apostles, and an exhibition of the first Christian churches* (also contains *A query on taking the Lord's Supper, answered by A. Campbell*), London 1836.

D.E. Harrell Jr, *Quest for a Christian America*, Nashville, Tenn. 1966.

D.E. Harrell Jr, *The social sources for division in the Disciples of Christ, 1865-1900*, Atlanta, Ga. 1973.

L. Hodgson (ed), *Convictions*, London 1934.

Hymns for Churches of Christ, Birmingham 1908.

Joint Committee for negotiations between Churches of Christ and the United Reformed Church, *Report for 1974*, Birmingham 1974.

Joint Committee for negotiations between Churches of Christ and the United Reformed Church, *Proposals for Unification*, Birmingham 1976.

J. Idwal Jones, *William Jones — a memoir*, Blaenau Festiniog, 1946.

W. Jones, *The Works of Mr Archibald M'Lean, with a memoir of his life, ministry and writings*, vol vi, London 1823.

W. Jones, *Primitive Christianity*, London 1837.

W. Jones, *Autobiography*, London 1846.

E.K.H. Jordan, *Free Church Unity*, London 1956.

L. King, *Memoir of David King, with various papers and addresses advocating the restoration in principle and in practice of primitive Christianity*, Birmingham n.d.

M.E. Lard, *Commentary on Paul's Letter to Romans*, Leicester 1887.

L.G. McAllister & W.E. Tucker, *Journey in Faith: A history of the Christian Church (Disciples of Christ)*, St Louis, Miss. 1975.

J. M'Cartney, *Can we co-operate with American churches? Some facts and suggestions*, Birmingham 1927.

J.W. McGarvey, *A commentary on Acts of Apostles*, Leicester 1887.

A. McLean, *The History of the Foreign Christian Missionary Society*, New York 1919.

W. Mander, *Can we co-operate with American churches? A reply*, 1927.

J. Miller, *Aberfan, A disaster and its aftermath*, London, 1974.

T.H. Milner, *The Messiah's Ministry*, Edinburgh 1858.

T.H. Milner, *The Gospel Guide*, Edinburgh 1860.

W.T. Moore, *The Life of Timothy Coop*, London 1889.

S. Mottershaw, *A history of the Church of Christ meeting in Long Hedge Lane, Nottingham*, Nottingham 1886.

D.B. Murray, *The first hundred years: the Baptist Union of Scotland*, Dundee 1969.

L. Oliver, *New Testament Christianity*, Birmingham 1911.

E.A. Payne, *The Baptist Union*, London 1959.

George C. Reid, *Our first evangelist*, Southport, 1885.

Reports of the World Conference on Faith and Order, Lausanne, Aug. 3-21, 1927; together with the Reply, prepared by the Union Committee and the Special Committee appointed under Res. 41 of the Annual Conference of 1928, and passed by the Annual Conference held at Wigan, Aug. 5-8, 1929, Birmingham n.d. (?1929).

Report of Discussions of Differences, n.d. (?1945).

Report of the Commission on the Ministry, set up by the Annual Conference of Churches of Christ, Glasgow, 1947, Birmingham n.d. (1954).

R. Richardson, *Memoirs of Alexander Campbell* (2 vols), Philadelphia 1868, 1870.

R. Roberts (revised C.C. Walker), *Dr Thomas, his life and work*, Birmingham 1925.

W. Robinson, 'History of the Churches of Christ in Furness', *Christian Monthly*, vol xviii (1920) pp 3-4, 21-22, 41-42.

W. Robinson, *Essays on Christian Unity*, London 1923.

W. Robinson, *Holy Ordinances*, Birmingham 1925.

W. Robinson, *What Churches of Christ stand for*, Birmingham 1926.

W. Robinson, *Christianity is Pacifism*, London 1933.

W. Robinson, *The Shattered Cross*, Birmingham 1945.

W. Robinson (ed), *Declaration and Address; by Thomas Campbell*, Birmingham 1951.

W. Robinson, *The Biblical Doctrine of the Church* (revised edition) St Louis, Miss. 1955.

J.B. Rotherham, *The New Testament critically emphasized*, London 1897.

J.B. Rotherham, *Let us keep the feast*, London, n.d.

J.B. Rotherham, *Reminiscences*, London n.d.

H.H. Rowdon, *The Origins of the Brethren*, London 1967.

Rules and Regulations of the Annual Conference of Churches of Christ, 1894, 1902, 1911, 1925, 1948, 1959, 1978.

W. Scott, *A discourse on the Holy Spirit* (also includes a letter on the same subject from John Thomas and Alexander Campbell's reply), London 1837.

G.A. Shepperson & T. Price, *Independent African*, Edinburgh 1958.

D.M. Thompson, 'Churches of Christ in the British Isles, 1842-1972', *Journal of the United Reformed Church History Society*, vol i (1973-74).

H. Townsend, *Robert Wilson Black*, London 1954.

A.C. Watters, *History of the British Churches of Christ*, Birmingham 1948.

G. Yuille, *History of the Baptists in Scotland*, Glasgow 1926.

INDEX